The Full Faith and Credit Clause

Recent Titles in
Reference Guides to the United States Constitution
Jack Stark, Series Editor

The Right to the Assistance of Counsel
James J. Tomkovicz

Prohibited Government Acts
Jack Stark

State Sovereign Immunity
Melvyn R. Durchslag

Constitutional Remedies
Michael Wells and Thomas A. Eaton

Privileges and Immunities
David Skillen Bogen

Searches, Seizures, and Warrants
Robert M. Bloom

The Supremacy Clause
Christopher R. Drahozal

Procedural Due Process
Rhonda Wasserman

Double Jeopardy
David S. Rudstein

Freedom of the Press
Lyrissa Barnett Lidsky and R. George Wright

The Taxing Power
Erik M. Jensen

Freedom of Speech
Keith Werhan

The Religion Guarantees
Peter K. Rofes

Limits on States
James M. McGoldrick Jr.

The Full Faith and Credit Clause

A Reference Guide to the United States Constitution

William L. Reynolds and
William M. Richman

REFERENCE GUIDES TO THE
UNITED STATES CONSTITUTION, NUMBER 15
Jack Stark, *Series Editor*

PRAEGER
Westport, Connecticut
London

Library of Congress Cataloging-in-Publication Data

Reynolds, William L., 1945–
The full faith and credit clause : a reference guide to the United States Constitution / William L. Reynolds and William M. Richman.
p. cm. — (Reference guides to the United States Constitution, ISSN 1539–8986 ; no. 15)
Includes bibliographical references and index.
ISBN 0–313–31541–8 (alk. paper)
1. Conflict of laws—United States—States. 2. Judgments, Foreign—United States—States. 3. Constitutional law—United States. I. Richman, William M. II. Title. III. Series.
KF417.R49 2005
342.73'042—dc22 2004028096

British Library Cataloguing in Publication Data is available.

Library of Congress Catalog Card Number: 2004028096
ISBN: 0–313–31541–8
ISSN: 1539–8986

First published in 2005

Praeger Publishers, 88 Post Road West, Westport, CT 06881
An imprint of Greenwood Publishing Group, Inc.
www.praeger.com

Printed in the United States of America

The paper used in this book complies with the Permanent Paper Standard issued by the National Information Standards Organization (Z39.48–1984).

10 9 8 7 6 5 4 3 2 1

For My Grandchildren
W.L.R.

For Carol
W.M.R.

Contents

Series Foreword

JACK STARK

One can conceive of the United States Constitution in many ways. For example, noting the reverence in which it has been held, one can think of it as equivalent to a sacred text. Unfortunately, most of its devotees have had less knowledge and even less understanding of the document than they have had reverence for it. Sometimes it is treated as primarily a political document and on that basis has been subjected to analysis, such as Charles Beard's *An Economic Interpretation of the Constitution of the United States*. One can plausibly argue that the Constitution seems most astounding when it is seen in the light of the intellectual effort that has been associated with it. Three brief but highly intense bursts of intellectual energy produced, and established as organic law, most of the Constitution as it now exists. Two of these efforts, sustained over a long period of time, have enabled us better to understand that document.

The first burst of energy occurred at the Constitutional Convention. Although some of the delegates' business, such as the struggle between populous and non-populous states about their representation in Congress, was political, much of it was about fundamental issues of political theory. A few of the delegates had or later achieved international eminence for their intellects. Among them were Benjamin Franklin, Alexander Hamilton, and James Madison. Others, although less well known, had first-rate minds. That group includes George Mason and George Wythe. Many of the delegates contributed intelligently. Although the Convention's records are less than satisfactory, they indicate clearly enough that the delegates worked mightily to constitute not merely a polity but a rational polity—one that would rise to the standards envisioned by the delegates' intellectual ancestors. Their product, though brief, is amazing. William Gladstone called it "the most wonderful work ever struck off."

Despite the delegates' eminence and the Constitution's excellence as seen from our place in history, its ratification was far from certain. That state of affairs necessitated the second burst of intellectual energy associated with that document: the debate over ratification. Soon after the Convention adjourned, articles and speeches—some supporting the Constitution and some attacking it—began to proliferate. A national debate commenced, not only about the document itself, but also about the nature of the polity that ought to exist in this country. Both sides included many writers and speakers who were verbally adroit and steeped in the relevant political and philosophical literature. The result was an accumulation of material that is remarkable for both its quantity and its quality. At its apex is *The Federalist Papers*, a production of Alexander Hamilton, James Madison, and John Jay that deserves a place among the great books of Western culture.

Another burst, not as impressive as the first two but highly respectable, occurred when the Bill of Rights was proposed. Some delegates to the Constitutional Convention had vigorously asserted that such guarantees should be included in the original document. George Mason, the principal drafter of the Virginia Declaration of Rights, so held, and he walked out of the Convention when he failed to achieve his purpose. Even those who had argued that the rights in question were implicit recognized the value of adding protection of them to the Constitution. The debate was thus focused on the rights that were to be explicitly granted, not on whether any rights *ought* to be explicitly granted. Again many writers and speakers entered the fray, and again the debate was solidly grounded in theory and was conducted on a high intellectual level.

Thus, within a few years a statement of organic law and a vital coda to it had been produced. However, the meaning and effect of many of that document's provisions were far from certain; the debates on ratification of the Constitution and the Bill of Rights had demonstrated that. In addition, the document existed in a vacuum, because statutes and actions had not been assessed by its standards. The attempt to resolve these problems began after Chief Justice John Marshall, in Marbury v. Madison, asserted the right of the U.S. Supreme Court to interpret and apply the Constitution. Judicial interpretation and application of the Constitution, beginning with the first constitutional case and persisting until the most recent, is one of the sustained exertions of intellectual energy associated with the Constitution. The framers would be surprised by some of the results of those activities. References in the document to "due process," which seems to refer only to procedures, have been held also to have a substantive dimension. A right to privacy has been found lurking among the penumbras of various parts of the text. A requirement that states grant the same "privileges and immunities" to citizens of other states that they granted to their own citizens, which seemed to guarantee important rights, was held not to be particularly important. The corpus of judicial interpretations of the Constitution is now as voluminous as that document is terse.

As the judicial interpretations multiplied, another layer—interpretations of interpretations—appeared, and also multiplied. This layer, the other sustained intellectual effort associated with the Constitution, consists of articles, most of them published in law reviews, and books on the Constitution. This material varies in quality and significance. Some of these works of scholarship result from meticulous examination and incisive thought. Others repeat earlier work, or apply a fine-tooth comb to matters that are too minute even for such a comb. Somewhere in that welter of tertiary material is the answer to almost every question that one could ask about constitutional law. The problem is finding the answer that one wants. The difficulty of locating useful guidance is exacerbated by the bifurcation of most constitutional scholarship into two kinds. In "Two Styles of Social Science Research," C. Wright Mills delineates macroscopic and molecular research. The former deals with huge issues, the latter with tiny issues. Virtually all of the scholarship on the Constitution is of one of those two types. Little of it is macroscopic, but that category does include some first-rate syntheses such as Jack Rakove's *Original Meanings*. Most constitutional scholarship is molecular and, again, some fine work is included in that category.

In his essay, Mills bemoans the inability of social scientists to combine the two kinds of research that he describes to create a third category that will be more generally useful. This series of books is an attempt to do for constitutional law the intellectual work that Mills proposed for social science. The author of each book has dealt carefully and at reasonable length with a topic that lies in the middle range of generality. Upon completion, this series will consist of thirty-seven books, each on a constitutional law topic. Some of the books, such as the book on freedom of the press, explicate one portion of the Constitution's text. Others, such as the volume on federalism, treat a topic that has several anchors in the Constitution. The books on constitutional history and constitutional interpretation range over the entire document, but each does so from one perspective. Except for a very few of the books, for which special circumstances dictate minor changes in format, each book includes the same components: a brief history of the topic, a lengthy and sophisticated analysis of the current state of the law on that topic, a bibliographical essay that organizes and evaluates scholarly material in order to facilitate further research, a table of cases, and an index. The books are intellectually rigorous—in fact, authorities have written them—but, due to their clarity and to brief definitions of terms that are unfamiliar to laypersons, each is comprehensible and useful to a wide audience, one that ranges from other experts on the book's subject to intelligent non-lawyers.

In short, this series provides an extremely valuable service to the legal community and to others who are interested in constitutional law, as every citizen should be. Each book is a map of part of the U.S. Constitution. Together they map all of that document's territory that is worth mapping. When this series is complete, each book will be a third kind of scholarly work that combines the macroscopic and the molecular. Together they will explicate all of the important constitutional topics. Anyone who wants assistance in understanding either a topic in constitutional law or the Constitution as a whole can easily find it in these books.

Acknowledgments

Professor Reynolds wishes to thank the University of Maryland School of Law and, especially, Dean Karen Rothenberg for their support of this project. Catie Napius provided excellent research assistance. Ryan Easley of the Maryland library staff was editor, researcher, and critic; he did a truly superb job. And Yvonne McMorris, his personal assistant was, as always, invaluable in all ways, and indefatigable above and beyond the call of duty. He also wishes to thank his family for their always continuing support and to honor the memory of his father, Austin.

Professor Richman is grateful for the generous support of the University of Toledo, the College of Law, and its dean, Phillip J. Closius, and associate dean, Beth A. Eisler. Much of the work on the book was accomplished with that support during a sabbatical leave in the fall semester of 2003. He also wishes to thank his family—Carol, Nathan, Emily, and Ben—for their love and support and to honor the memory of his parents, Bernice and Jacob.

Introduction

Article IV of the United States Constitution represents the attempt by those who drafted the federal constitution to alleviate some of the stresses that would occur frequently as the states dealt with one another on matters less grand than most of those discussed during the long debates in that Philadelphia summer of 1787. Thus, the first two sections of Article IV contain the Extradition Clause (requiring the return of fugitives, including fugitive slaves, to the state from which they had fled) and the Privileges and Immunities Clause (ensuring that one state's citizens will not be discriminated against by another state when they move to or travel through that second state). That article, which might also be called the Interstate Comity Article, also contains the Full Faith and Credit Clause, the subject of this book.

Article IV tries to lessen the frictions inevitably caused by everyday interstate transactions by using mandatory language in each of its provisions. ("Full Faith and Credit *shall* be given. . . ."; "The citizens of each state *shall* be entitled. . . ."; "A [fugitive] . . . *shall* on demand . . . be delivered up. . . .").[1] The apparent linguistic removal of discretion in application of the Article IV mandates reveals the importance that the drafters gave to the goal of interstate comity. As a general rule, the drafters achieved their goal, and the workings of the interstate comity provisions have not proven controversial (although the Fugitive Slave Clause did prove to be very controversial in the years immediately preceding the Civil War).

The Full Faith and Credit Clause has proven to be far and away the most important of the mandates of Article IV in constitutional practice.

It provides:

> Full Faith and Credit shall be given in each State to the public Acts, Records, and judicial Proceedings of every other State. And the Congress may by general Laws prescribe the Manner in which such Acts, Records and Proceedings shall be proved, and the Effect thereof.

Although certainly an important provision to the framers of the 1787 federal constitution (the provision has roots extending at least as far back as the English

Civil War), the Full Faith and Credit Clause, as it is generally known, comes down to us burdened with relatively little original legislative history. Moreover, Congress has basically left unexercised the power to legislate given it by the clause; apart from the original implementing legislation in 1790, the only statutory provisions dealing with full faith and credit have been a few pieces of legislation dealing with interstate family problems enacted only in the past quarter century. As a result, the courts have been left free to interpret the full faith and credit mandate as they see fit, unguided and unhampered either by evidence of the original understanding of that clause, or by legislative guidance from drafters of any era. That judicial jurisprudence, however, has proven remarkably rich, and it has played a key role in the peaceful development of the United States. The Full Faith and Credit Clause, in other words, has proven to be largely a product of the common-law style of constitutional decision making.

It should not be surprising that the development of the clause has been left in the hands of lawyers and the judiciary (so much so that Justice Robert Jackson once referred to it as "The Lawyer's Clause of the Constitution")[2] and it has been used primarily—even overwhelmingly—to resolve "technical" problems in litigation. Those "technical" resolutions, however, can have profound consequences. To cite but one example, the need to decide whether the validity in North Carolina of an ex parte Nevada divorce decree was covered by the Full Faith and Credit Clause helped spark the divorce revolution of the 1960s and 1970s. Today, the resolution of the problems presented by the question of whether states are required to recognize same-sex civil unions and marriages entered into in other states holds the possibility of full faith and credit leading the nation into another era of sweeping change.

From the earliest decisions involving the Full Faith and Credit Clause, the Supreme Court has been clear and consistent about the basic purpose of the provision, although it is true, as it is of any legal topic, that the Court's applications of the clause at times may lack constancy. As noted earlier, the Full Faith and Credit Clause is part of Article IV, which governs relations among the states. And the Full Faith and Credit Clause was designed by the Framers to achieve that critical goal making one sovereign out of many, "*e pluribus unum*," as can be seen in what is perhaps the most quoted explanation of the purposes of the clause:

> The very purpose of the full faith and credit clause was to alter the status of the several states as independent foreign sovereignties, each free to ignore obligations created under the laws or by the judicial proceedings of the others, and to make them integral parts of a single nation throughout which a remedy upon a just obligation might be demanded as of right, irrespective of the state of its origin.[3]

No longer, in other words, would a state be free to indulge in one of the prerogatives of a sovereign—that is, "to ignore obligations" of other sovereigns; instead, each state would be an "integral part [ ] of a single nation . . . , "no longer free to ignore a "just obligation" from another state. The history of the Full Faith and Credit Clause is largely the accommodation of that policy to the changing needs of a rapidly evolving nation. That is the story we tell here.

This book begins by discussing the legislative history of the Full Faith and Credit Clause, along with some of the early jurisprudence and commentary on the clause. We then examine separately the history and current status of its three components: respectively, the respect one state owes another state to its "Public acts," to its "public records," and to its "judicial proceedings." A final section is devoted to family law, a full faith and credit category with unique and transcendent problems.

We shall show that the public records provision has been eclipsed by developments in procedural and evidentiary law; that the public acts provision has little significance today; and that, in contrast, the judicial proceedings mandate has had a rich history and has done much to fulfill its goal of making "one out of many." The family law provision, however, has had a great deal of impact on the lives of ordinary Americans.

NOTES

1. U. S. Const. art. IV, (Emphasis added).
2. Robert Jackson, *Full Faith and Credit: The Lawyer's Clause of the Constitution*, 45 Columbia L. Rev. 1, 9 (1945).
3. Milwaukee County v. M.E. White Co., 296 U.S. 268, 276–77 (1935).

1

History

The origins of the Full Faith and Credit Clause are somewhat murky. The concept of full faith and credit was not new at the time of the Constitutional Convention in 1787, but the debates there make scant reference to the clause, and the discussion in the states over ratification of the Constitution refer even less to it. The debates over the clause at the convention do make clear, however, that it was designed to make it easier to enforce judgments entered by courts in other states.

BACKGROUND

International trade requires, among other things, that the judgments of the courts of one nation can be enforced in the courts of another. In the early stages of economic development, this need may not have been so pressing; after all, a disappointed party could always simply refuse to deal with the defaulting debtor. As international commercial transactions increased dramatically during the eighteenth century, the need for an effective solution to the problem became more important.

The obvious answer, of course, was for a court asked to enforce a foreign judgment (that is, a judgment rendered by a court located in another country) to accord that judgment full preclusive effect; to treat the judgment in other words, the same way that an enforcing court would treat one of its own judgments. Unfortunately, there were obvious drawbacks to this solution. Among them were three very important concerns: the judgment may have been rendered by an unfair tribunal; the defendant may not have had notice of the proceedings or an opportunity to defend itself; and the alleged record of the original proceeding may not have been accurate (we call this the attestation problem). Those problems were, of course, more acute than they are today with our widespread acceptance of the norm of impartial justice and the ease of travel even to places thousands of miles away. But in the late eighteenth century these were real issues.

Viewed more broadly, any attempt to regulate the enforcement action had to deal with two main questions: First, is the judgment entitled merely to prima facie (sometimes called comity) effect or is it entitled to preclusive effect? If the latter, then it will be enforced, subject only to a discrete number of limited defenses. If the judgment is classified as prima facie, however, then it is essentially open to relitigation on motion by the judgment debtor. The second question is an evidentiary one: How does the judgment creditor establish the authenticity of the decree that it is seeking to enforce?

English law at the time of the 1787 Constitutional Convention had long been concerned with the problem of enforcement; the phrase "full faith and credit" can be found in English records as far back as 1585.[1] The common law, along with international law generally, evolved eventually to the point that the judgment of a court in another country was presumptive evidence of a debt owed to the judgment creditor; in other words, the first decree was entitled to prima facie effect.[2] Thus, in order to recover on the judgment in England, the foreign creditor had to file an original action there to enforce the judgment; in that action, the debtor could introduce evidence to rebut the presumption of validity. That procedure—involving the possible introduction of new evidence by the judgment debtor, of course—could lead to a relitigation of the underlying case, hardly a satisfying process to the judgment creditor.

It is not surprising that the colonies adopted the English procedure when dealing with judgments of courts from other colonies. Not only was English law the law with which they were most familiar (and that was most available), but the colonial courts were also subject to review by the Privy Council back in London. Although that adoption was natural enough, it created a recurrent problem that the English courts had not had to face. That problem was the migratory debtor, who, in the vast and open areas of colonial America, could easily avoid his creditors simply by moving to another colony where enforcement procedures would have to be initiated against him. The debtor, however, could delay enforcement by contesting the enforcement on the merits. That tactic could buy him considerable time. When the time to pay came in the new colony, however, he often would move on again. The problem of the migratory debtor was a major impetus behind the drafting and adoption of the Full Faith and Credit Clause.

Enforcement issues created another problem, one the English had not had to address, but one that had become important by the time the Constitution was drafted. This problem was unity. The tension and discord prompted by the refusal of a court to enforce another state's judgments could prove a major stumbling block in the effort to unify thirteen independent states.

The colonists had recognized both of these problems from the beginning; as early as 1644, there had been isolated and unsuccessful attempts to deal with the enforcement issue. The most important American reform was adopted in Massachusetts in 1774. The preamble to that law referred to the problem of the migratory debtor ("honest creditors are often defrauded . . . by negligent and evil-minded debtors"); to remedy that problem, the law stipulated that a judgment rendered in another colony, upon introduction of "a true copy of the record and proceedings," the copy shall be "good and sufficient evidence of what had been decided," that the foreign judgment was to have the "same effect and operation" in Massachusetts as in the jurisdiction where it was made, and that it was "proper," therefore, to use the foreign judgment in an action for debt recovery in Massachusetts.[3] The 1774 law was quite far-reaching in its effect; not only did it solve the attestation problem for foreign records, but it also gave preclusive effect to the foreign judgment by treating it as a domestic judgment. In other words, it killed two birds—attestation and effect—with one stone.

The Articles of Confederation

No doubt the Massachusetts law was known to the drafters of the Articles of Confederation in 1777, and those articles also contained a provision addressing the problem posed by foreign judgments. The articles, however, were a step backward from the Massachusetts law. Article IV of the Articles of Confederation was remarkably similar to Article IV of the 1787 Constitution, the clause we referred to in the introduction as the Interstate Comity Article. Both articles contain a Full Faith and Credit Clause, a Privileges and Immunities Clause, a guarantee of free travel across state lines, and a provision for interstate extradition. The Confederation's Article IV was designed to smooth friction among the several states, as is clear from the preamble of the Privileges and Immunities Clause, which could well serve as an introduction to all of Article IV. The preamble stated the purpose: "The better to secure and perpetuate mutual friendship and intercourse among the people of the different States in this Union." The Full Faith and Credit Clause itself stated that, "full faith and credit shall be given in each of these States to Records, Acts and Judicial Proceedings of the Courts and Magistrates of every other State."[4]

The Confederation's Article IV was a less successful attempt at correcting the enforcement problem than was the Massachusetts law. Further, it was ineffective in practice. None of the few reported decisions involving the Full Faith and Credit Clause in the Articles of Confederation treated the out-of-state judgment as mandating a rule of preclusion. Those cases, rather, treated the clause as a rule of evidence and made the judgment subject to attack by the judgment debtor. Although those decisions tracked the prevailing rule in English and international law, they did little to foster greater unity among the states.

The Constitutional Convention

The group of delegates that gathered at Philadelphia in the summer of 1787 to establish our government consisted of practical men who wanted to establish a system that would work, one that would help achieve the ends eventually set forth in the preamble to the Constitution. The great debates at the convention, of course, involved weighty political issues such as state sovereignty and the relationship between the states and the federal government. But relations among the states also demanded critical attention. The debates about the Full Faith and Credit Clause, limited as they were, therefore, shed light not only on that clause, but also on the larger questions of what was expected of the states in their dealings with one another.

Although two of the four drafts submitted at the start of the convention had contained full faith and credit provisions, it was not until relatively late in the proceedings that full faith and credit made its way into the records of the convention. On August 6, 1787, the Committee on Detail reported its first draft of the constitution to the delegates. That draft provided this version of the Full Faith and Credit Clause:

> Full faith shall be given in each State to the acts of the Legislatures, and to the records and judicial proceedings of the courts and magistrates of every other State.[5]

That draft essentially mirrored the full faith provision in the Articles of Confederation with the addition of "the acts of Legislatures" to the list of items to which full faith and credit was due. The draft, however, did not expressly provide that preclusive effect be given to earlier judgments, the Achilles' heel of the Confederation's clause.

The Committee on Detail's draft came up for consideration by the delegates on August 29. After some preliminary discussion concerning coverage of legislative "acts" that did the work of judgments in some states,[6] Charles Pinkney moved to commit (for work by a committee) the draft full faith and credit proposal. James Madison agreed with Pinkney and then went further, suggesting that Congress "might be authorized to provide for the *execution* of judgments in other States."[7]

This went a bit too far for Edmund Randolph, who responded that, "there was no instance of one *nation* executing judgments of the courts of other *nations*."[8] Randolph then made his own proposal:

> Whenever the Act of any State, whether Legislative Executive or Judiciary shall be attested & exemplified under the seal thereof, such attestation and exemplification, shall be deemed in other States as full proof of the existence of that act—and its operation shall be binding in every other State, in all cases to which it may relate, and which are within the cognizance and jurisdiction of the State, wherein the said act was done.[9]

Randolph's proposal was somewhat radical, for it would have required states to treat the "acts" of other states as "binding." Professor Whitten comments that, if the Randolph proposal had been adopted, it would have introduced a "conflict of laws and jurisdictional limit on the operation of state laws and judgments in other states."[10] Randolph's proposal, ultimately rejected without discussion or vote, is the only time during the convention that the question of giving extraterritorial effect to statutes enacted by other states surfaces.

Gouverneur Morris (one of the most influential of the delegates) then ended the floor debate with the following proposal:

> Full faith ought to be given in each State to the public acts, records and judicial proceedings of every other state; and the Legislature shall by general laws, determine the proof and effect of such acts, records and proceedings.

The Morris motion resembled the draft that had been provided by the Committee on Detail, with the important addition of a grant of power to Congress to prescribe the "effect" of "acts, records and proceedings." The Morris draft did not go as far as the 1774 Massachusetts statute in terms of giving domestic effect to a foreign judgment, but it did permit *Congress* to go that far.

Both the Randolph and Morris motions were sent to a select committee for closer examination. That committee reported back to the Convention on September 1787, with a proposal similar to the one that had been made by Morris:

> Full Faith and Credit ought to be given in each State to the public acts, records, and Judicial proceedings of every other State, and the Legislature shall by general laws prescribe the manner in which such acts, Records, & proceedings shall be proved, and the effect which Judgments obtained in one state, shall have in another.[11]

The September 1 draft, therefore, provided first that Congress could establish the manner of authenticating official events in other states; and, second, Congress could determine the effect of out-of-state judgments.

The delegates considered the committee's draft on September 3. Morris moved to amend the draft by placing the word "thereof" after the word "effect" in the last clause of the draft and then eliminating the rest of that last clause. If that amendment had been adopted, state acts, records, and judicial proceedings all would have fallen equally under Congressional authority. James Wilson then observed that, "if the Legislature were not allowed *to declare the effect*, the provision would amount to nothing more than what now takes place among all Independent nations."[12] Wilson was concerned apparently that the first sentence of the draft required that the states give only prima facie effect to judgments from other states—the same rule as that provided by English law. After a bit more debate, the motion by Morris was adopted.

Madison then moved two significant changes (both of which were adopted without dissent) to the proposal made by Morris. First, the word *ought* in the initial clause was replaced by *shall*. (Thus, eventually edited, "Full Faith and Credit *shall* be given . . .") The importance of this change should be obvious: The clause is not optional, but binds the states by its terms. This corrected the primary shortcoming of the Articles of Confederation; the principles enacted would no longer be theoretical models of governance but would have teeth in order to enforce compliance.

In addition, the phrase in the draft granting power to Congress to legislate was changed by Madison's motion in the other direction—from *shall* to *may*. This second change ultimately was edited to read: "And the Congress may by general Laws prescribe the Manner in which such Acts, Records and Proceedings shall be proved, and the Effect thereof." Should the states refuse to honor the clause, Congress would have the power to enforce compliance.[13]

The adoption of Madison's two changes ended the legislative debates of the clause. It was later reported out by the Committee on Detail with only minor changes, and it was ratified with the rest of the Constitution.

In the end, however, the clause did not go as far as some might have wished. It did not require the second state to execute directly a judgment entered by a court of another state. Instead, it established an ironclad rule of preclusion—the matters covered in the first litigation could not be litigated again elsewhere. The judgment creditor, however, still had to file a separate action in the second state to enforce the judgment entered in the first. The important thing, however, was that at last there was a constitutional mandate that could lead to the establishment of a preclusive method of enforcement. No more could debtors roam the states seeking to avoid their fate.

Madison summed up the impact of the Full Faith and Credit Clause in Federalist number 42:

> The power of prescribing by general laws the manner in which the public acts, records and judicial proceedings of each State shall be proved, and the effect they shall have in other States, is an evident and valuable improvement on the clause relating to this subject in the articles of confederation. The meaning of the later is extremely indeterminate; and can be of little importance under any interpretation which it will bear. The power here established, may be rendered a very convenient instrument of justice, and be particularly beneficial on the borders of contiguous States, where the effects liable to justice, may be . . . translated in any stage of the process, within a foreign jurisdiction.[14]

What do we learn from all of this? First, the attestation problem, although a real one, could be easily solved—by delegating the problem, one that needed only a technical fix, to Congress. Second, full faith and credit to the laws of other states (the choice of law problem) surfaced only briefly and quietly disappeared from the scene. Third, judgments from other states were to be given preclusive effect.

We also can infer the following. First, and most important, the delegates believed that the new nation could trust the quality of the justice dispensed by the courts in each state. By giving the judgments of each state preclusive effect, the Framers must have expected that all state judicial proceedings would be reasonably fair. Second, the absence of *any* discussion about how Congress would exercise its implementing powers suggests that the delegates believed they were only giving Congress incremental power to deal with details and legislate at the edges, rather than lawmaking power (that is, to change materially the meaning of full faith and credit).

THE EARLY JUDICIAL HISTORY OF THE CLAUSE

During the half century or so following the ratification of the Constitution, the Full Faith and Credit Clause had a history almost as sparse as its history during the 1787 Convention. Although the first Congress passed an implementing statute in 1790, and modified it slightly in 1804, there was no other full faith and credit legislation until 1948. There were a number of state and lower federal court decisions in that early period, but the Supreme Court did not render its first decision under the clause until 1813, and rendered few others in the ensuing decades. Sparse as this history is, it does confirm the central role that the Framers had intended the Full Faith and Credit Clause to play.

The Implementing Statute

In 1790, in the second session of the First Congress (a group containing a sizable number of former delegates to the Constitutional Convention), Congress passed legislation implementing the Full Faith and Credit Clause. That statute read:

> That the acts of the Legislatures of the several States shall be authenticated by having the seal of their respective States affixed thereto; that the records and judicial proceedings of the courts of any State shall be proved or admitted in any other court within the United States by attestation of the clerk, and the seal of the court annexed, if there be a seal, together with a certificate of the judge, chief justice, or presiding magistrate, as the case may be, that the attestation is in due form. And the said records and judicial proceedings shall have such faith and credit given to them in every court of the United States, as they have by law or usage in the courts of the State from whence the said records are, or shall be taken.[15]

Virtually no legislative history of that statue survives but it is clearly not a radical document.[16] Apart from restating the Constitutional provision, the first part of the 1790 law merely prescribes the method (by using the ever popular seal) of authenticating not only a judicial judgment, but also a legislative enactment, as well as other state records. Of more practical importance, the 1790 law seems to make clear the most fundamental point—it requires that judgments from other states shall be given preclusive effect. The statutory language on that point is difficult to read in any other way: "said records and judicial proceedings shall have such faith and credit given to them in every court of the United States, as they have by law or usage in the courts of the State from whence the said records are or shall be taken." We shall see shortly, however, that some courts had trouble realizing the import of that language.

In 1803, a committee was appointed by Congress to study whether any changes should be made in the 1790 legislation. A bill, adopted in 1804, made two minor changes: broadening slightly the coverage of the earlier authentication provision, and extending its coverage to territories of the United States.[17] The law did not address the question of whether the prima facie or conclusive readings of the Full Faith and Credit Clause should be adopted, even though, by then, that question had been asked in the lower courts.

Although the implementing legislation did not clear up all problems that have arisen in the more than two centuries since its adoption, perhaps it was wise, as

David Currie has observed, "not to attempt to resolve all the problems of interstate choice of law while it was wrestling with the difficulties of setting up the Government."[18] In any event, the Supreme Court has had little difficulty over the years in making reasonable and sensible pronouncements concerning the clause. So perhaps it was just as well that Congress never attempted to answer all full faith and credit questions.

The Early Decisional Law

It seems fairly clear that the language of the full faith and credit implementing statute adopts the preclusive rather than prima facie interpretation of the effect to be given judgments issued by the courts of other states. (Remember that the legislative history of those statutes has been lost.) Nevertheless, in the first quarter century following its adoption, there was considerable controversy in the courts over that proposition. Famous judges could be found on both sides of the divide. Here are two examples.

First, in Armstrong v. Carson (1794)[19], Justice James Wilson (a member of the Constitutional Convention who had been active in the debate over the Full Faith and Credit Clause there and who was also a great legal scholar and judge), sitting on Circuit (that is, as a lower court judge), opined that an action on a New Jersey judgment, unenforceable in that state, could not be enforced in Pennsylvania, because the 1790 act made clear that the judgment should have the same effect in both states. His explanation was quite clear:

> [W]hatever doubts there might be on the words of the Constitution, the act of Congress effectually removes them; declaring in direct terms that the record shall have the same effect in this Court as in the Court from which it was taken.[20]

Wilson, in short, opted for the preclusive interpretation.

On the other hand, a divided (and distinguished) Supreme Court of New York reached the opposite result in Hitchcock v. Aicken (1802).[21] Chancellor Kent (one of the greatest figures in American legal history), a member of the majority, took the view that the Full Faith and Credit Clause adopted the prima facie interpretation, while the two dissenters, Justices Brockholst Livingston and Smith Thompson (both of whom were later to serve on the Supreme Court) adopted the preclusive approach.

We have mentioned only two of a number of early cases in which courts disagreed as to whether to adopt the prima facie or preclusive readings of Full Faith and Credit. The cases include different results reached by Supreme Court justices riding circuit (that is, as trial judges). It was time for the whole Court to clarify the law.

The Supreme Court's Early Decisions

Mills v. Duryee (1813)[22] was the first full faith and credit case to reach the Supreme Court. It was argued that full faith and credit to judgments demanded only that the decision in the first tribunal be admitted as evidence in the second; and further, that the second tribunal could decide whether to enforce the earlier judgment—that is, what "effect" should be given that judgment.

The Court, speaking through Justice Joseph Story, rejected that view emphatically. Although almost bereft of reasoning, Story's opinion relied on the implementing legislation:

> Were the construction contended for . . . to prevail . . . this clause in the constitution would be utterly unimportant and illusory. The common law would give judgments precisely the same effect. It is manifest, however, that the constitution contemplated a power in congress to give effect to such judgments. And we can perceive no rational interpretation of the act of [1790] unless it declares a judgment conclusive.[23]

The Full Faith and Credit Clause, in other words, had rejected the common-law or prima facie approach to enforcement; any other reading would render it "utterly unimportant and illusory." The importance of the emphatic rejection in *Mills* of the prima facie interpretation of the full faith and credit mandate is heightened by the fact that it was issued over a dissent, a rare event in those days, by Justice William Johnson. The rejection of Justice Johnson's closely reasoned argument on behalf of the prima facie interpretation of the mandate demonstrated that the Court was firmly committed to a more expansive reading of its meaning.

Five years later, in Hampton v. McConnel (1818),[24] the Court, in a very brief opinion by Chief Justice Marshall, reiterated the preclusive effect in *Mills*:

> The doctrine there held [that is, in *Mills*] was that the judgment of a state court should have the same credit, validity and effect, in every other court of the United states, which it had in the state where it was pronounced, and that whatever pleas would be good to a suit thereon in such state, and none others, could be pleaded in any other court in the United States.[25]

Thus, the Court adopted what we later refer to as the "Iron Law of Full Faith and Credit Clause" (see Chapter 4): A judgment must be given as much preclusive effect in the enforcing state as it would be given in the state in which it was rendered.

Finally, in M'Elmoyle v. Cohen (1839),[26] the Court, in an opinion by Justice Wayne, made clear that it stood by its earlier rulings. The unanimous opinion began with a historical analysis and concluded with a ringing affirmation of the preclusive version of the Full Faith and Credit Clause:

> When our revolution began . . . it was seen by the wise men of that day, that the powers necessary to be given by the confederacy, and the rights to be given to the citizens of each state . . . would produce such intimate relations between the states and persons that the former would no longer be foreign to each other in the sense that they had been, as dependent provinces.[27]

These early cases show that the Court had little difficulty in giving the law of full faith and credit a preclusive reading. Although the Court in both *Mills* and

M'Elmoyle refer to the 1790 statute, neither seems to make much of that reference; the act was thought to be declaratory of the clause itself, and merely executed the clause and provided the method for its enforcement. Finally, none of the early case law showed any notion that the provisions mentioning "public acts" in either the clause or the implementing statute in any way were meant to effect choice of law questions. That idea did not surface until the end of the nineteenth century, had a few moments in the sun in the early part of the twentieth century, and lingers on in very abbreviated form today, albeit intermingled with the Due Process Clause.[28] (See our discussion of this problem in Chapter 3.) Those who drafted the clause and those who enforced it were concerned with only two issues: how to authenticate foreign records and whether judgments should be given prima facie or preclusive effect.

FULL FAITH AND CREDIT IN THE CONTEXT OF ARTICLE IV

One of the key objectives of most of the Framers was to forge a unified system of government. There was a national need for certainty and uniformity in the results of the states' legal systems. The primary purpose behind the several provisions of Article IV was to extend social and economic integration and to provide a structure that would unify the states in the administration of justice. The Full Faith and Credit Clause has helped achieve those ends, admirably carrying out the wishes of those who drafted it.

From early in the nineteenth century, when the first full faith and credit cases were decided, to the present day, the Supreme Court has been adamant in reading the clause in such a way as to minimize the friction inherent in multistate problems of the enforcement of laws and judgments. To that end, the court has insisted that each state must trust the integrity of the activities of other states. This is not an altogether easy task to perform and the Court has had to back and fill from time to time but, since the Civil War, at least, the areas covered by the Full Faith and Credit Clause have not threatened seriously the tranquility of American life.

NOTES

1. Kurt H. Nadelman, *Full Faith and Credit to Judgments and Public Acts: A Historical—Analytical Reappraisal*, 56 Michigan L. Rev. 33 (1957).
2. Walker v. Witter, 99 Eng. Rep 1 (K.B. 1778).
3. The 1774 Massachusetts law is discussed in Nadelman at 39–41.
4. Articles of Confederation art. IV.
5. 3 Max Farrand, The Records of the Federal Convention of 1787 188 (1911). Farrand, of course, contains the full record of the convention. Nadelman at 87-88 provides a useful set of extracts from Farrand concerning the full faith and credit debates.
6. In some states, the legislature could discharge insolvent debtors, in other states discharge was the result of a judicial proceeding. The same diversity in practice was true of divorce. Nadelman at 54–56 has a good discussion of the problem.

7. Farrand, *supra* note 5, at 447.

8. *Id.* at 447. The question of execution of a foreign judgment—that is, should it be automatic and in the same way that it would be executed in the rendering state is discussed in Part V. A somewhat definitive resolution by the Supreme Court had to wait until the 1998 decision in Baker and Thomas v. General Motors Corp., 522 U.S. 222 (1998), also discussed in Part V.

9. *Id.*

10. Ralph U. Whitten, *The Original Understanding of the Full Faith and Credit Clause and DOMA*, 32 Creighton L. Rev. 255, 290 (1998).

11. Farrand, *supra* note 5, at 485.

12. *Id.*

13. The word *faith*, defined as confidence or trust, apparently had the same meaning to the Framers as the word *credit*. As such, there appears to be a redundancy as the two words convey the same idea. It is possible that the Framers retained the phrase of *full faith and credit* because it had been used in the Articles of Confederation. Deleting a word from the clause may have implied a constitutional prescription weaker than the corresponding clause of the Articles of Confederation. That was certainly not the message the Framers wished to convey.

14. The Federalist No. 42 (James Madison) (1961 ed.) 287.

15. 2 *Statistics at Large of USA* 298 (1804).

16. It has been suggested that the legislative records were lost when the British burned Washington in 1814. Nadelman, *supra* note 1, at 60, n. 124.

17. 2 *Statistics at Large of USA* 298 (1804).

18. David P. Currie, The Constitution in Congress: The Federalist Period, (Chicago: The University of Chicago Press, 1997) 102.

19. Armstrong v. Carson, 1 F. 543 (C.C. Pa. 1794).

20. *Id.*

21. Hitchcock v. Aicken, 1 Cai. R. 460 (N.Y. 1804).

22. Mills v. Duryee, 11 U.S. 481 (1813).

23. *Id.*

24. Hampton v. McConnel, 16 U.S. 234 (1818).

25. *Id.*

26. M'Elmoyle v. Cohen, 38 U.S. 312 (1839).

27. *Id.* at 325.

28. The Whitten article contains the best discussion of the history of the public acts provision. Nadelman, *supra* note 1, at 79 reports that future Chief Justice John Marshall, speaking before the Virginia Ratifying Convention, scoffed at the notion that the Full Faith and Credit Clause in any way carried choice of law possibilities.

2

"Public Records": The Clause and the Statute

The Full Faith and Credit Clause applies not only to judicial proceedings and to public acts, the areas where it has had the greatest impact, but also to public "Records."[1] However, the meaning of the term full faith and credit shifts as the focus changes from *judicial proceedings* and *acts* to *records*. To give full faith and credit to another state's judicial proceedings is to give them preclusive effect according to the law of the rendering state.[2] Full faith and credit to the positive law of another state requires, in very narrow circumstances, the application of that other state's law rather than the forum's own law.[3] By contrast, to give full faith and credit to "records" means simply to admit them routinely into evidence in the courts of the forum.

To understand the significance of the application of the clause to records, it is useful to consider the status of foreign records at common law. According to the common-law approach, the laws and records of foreign sovereigns were treated as questions of fact to be decided by the trier of fact (usually the jury) just as were other factual questions. Common-law courts, in other words, did not take judicial notice of the law or records of foreign sovereigns.

Given the common-law position, it is easy to understand why the Framers included a provision for records in the Full Faith and Credit Clause. Without it the authentication of sister-state records would have been a particular nightmare. Would an official from say, Rhode Island, have to be brought into a court in Massachusetts to authenticate a judgment entered by a court in the former state? Important as the clause is for authentication purposes, its even more vital purpose was to keep the jury away from the authenticity question. Interstate friction of a high order would be inevitable under the common-law approach, where a jury's caprice could nullify a record of judgment or a statute from another state. The resulting uncertainty could have been disastrous for the young nation, which needed to protect settled expectations in order to foster economic growth.

The Full Faith and Credit Clause *itself* works no change in the common law; it does not require the courts of one American state to give judicial notice to the laws and records of another state. Rather, it permits the courts of the second or enforcing state (F-2) to insist on traditional evidentiary proof of the law and records of the first or rendering state (F-1).[4]

The full faith and credit *statute*, however, does simplify and make routine the process of proving the law and records of F-1 in the courts of F-2. (The statutory language does not include reference to the records of federal courts, but the courts have read the statute to apply to proof of those records as well.) Adopted by the first Congress in 1790 and last reenacted in 1948, the statute provides that sister-state records "shall be proved . . . by the attestation of the clerk . . . together with a certificate of a judge of the court that the said attestation is in proper form." Once authenticated, the statute decrees that state court records "shall have the same full faith and credit in every court within the United States . . . as they have by law or usage in the courts . . . from which they are taken."[5]

As a result of the statute, the procedure for proving the records of the F-1 court in the courts of F-2 is simple enough; the clerk of the rendering court must attest to the genuineness of the record, and then a judge of that court must certify that the attestation is in proper form. By and large, the courts have applied the procedure faithfully, and some have not even insisted on total technical compliance. Proof has been permitted by the production of a photocopy of the original record but seldom by oral testimony. Other than extending the reach of the recognition directive to cover federal court records, the courts have read the statute in accord with its plain meaning as applying only to records from American courts, and not as applying to the records of courts from another nation, or to the records of administrative bodies.

While the courts and commentators have lavished attention on the effect of the clause and the statute on public acts and judicial proceedings, they have almost ignored their application to records. The case law is sparse and old, and the commentary nonexistent. Thus, there is little more to say about the application of the Full Faith and Credit Clause and its implementing statute to judicial records. In a way, the very dearth of material on these questions reveals how well the system works in practice: If the system did not work well, we would expect to see many, many cases. Interstate enforcement of both statutes and judgments is, after all, a common problem.

This absence of controversy also reveals important trends in the development of the state and federal law of civil procedure and evidence. The Full Faith and Credit Clause and the implementing statute are pieces of national law that compel state and federal courts to admit into evidence any record that meets the statutory criteria. Thus, cases calling for their application will arise only when the evidence and procedure rules governing state and federal courts are less favorable to the proof of official records than the requirements of the Full Faith and Credit Clause and statute. In fact, however, today the opposite is the case; every state and federal court now operates under procedural rules that are even more favorable to the admission of official records than is the law of full faith and credit. A brief description of the most important of these provisions follows.

THE FEDERAL RULES OF CIVIL AND CRIMINAL PROCEDURE

Records

Rule 44 (a) (1) of the Federal Rules of Civil Procedure and Rule 27 of the Federal Rules of Criminal Procedure (which also incorporates the Civil Rules by reference) permit easy and efficient proof of official records of sister states. Departing from prior law, they allow authentication of such records by an official publication of the record. An alternative approved by the rules is an attestation and certification procedure similar to the one dictated by § 1738. Presumably, litigants usually will choose the official publication method. The availability of the two methods in federal courts and in the many states that have rules modeled on the federal rules, insures that there seldom will be a need to force admission by resort to the external mandate of § 1738. Note that the rules do not mean that an appropriately authenticated sister-state record necessarily will be admissible; such records might be excluded on relevance, hearsay, or privilege grounds. The rules' effect is only to satisfy the authentication requirement.

Another section of Rule 44 permits proof of the official records of *foreign nations* by official publication or by a variation of the attestation and certification procedure provided by § 1738. Again, the Rules of Criminal Procedure incorporate these provisions by reference.

Laws

Until fairly recently, proof of sister-state and foreign-nation *law* in state and federal courts was treated as a question of fact, a characterization that had many unfortunate consequences. Thus, traditionally foreign law had to be raised in the pleadings, was proved according to the formal rules of evidence (usually by expert witnesses), was argued to the jury, and was not subject to meaningful appellate review.[6]

Fortunately, now both Federal Civil Rule 44.1 and Federal Criminal Rule 26.1 have reversed that practice in the federal courts. According to those rules, parties need not plead foreign law, but must notify other litigants of their intent to rely on it in their pleadings or some less formal type of written notice. The rules permit proof of foreign law by "any relevant material or source"[7] whether offered by a party or discovered by the court during its own research. Typically, parties offer and the court investigates foreign primary and secondary sources; expert testimony on the content of foreign law can be offered as well. Although the rules do not address the issue explicitly, courts have held that the decision on the content of the foreign law is for the judge, not the jury; and the rules explicitly treat the issue as a question of law, thus providing for the same level of appellate review as would be appropriate for a decision on an issue of domestic law.

In the state systems, the trend is also toward the modern method for proving sister state and foreign nation law. About half of the states have adopted the Uniform Judicial Notice of Foreign Law Act,[8] which mandates judicial notice of the law of sister states but not foreign nations. Some states have extended the reform to foreign-nation law as well. A few have done so by modifying the provisions of the Uniform Act. In others the same result is achieved by the adoption of the Uniform Interstate and International Procedure Act,[9] whose provisions closely resemble those of the federal rules.

MODERN EVIDENCE CODES

Modern evidence codes provide special authentication, hearsay, and best evidence rules that simplify the proof of official records. The following subsections treat each of these issues:

Authentication

In order to authenticate a document, the proponent must show that the document is genuine, that is, that the document is what the proponent claims that it is. Otherwise the document is irrelevant, and thus inadmissible. The standard of proof for authentication is not very strict; the authenticating evidence, under the federal evidentiary rules, must be "sufficient to support a finding."[10] That means that the judge does not have to believe that the document is genuine, but only that a reasonable juror could believe it to be so. The judge's preliminary finding of authenticity serves only to allow the document to be admitted into evidence and does not bind the fact finder, which must make its own determination of genuineness in reaching its ultimate verdict.

The background against which the federal authentication rules operate is the common law's presumption of inauthenticity for records. Justified or not, the common-law rule was that a signature, letterhead, or recitation of authorship on the face of a document was not sufficient proof of authenticity to admit the document into evidence. In the typical case, the proponent of the document's authenticity would need to offer the testimony of a witness who executed the document, saw it being executed, or recognized the signature of the purported author.

When the offered document is an official record, however, the Federal Rules of Evidence and other modern evidence codes go far toward reversing the common law presumption of inauthenticity. Rule 901 (b) (7) of those Rules permits the authentication of a public record or report by evidence that the document was found in the public office where such items are kept. Rule 902 goes farther and makes several classes of public documents self-authenticating, thus reversing the common-law presumption. These include, among others: (1) documents bearing the seal of the United States or of any state or territory, or of an officer or employee of those governmental bodies; (2) documents issued by foreign governments accompanied by a final certification of genuineness made by appropriate American or foreign diplomatic officials; (3) books, pamphlets, or other publications purported to be issued by public authorities.

Very often, even these liberalized authentication devices are unnecessary because the parties have used the liberal discovery devices of the civil rules (e.g., interrogatories, requests for admissions, depositions), or stipulations in criminal cases to obtain their opponents' admissions of the authenticity of documents that they plan to offer into evidence.

The Original Document Rule

Because documents are exceedingly rich in detail, and often crucial to the parties' rights and duties under the substantive law, the common law insisted on extremely accurate proof of their authenticity and accuracy. Thus, under the common law "best evidence rule" one who wished to prove the content of a document had to offer the original of the document unless it was unavailable for some reason other than the serious fault of the proponent.[11] The Federal Rules of Evidence have liberalized the common law considerably. Providing for the routine admissibility of copies produced by modern superaccurate technologies (photocopies, computer printout), Rule 1003 is the most important generally applicable innovation in the rules. Also important, especially in this discussion, is Rule 1005, which admits copies of public records, which are certified correct by the custodian of the record or testified to be correct by a witness who has compared the copy with the original.

The Hearsay Rule

The usual definition of hearsay evidence is that it is an out of court statement offered to prove the truth of the matter asserted in the statement. Subject to a long list of exceptions, the common law generally excluded hearsay evidence. The reason for the exclusion was the inability of the opponent of the evidence to place the out of court witness (known as the "declarant") under oath, cross-examine her, and display her demeanor to the fact finder. Without these safeguards, the fact finder (jury or judge) could not evaluate the declarant's perception, memory, sincerity, and ability to communicate.

When a document is offered into evidence for the truth of the matters asserted in it, the document is considered to be hearsay because it is the out of court statement of its author. Without appropriate exceptions, the result would be the exclusion from evidence of the statements in many sister-state records. The document might be admissible to show its existence or its legal effect, but statements of fact contained in it would be hearsay and thus inadmissible.

The response of the Federal Rules of Evidence to the harsh rule of the common law is a series of liberal exceptions to the hearsay rule for a number of types of government records. Probably the most important is Rule 803 (8), which admits records, reports, statements, and data compilations from public offices or agencies, which set forth the agency's or office's activities, matters observed by public officials, and factual findings resulting from investigations conducted by public agencies or officials. Also prominent is Rule 803 (9), which provides an exception for records or data compilations of births, deaths, marriages, and the like, if the report was made to a public official pursuant to legal requirement. Another provision relevant to recidivist statutes, felony disqualifications, and sentencing is Rule 803 (22), which provides an exception for judgments of criminal convictions.

The upshot of the liberal admissibility and judicial notice provisions of modern civil, criminal, and evidence rules is that the law of the recognizing state is usually more hospitable to sister-state records than is required by the "records" provisions of the Full Faith and Credit Clause and statute. Accordingly these two provisions are seldom litigated, and thus they are seldom interpreted by the courts or considered by the scholars.

NOTES

1. The *Constitution of the United States*, art. IV, § 1 provides, "Full Faith and Credit shall be given in each State to the public Acts, *Records*, and judicial Proceedings of every other State." (Emphasis added.)

2. *See* Parts IV and V, *supra*.

3. *See* Part III, *supra*.

4. This is the traditional notation used in this area; "F-1" refers to the first court to issue a judgment in the case, and "F-2" refers to the second court to do so.

5. 28 U.S.C. § 1738 (1948).

6. *See* 3 William M. Richman and William L. Reynolds, *Understanding Conflict of Laws* 175–76 (2002).

7. Federal Rules of Civil Procedure, Rule 44.1; Federal Rules of Criminal Procedure, Rule 26.1.

8. 9A Uniform Laws Annotated 553 (1965).

9. 13 Uniform Laws Annotated 355 (1986).

10. Federal Rules of Evidence 901(a).

11. *See* Federal Rules of Evidence 1004 for a modern treatment of excuses for non-production of the original writing.

3

"Public Acts"

INTRODUCTION

The first part of the Full Faith and Credit Clause mandates that full faith and credit be given to the "public acts" of other states. Questions concerning this part of the clause primarily arise in choice of law cases. The basic problem in choice of law is this: When the forum applies its own law to a multistate problem, has it denied full faith and credit to the laws of the other state; that is, has it denied full faith and credit to one of the other state's "public acts"? The answer to this question, of course, is an important one in modern America. Our vibrant economy and mobile society create a myriad of legal problems every day where it would be plausible to have the laws of two or more states apply. Chapter 3 examines how the Full Faith and Credit Clause has been applied in this area. That is, the question of how courts react when asked to enforce another state's law is the subject of this section.

The public acts section has had a long and checkered history. At times, the Supreme Court has come very close to using this provision to make choice of law decision making subject to serious constitutional restrictions. Now, however, it is clear that the Full Faith and Credit Clause does not compel "a state to substitute the statutes of other states for its own statutes dealing with a subject matter concerning which it is competent to legislate" Sun Oil Co. v. Wortman (1988).[1] Instead, the Supreme Court reads the public acts portion of the Full Faith and Credit Clause together with the Due Process Clause and derives from both a single and minimal constitutional limitation on the forum state's authority to apply its own law to a dispute in its courts. In short, the states have been left to deal with interstate comity problems largely on their own.

THEORETICAL ANALYSIS: FULL FAITH AND CREDIT AND CHOICE OF LAW

What then is the content of that modest federal constitutional limit on state courts' choice of law decision-making autonomy? A useful prelude of any investigation of this question requires a summary discussion of the way courts make the choice of law decisions that the constitution might limit. Today, five methodologies account for almost all choice of law decisions made by American courts: the traditional system (in other words: the methodology reflected in the Restatement (First) of Conflict of Laws; the center of gravity theory; interest analysis (including its many variants); the better law theory; and the Restatement (Second) of Conflict of Laws).

The Traditional System

The traditional system, eventually codified in the Restatement (First) of Conflict of Laws (adopted in 1934), dominated American choice of law thinking until relatively late in the twentieth century, and it is still used in about 20 percent of the states.[2] The traditional system was based on the vested rights theory, the idea that an event occurring in a foreign state created a right that "vested" at the occurrence of the event. For example, when a contract was entered into (that is, signed or otherwise agreed upon) in Kansas, the obligations of the contracting parties (their rights and duties) "vested" according to Kansas law. When the plaintiff brought suit, the forum court simply enforced the right that already had vested elsewhere in the state where the contract had been signed (in the example, Kansas). The practical result of the vested rights theory is a choice of law system composed of a few broad, single contact, jurisdiction selecting choice of law rules. The rules of the traditional system of the First Restatement are few and broad in that they cover large areas of the law; thus, there is one rule for torts, one for contracts, one for procedural issues, and one each for movable (personal) and immovable (real) property. The rules are "jurisdiction selecting,"[3] which means that they select the applicable law by first selecting a place or jurisdiction, and then applying that place's substantive law rule. In other words, the rules are, by and large, content blind in that their choice is not interested, at least in theory, in the substantive policies involved in the problem. Thus, the substance of the rule and its motivating policy are not relevant in the selection process. Finally, the rules are single contact rules; that is, they select the applicable law by locating a single contact or event in a state, and then apply that state's law to all substantive issues. Thus, the rule for torts was the law of the place where the injury occurred; the rule for contracts, the law of the place of making of the contract; the rule for procedure, the law of the forum; and the rule for real property, the law of the situs of the property.

The virtues claimed for the traditional system are clear: simplicity, predictability, and forum neutrality, that is, the same result will be reached regardless of where the plaintiff brings suit. Unfortunately, the system sometimes produces unhappy results, such as the choice of a substantive law rule that violates the parties' expectations or is harsh or anachronistic, or that represents the policy of a state that has no real interest in the parties or in the dispute. Although not satisfied with these results, the traditionalist courts have been unwilling to break faith with their unwieldy system and articulate the reasons why the practical choice is unsatisfactory; instead, courts using the vested rights theory have adopted "escape devices"—conceptual strategies that are consistent with the traditional system but that nevertheless permit a different choice of law. These escape devices, it must be emphasized, do not involve policy choices, at least on the face of things; rather, they permit the court to manipulate among supposedly readily apparent choices in order to reach a desired result.

One escape device is recharacterization of the problem: This device works marvelously well because each First Restatement rule applies to a single category of cases. Thus, if the situs rule used in a case involving real property dictates a harsh result, the court can recharacterize the land transaction as a contract problem and apply the more congenial law of the place of making of the contract. Similarly, if the contract place of making rule frustrates the expectations of the parties, the court can recharacterize the issue as one of procedure and apply instead the law of the forum. Precedent and intellectual honesty may suffer, but the recharacterization does work to change the choice without abandoning the theory.

Another escape device is *renvoi*—reading the forum's choice of law rule to refer the dispute not to the internal law of the foreign state (in other words, to its substantive law), but to the "whole" law of the other state, a reference which includes the foreign state's rules for choice of law. Thus, if the forum's law of the place of making rule selects the law of state X, and that law makes a widow a pauper, the court can read the forum's choice of law rule to refer instead to the whole law of X, including its choice of law rule, which refers the problem back to the more humane law of the forum.

A final and more candid escape device is "public policy." Its rigid rules notwithstanding, the First Restatement does not compel the choice of a law that egregiously violates the important public policy of the forum. Thus, if the choice of law rule of the forum, a free state, referred to the personal property law of a slave state, the forum could refuse to apply the law selected by the system and apply its own instead.[4] This escape device may look quite open ended; but, in theory, at least, there is a tight limit on the judge's discretion in that the foreign law must be "vicious, wicked or immoral, and shocking to the prevailing moral sense."[5] Had it been so limited, the public policy device would function as a crucial escape valve, but, in practice, First Restatement courts used it often to escape the choice of substantive law rules that seem relatively benign, such as rules providing for spousal tort immunity or limitation of wrongful death damages.

Although the escape devices add some needed flexibility to the traditional system, they rob the traditional system of its supposed virtues—simplicity, predictability, and forum neutrality. It is easy to see how that would happen. Because the courts that use escape devices do not articulate the real reasons for their decisions (remember: the vested rights theory is not based on policy analysis), a lawyer reading the written opinions will not be able to predict when a court will apply the rule right out of the box, and when instead it will apply one of the escape devices. Worst of all, perhaps, the court will not think through the problem carefully because the simplicity of the system has lulled it into mechanical categorization. Thus, a court that does not like the result reached by treating an employee's job-related injury as a "contract" problem, can treat the issue as one sounding in tort (e.g., injury caused by the negligence of another employee). The problem is that the availability of a simple recharacterization that achieves the desired results lets the court off the hook too easily. It is not forced to inquire into the reasons why the employee should or should not recover. The focus, in other words, is not on legislative purpose, but on intuitive decision making. These problems, unfortunately, were all too common with courts applying traditional choice of law analysis.

The Center of Gravity Theory

The first step toward modern choice of law theory, the center of gravity or grouping of contacts theory, continues in use today in a few states. Some courts apply it self-consciously, while others apply it in practice even though they purport to use some other methodology (usually that of the Second Conflicts Restatement). The method requires the court to enumerate the contacts that the case has with each state, and then to apply the law of the state whose connection with the parties and the dispute is greater. The theory is similar to that of the First Restatement in that it is "jurisdiction selecting"; it chooses the applicable law by first choosing a place without regard to the content of that state's law or, indeed, the content of any other competing state's law. It is an advance, however, over the First Conflicts Restatement in that the center of gravity theory encourages courts to consider all the contacts the case has with the involved states in lieu of fixating on just one.

In practice, however, the center of gravity theory has proved to be subject to easy manipulation because it provides no mechanism for determining what should count as a contact, and how much each contact should count. The latter point is critical, for it means that there is no method in the theory to prevent a court from placing its thumb on the scale by manufacturing additional contacts for the state whose law it favors. For instance, in a contract case, the place of making, the place of performance, and the domiciles of the parties ordinarily would be significant contacts, but nothing prohibits the court from tilting the balance by considering additional, marginally relevant contacts such as the domicile of the parties' attorneys, the place where the promisor would secure the income needed to perform the contract, or the place where the parties first met.

Interest Analysis

The first truly modern choice of law theory, interest analysis is the dominant choice of law methodology in a few states, but its impact has been much greater because of its influential role in the drafting of the Second Conflicts Restatement.

Interest analysis is generally credited to the scholarship of Professor Brainerd Currie who wrote in the late 1950s and early 1960s. Its importance lies in the fact that it forces the court to go beyond its "jurisdiction selecting" predecessors by considering the content (or purpose) of the competing states' internal laws. The method, like the center of gravity approach, requires the court to enumerate the contacts that the dispute has with each state, but then it makes a radical departure. Recognizing that law is a purposive endeavor, interest analysis asks the court to consider the policies that motivate each state's internal law, and then determine the relationship of those policies to the contacts that each state has with the parties and the dispute. The contact/policy relationship is what determines the court's choice.[6]

There are three possible permutations in interest analysis: false conflicts, true conflicts, and the "unprovided for" case. In the false conflict case, the policies and contacts are arranged so that only one state's policy can be advanced by the application of its law. Suppose for instance an automobile owner/driver (defendant) and his guest/passenger (plaintiff) are both domiciled in state X, which has no limit upon tort damages for pain and suffering. They are involved in a one-car accident that occurs in state Y, a state that has a "tort reform" statute that limits recovery for pain and suffering to $100,000. The First Conflicts Restatement would choose to apply the law of Y as the place of injury, and the center of gravity test can be manipulated to produce either result. But interest analysis requires more data; its result depends in part on the reasons why Y has and X does not have a damage limitation. Suppose the court determines that X retains the traditional rule in order to compensate victims fully, and that Y's rule is designed to reduce insurance premiums. Because the plaintiff is domiciled in X, application of X's law will advance its policy goal (compensation); by contrast, application's of Y's law will not advance its policy goal because the insurance policy was not written there. Thus the policy-contact relationship is such that Y's policy would not be advanced by the application of its law, while X's would be. Quite sensibly, in this false conflict case, interest analysis chooses the law of X, the only interested state.

In a true conflict case, each state's policy would be advanced by the application of its law. Suppose in the example just cited, that the defendant is domiciled in state Y. Application of the law of X still would advance X's full compensation policy, but now, application of the law of Y would also advance its premium reducing policy. The case is a true conflict, and there is no obvious solution. Some proponents of interest analysis suggest applying the law of the forum;[7] others resort to the place of injury rule;[8] and still others recommend application of the law of the state whose policy would be more impaired if the other state's law were applied.[9]

In the final permutation of interest analysis, usually referred to as the "unprovided for case," neither state's policy would be advanced by the application of its law. Suppose the same hypothetical, but this time assume that the defendant is domiciled in state X, and that the plaintiff is domiciled in state Y. The policy goal of state X will not be advanced by the application of X law; no X resident will receive more complete compensation. Nor will the policy goal of state Y be advanced by using its law because protecting an X resident from ruinous damages will not affect insurance premiums in state Y. Once again there is no obvious solution.[10]

The Better Law Option

Professor Robert Leflar advocated using five "choice-influencing considerations" to guide choice of law of decision making: (1) predictability of result, (2) maintenance of interstate and international order, (3) simplification of the judicial task, (4) advancement of the forum's governmental interest, and (5) application of the better rule of law.[11] Courts using the system often find the first four considerations inconclusive, and so the better rule of law often dictates the result. This theory wears its virtue and its vice on its sleeve. It is simple and flexible and needs no manipulation to produce felicitous results, but it fails to guide the court significantly, requiring it instead to "do the right thing." Another obvious objection is its subjectivity; a member of the insurance defense bar, and a plaintiff's personal injury lawyer, for example, are unlikely to agree upon the "better rule of law" in a products liability case. For that matter, in our polarized times, a garden-variety Democrat is unlikely to agree with a neoconservative Republican very often. Another worry is that the better rule of law system is simply a disguised version of the "law of the forum" option.

The Second Conflicts Restatement

Components

The Second Conflicts Restatement, although published in 1971, was the product of key decisions made as early as 1956. In that year, its drafters decided by a single vote (13–12) to junk the vested right approach to choice of law and adopt a functional system based on the notion that law should seek to serve substantive ends. Thus, the Second Conflicts Restatement in a sense led rather than followed the revolution. The great prestige of the American Law Institute, of course, helped the revolution to succeed. On the other hand, the primary drafting of the Second Restatement was done before there was much guidance in the form of commentary and case law. As a result, it does have rough edges, and they do show. Nevertheless, the Restatement (Second) of Conflict of Laws today is followed in about half the states.

The Second Restatement is much more complicated than its rivals, consisting of three separate choice of law strategies. Like the First Restatement of Conflicts, it contains numerous specific sections to regulate particular cases and issues. Most of those rules are jurisdiction selecting presumptions of varying strengths; they range from conclusive presumptions in cases involving real property to merely suggestive ones in many contract and tort situations. Some Second Restatement rules are not jurisdiction selecting, but, rather, substantivist; that is, they select the applicable law by its result rather than its location. Thus, the rule for usury is a validating rule that rejects the usury defense as long as the interest rate is permissible in any state that the contract is connected with. Other rules are party autonomy rules, permitting the parties to consensual transactions to choose for themselves the law that will govern their transaction.

The Second Restatement does not have a rule to govern every type of case or legal issue that could possibly arise, so it needs a mechanism to resolve cases that do not fall within the scope of its particular rules. That mechanism is based on grouping of contacts sections that apply to broad areas of law such as torts or contracts. Each of these supplies a list of contacts that are to be "taken into account" in cases in that general area of law. When a case falls outside the scope of a particular rule, the court looks to the general grouping of contacts section that covers the broad type of case before it.

The final and most important component of the Second Restatement system is found right at the beginning; this is § 6, which enumerates a list of seven choice of law factors for a court to keep in mind when analyzing a choice of law problem: the needs of the interstate and international systems; the relevant policies of the forum; the relevant policies of other interested states and the relative interests of those states in the determination of the particular issue; the protection of justified expectations; the basic policies underlying the particular field of law; certainty, predictability, and uniformity of result; and ease in the determination and application of the law to be applied. These are reminiscent of Professor Leflar's choice influencing considerations, with the notable absence of a "better rule of law" provision. Choosing the applicable law bearing these factors in mind will result in applying the law of the state with "the most significant relationship to the parties and the transaction"[12] in question. Among the most important features of § 6 is that factors two and three clearly require an interest analysis in nearly every case.

Section 6 serves several different functions in the scheme of the Second Restatement. In the general grouping of contacts sections, it functions as a choice of law directive. Thus the grouping of contacts section for torts directs the court to apply "the . . . law of the state which . . . has the most significant relationship to the occurrence and the parties under the principles stated in § 6." The list of contacts that follows is simply to be "taken into account" in applying § 6.[13] In many of the specific sections (jurisdiction selecting, substantivist, and party autonomy) it functions as an escape valve or override. Thus, § 193, dealing with fire and casualty insurance questions, chooses the law of state that the parties understood would be the principal location of the risk, "unless . . . some other state has a more significant relationship under the principles stated in § 6" to the case.

Application: In Theory

The Second Restatement does not indicate explicitly how the courts should apply its several different components to produce a result in a choice of law case.

The drafters probably intended the court first to apply any specific section that specifically treats the issue before the court. Some of these sections provide jurisdiction selecting rules and some use other choice of law strategies. Nevertheless, almost all sections include a reference to § 6, at least as an escape valve. If the case or issue is one of the many not covered by a specific section, the court should refer to the general, area-wide grouping of contacts section relevant to the case. These sections, of course, also include a reference to § 6. Eventually, therefore, whether the court applies a specific section or a general grouping of contacts section, it will be directed to apply the factors of § 6.

Factors two and three of § 6 clearly direct the court to perform an interest analysis. In most cases, if that analysis reveals a false conflict, the court should apply the law of the only interested state. Otherwise, the court should use the remaining factors in § 6 to resolve the true conflict or unprovided for case. The drafters clearly did not intend the court to use the grouping of contacts to perform a crude center of gravity or contact counting analysis. Rather the enumerated contacts are simply to be "taken into account" in applying the factors of § 6.

Application: In Practice

Some courts apply the methodology of the Second Conflicts Restatement as the drafters intended, but many courts that have "adopted" the Second Restatement misapply it completely. Most courts simply ignore the specific territorial presumptions even in cases that fit them well. Thus, a recent empirical study showed that in Second Restatement judicial opinions, citations to the two most popular area-wide, grouping of contacts sections (i.e., § 145 concerning torts and § 188 dealing with contracts) significantly outnumbered the total citations to all the specific sections combined.[14] Further, about half of the judicial opinions purporting to "apply" the Second Restatement misconstrue completely the relationship between § 6 and the grouping of contacts sections. These courts ignore the mandate of § 6 to conduct an interest analysis, that is, to identify the policies behind the competing states' laws and classify the case as a true conflict, false conflict, or unprovided for case. Instead these courts read the grouping of contacts section to sanction a crude contact counting analysis. The factors of § 6 are read to require only a "balancing" of state interests, which often cancel each other out. The result is a system that, although called the Second Restatement, in fact, is more or less indistinguishable from the center of gravity method. (A particularly egregious example is Nationwide Mutual Ins. Co. v. Black (1995).)[15]

Choice of Law Theory and the Constitutional Test

The usefulness of considering choice of law theory in the context of this book is that it provides the necessary background for the Supreme Court's case law on the limits that the Due Process and Full Faith and Credit Clauses place on state court choice of law decisions. Briefly stated, the standard is this: A state court can apply its own state's law to a dispute if the state "[has] a significant contact or significant aggregation of contacts, creating state interests, such that choice of its law is neither arbitrary nor fundamentally unfair."[16]

Viewed through the lens of this test, most of the modern choice of law methodologies are unlikely to produce unconstitutional results. The center of gravity theory, interest analysis, and the Second Restatement, for example, are very unlikely to produce choice of law results that could violate the constitutional standard. Each of these methods focuses to a greater or lesser extent on contacts and state interests, the very considerations that the constitutional test makes paramount. Therefore, if a state court makes a conscientious (i.e., not disingenuous) attempt to apply one of those theories, it is almost guaranteed to produce a constitutional result.

That leaves the First Restatement and the better law theory, each of which has the potential to choose the law of a state with relatively little interest in or contact with the dispute. In the early part of the twentieth century, the *Lochner*-era Supreme Court[17] had come close to holding the vested rights theory and traditional choice of law practice to be constitutionally mandatory. But under its current contacts/state interests jurisprudence, the First Restatement method seems vulnerable to constitutional attack. A First Restatement court, for instance, might apply the forum's more permissive statute of frauds in a case where the prelitigation facts have nothing to do with the forum. Arguably such a result could violate the constitutional test, the forum having no interest in or contact with the dispute, at least before suit is filed. Similarly, a better law court might apply the law of an unconnected, uninterested state if its law were significantly "better" than the law of a state with significant contacts with the dispute.

Ironically, both of these situations have occurred, and the Supreme Court has blessed the questionable state court choice in each one. In Allstate Insurance Co. v. Hague (1981),[18] the Minnesota forum, allegedly using the better law theory of Professor Leflar, applied its own law permitting stacking of insurance benefits, as opposed to Wisconsin's contrary law, even though Minnesota had relatively insignificant contacts with the dispute. To be sure, Minnesota was the place of employment of the insured, but the question of automobile insurance stacking was unrelated to employment. Minnesota was one of fifty states in which the insurer did business, but such a ubiquitous contact has little significance. Finally, Minnesota was the post-accident home of the insurance beneficiary, but heavily weighing such a contact provides a dangerous incentive for forum shopping. Nevertheless, the Supreme Court magnified the importance of those meager contacts and upheld the Minnesota court's choice of its own law.

In Sun Oil Co. v. Wortman,[19] a Kansas court applied its own longer statute of limitations to cases that had nothing else to do with Kansas. Even though the Supreme Court had struck down the Kansas court's application of its own substantive law,[20] it upheld the application of the longer Kansas limitations provision. Justice Antonin Scalia's majority opinion relied heavily on the history of choice of law and of the Full Faith and Credit Clause itself: "The historical record shows conclusively . . . that the society which adopted the Constitution did not regard statutes of limitations as substantive . . . but rather as procedural restrictions fashioned by each jurisdiction for its own courts."[21] In language broader than the case required, the opinion seemed almost to insulate any First Restatement choice of law decision from constitutional attack.

> In sum, long established and still subsisting choice-of-law practices that come to be thought, by modern scholars, unwise, do not thereby become unconstitutional. . . . It is not the function of this Court . . . to make [such] departures from established choice-of-law . . . practice constitutionally mandatory.[22]

The ease with which the Supreme Court manufactures state contacts and interests and its veneration of choice of law traditions make it quite unlikely that it will strike down any decision rendered by a state court that has conscientiously applied any of the dominant choice of law methodologies. The only candidates that remain for Supreme Court disapproval are those where the state court outrageously misapplies one of the theories or fashions a nontheoretical or pragmatically ad hoc solution in an unusual situation.[23]

That leaves the states with a great deal of freedom in making choice of law decisions, a discretion that places a potential strain upon notions of interstate comity. A review of the various choice of law methodologies shows that neither the common law nor the state legislatures have developed efficient, predictable, and just methods of resolving multistate legal disputes. The vested rights approach of the First Restatement, at least in theory, does pretend to be efficient and predictable. But achieving those goals under the vested rights methodology has been illusory, primarily due to the many escape devices, which permit judges to reach results they believe to be just without the need to engage in any rigorous analysis of the problem. The more modern methods of choice of law analysis purport to achieve justice, but at the cost of efficiency and predictability. Although those methods require judicial analysis, they can be easily manipulated in close cases. Certainty in choice of law, in other words, is not the destiny of our judiciary.

And yet, there has been no uproar over a loss of interstate comity. There are several reasons why that is true. First, judges seem to do a pretty good job on choice of law issues, although academics do an awful lot of grumbling about the results. The professors only see the tip of the reported case law iceberg: appellate cases that judges thought interesting and important enough to submit for publication. The far greater number of cases that are filtered out before trial must represent, as a group, the easier cases whose resolution is relatively less controversial. If that is so, the current system works far better than one would realize from reading the work of law professors.

Second, most real choice of law disputes involve either tort law or regulatory statutes. In yet other areas, such as contracts, the law is pretty much the same everywhere (and, if it is not, routinely enforceable choice of law clauses can handle the problem). In other areas, there is general agreement on how to handle interstate problems (apply the *lex sitae* in real property cases), or uniform laws (e.g., the Uniform Probate Code) have eliminated most problems.

This is not to say that choice of law decisions, especially in areas like products liability, do not raise an occasional hackle. But because those decisions are rarely directed at the government of another state, but rather at some private actor located in another state, there has not been a great deal of strain placed upon the principle of interstate comity.

TEXTUAL ANAYLSIS: WHAT IS A "PUBLIC ACT"?

This question of what constitutes a "public act" is slightly more complicated than it might seem initially. The history of the adoption of the Full Faith and Credit Clause and Congressional implementation of the clause are of little help on this topic, so once again the student must rely on case law and judgment. There are many candidates for inclusion in the "public act" category because all sorts of positive law pronouncements by a state—its statutes, common-law decisions, and administrative regulations—might be styled "public acts."

In answering the question, it is important to remember that the purpose of the Full Faith and Credit Clause was to advance interstate comity. Thus, the key issue might seem to be, what enforcement does F-1 give to what might plausibly be styled its own public acts? If F-1 treats its own acts as deserving of special protection, then it would seem that other states should give those public acts the same special protection. And that is how the law in this area has developed.

At a minimum, any statute or state constitutional provision satisfies the constitutional test. Thus, any legislative adoption carrying the force of law is entitled to "full faith and credit"—whatever that term might mean (see Chapters 4 and 5). There appears to be no disagreement on the inclusion of statutory and constitutional provisions under this heading, and the Court has squarely so held on a number of occasions (*See, e.g.*, Carroll v. Lanza, 1955).[24] It is also clear that judicial opinions constitute public acts as they too are expressions made by a coordinate branch of the state government (Smithsonian Institution v. St. John, 1943).[25] Because the purpose of Article IV was to ease relations among the states, it is easy to appreciate the application of full faith and credit to both statutes and judicial precedents.

Administrative regulations also are public acts (Magnolia Petroleum Co. v. Hunt, 1943).[26] The reasoning is simple. Because administrative agencies, at least in theory, exercise responsibility delegated to them by the legislature, agency actions are effectively actions of the legislature and should be protected by the Full Faith and Credit Clause.

Finally, federal law—statutory or decisional—is not covered by the Full Faith and Credit Clause for a very simple reason: If the federal law, properly construed, applies to the action, then the federal law must displace any state law that might otherwise be applied. This result, of course, is required by the Supremacy Clause found in Article VI of the Constitution. In other words, federal "acts" control competing state laws by virtue of the Supremacy Clause, not because of the Full Faith and Credit Clause.

TEXTUAL ANALYSIS: FULL FAITH AND CREDIT TO A "PUBLIC ACT"

Although it is relatively easy to determine what is a "public act," it is a far more difficult project to determine the effect of such a finding. In other words, what does it mean to give full faith and credit to a public act? Must a court in state A apply the common law and statutory law of state B—rather than its own—to a problem involving both states? And when might the requirement to subordinate forum law to the law of a sister state apply, if it ever applies? In other words, must the forum ever subordinate its own law? When the other state is the locus of some key factual contact or has some privileged interest in the transaction; when the sister state has more contact with and interest in the case than the forum state; or only when the forum state has no appreciable interest in or contact with the dispute? In still other words, can we find a pattern that will tell us when a court must, may, and cannot apply a particular law? What follows is a discussion of the Supreme Court's decisions in the area.

Full Faith and Credit Clause and Choice of Law: The Supreme Court's Jurisprudence

A choice of law problem arises every time the law of more than one state might apply to a situation. An easy example is an automobile accident in state X between drivers from states Y and Z. When suit is brought in a court in state A, which law should the A court apply: its own law, or that of X, Y or Z? That sounds like an easy enough question when the problem is a simple one involving the rules of the road, but what if the operative issue is spousal immunity, a doctrine that has been abolished in some states and retained in others?

The analysis of such seemingly simple problems can become complex enough; imagine the difficulty when the multistate issue involves hazardous waste spillage and whether the "event" is covered by the polluter's liability insurance policy. Exceedingly learned articles and books have been written on these topics, and many a professor has received tenure for writing them. Fortunately, the vast majority of those incredibly interesting (or tedious, depending on your choice of word) issues are beyond the scope of this book. Our purpose here is to examine only whether the Full Faith and Credit Clause ever federally compels a particular choice of law result.

Beginning in 1897, in Allgeyer v. State of Louisiana (1897),[27] the Supreme Court developed a highly conceptual approach to answer that question. *Allgeyer* involved an insurance contract made in New York; the insurer then mailed a letter to the insured in Louisiana stating what property was covered by the policy. The state of Louisiana prosecuted the insurance company for violating a statute that required every foreign corporation doing business in Louisiana to appoint an agent for service of process in that state.

The Supreme Court held for the insurer, reasoning that each state's law created, in the proper circumstances, certain "rights" in persons (either natural or corporate), and that an unjustified refusal to enforce those rights raised serious constitutional concerns. Phrased in that manner, the question is one about the deprivation of "vested rights," a question that looks as if it should be resolved pursuant to the Due Process Clause. If, however, the question were to be seen as one involving the proper application of one state's law (that is, the application of a "public act") in the courts of another state, the problem looks more like one suited for resolution under the Full Faith and Credit Clause. After all, if the A courts (in the hypothetical) do not give proper respect to (and application) of, say, an X statute, then it could be said that the A court has denied full faith and credit to the X statute. The logical conclusion to all of this, at least to the Supreme Court in those days, was that one and only one state's law should be applied to the substantive aspect of a problem (although the forum could—and still can—always apply its own law to procedural questions).[28] Failure to apply the correct law, therefore, either denied "vested rights" (as they were known), or denied proper respect to the laws of another state. In other words, there was either a due process problem or a full faith and credit problem lurking in any choice of law question. Thus, in *Allgeyer* itself the question was where the insurance contract had been "made." Because the Court found that the contract had been made in New York, the parties' rights had "vested" under the laws of that state. For that reason, the Louisiana Insurance Commissioner lacked authority to regulate the contract in question.

Following *Allgeyer*, the Court tended to favor the use of the Due Process Clause in choice of law cases. The notion of vested rights nicely dovetailed with the prevalent substantive due process ideology of that era, a philosophy that conveniently favored the interests of the powerful. Indeed for a time, it seemed as if choice of law decisions had come close to being constitutionalized as part of the Due Process Clause.[29]

Nevertheless, the Full Faith and Credit Clause still had a role to play, and eventually it came to dominate constitutional decisions involving choice of law. That process began with a famous trilogy of workers' compensation cases decided in the 1930s.

The 1930s Trilogy

Between 1932 and 1939 the Supreme Court decided three cases involving the relationship between state choice of law decisions and the Full Faith and Credit Clause. The first of the cases followed the *Allgeyer* vested rights approach, the second was transitional, and the third showed an apparent reversal of doctrine.

Bradford Electric Light Co. v. Clapper

The first case of the trilogy was Bradford Electric Light Co. v. Clapper (1932).[30] Clapper had been hired in Vermont and then was assigned to temporary duty in New Hampshire, where he was killed while on the job. Clapper's widow sued his employer in New Hampshire, the state of injury, alleging negligence. Under the *Allgeyer* vested rights approach, the case was simple: Because the worker's contract when entered into was a wholly "Vermont" contract (that is, Clapper had been hired there), all rights—by either party—had to be determined by Vermont law. In other words, the New Hampshire statute could not alter the rights that had already vested under Vermont laws. Unfortunately for the plaintiff, the Vermont workers' compensation statute provided that it was the exclusive remedy for any injury, wherever it occurred, arising out of a Vermont contract of employment.

The Supreme Court held that the Vermont workers' compensation statute, a public act under the Full Faith and Credit Clause, created "rights" in the employer. New Hampshire could not refuse to enforce those rights without violating the Constitution. It was irrelevant, the Court noted, that the injury occurred in New Hampshire and that the plaintiff had sued there; the Full Faith and Credit Clause required enforcement of the employer's Vermont-created "rights" extraterritorially (in New Hampshire, in other words), and required application of the statute to control events that took place in another state (here, New Hampshire).

Alaska Packers Association v. Industrial Accident Commission

The next case, Alaska Packers Association v. Industrial Accident Commission, (1935), decided only three years after *Clapper*, changed the rules of the game considerably. *Alaska Packers* involved an employment contract made in California for work to be done in Alaska. The employee, who had been injured in Alaska, filed a claim for workers' compensation in California. Although the employment contract stated that it would be governed by the Alaska workers' compensation law, and under Alaska law the statute provided the exclusive remedy for a covered worker, the Supreme Court permitted the California courts to apply their own law to the problem. In an about-face from the vested rights approach of *Clapper*, the Court reasoned that the forum need apply foreign law only when the forum's interests are not as strong as the interests of the other state. In *Alaska Packers* itself, the Supreme Court found that California's strong interest in compensating its domiciliaries could constitutionally overcome the legitimate Alaskan interest in having its workers' compensation law applied to an Alaskan accident. Moreover, the *Alaska Packers* Court held that it—the Supreme Court of the United States—would perform the required balancing of competing state interests. (That part of the *Alaska Packers* holding, which imposed an impossible supervisory burden on the Supreme Court, was fortunately discarded in Pacific Employers Ins. Co. v. Industrial Accident Commission (1939), decided four years later.)

Finally, relying on a suggestion that it had made earlier in *Clapper*, the *Alaska Packers* Court also held that California could apply its own law if it found the Alaskan law "obnoxious," a term the court conspicuously failed to define. In addition, the Court failed to explain why a court could choose to refuse to enforce a law merely because it found the law "obnoxious." After all, the Full Faith and Credit Clause itself suggests that recognition of another state's laws should be a routine occurrence. (The Court in *Alaska Packers* also did not explain why a New Hampshire court could not find the Vermont compensation statute in *Clapper* "obnoxious," but a California court could make that finding concerning the Alaska workers' compensation law.)

Pacific Employers Ins. Co. v. California

The last case in the 1930s trilogy, *Pacific Employers*, (1939)[31] involved a Massachusetts employment contract and a worker injured in California; the worker brought suit in California under that state's workers' compensation statute. Thus, the facts closely resembled those of *Clapper* and, therefore, presented the flip side of those presented in *Alaska Packers*. That factual difference did not matter. Again, California was permitted to apply its own workers' compensation law, although the court found that Massachusetts had a legitimate interest in applying its own law.

The holding raises an obvious question: How was *Pacific Employers* different from *Clapper*? Or, expressed differently, how could the court refuse to follow a precedent that seemed squarely on point? The Court, unfortunately, did not bother to tell us. It merely held that the Full Faith and Credit Clause does not require the forum to apply the law of another state to the detriment of the forum's policy in favor of providing compensation for employees injured within California and paying those who provided the employees' medical care.

The Court explained that its decision furthered the purpose of the Full Faith and Credit Clause, describing that purpose in this way:

> While the purpose of that provision was to preserve rights acquired . . . under the public acts . . . of one state by requiring recognition of their validity in other states, the very nature of the federal union of states, to which are reserved some of the attributes of sovereignty, precludes resort to the full faith and credit clause as the means for compelling a state to substitute the statutes of other states for its own statutes dealing with a subject matter concerning which it is competent to legislate. . . .
>
> Full faith and credit does not here enable one state to legislate for the other or to project its laws across state lines so as to preclude the other from prescribing for itself the legal consequences of acts within it.[32]

In short, one state cannot control events that take place in another state. If the first state could do so, the sovereignty of the second state would be at peril.

Thus, even though both California and Massachusetts had legitimate interests in the resolution of the workers' claims, California could properly apply its own law without performing the balancing of competing state interests seemingly required by *Alaska Packers*. In other words, because California was "competent" to legislate concerning workers in that state, Massachusetts could not "project" its law and "preclude" California from legislating on the matter. California could defer to the Massachusetts legislation if it so chose, but deference was not required.

In other words, it was clear by the end of the 1930s that the Constitution did not prescribe a significant rule of decision in the routine choice of law case. When either state's law could plausibly be applied, that is, when both states had a legitimate interest in the outcome of the litigation, the forum could choose to apply whichever law seemed better fitted to achieve justice.

A Bit of Relevant Constitutional History

The progression of the *Clapper/Alaska Packers/Pacific Employers* trilogy mirrored the Supreme Court's shift in ideology in 1937, caused by the conversion of Justice Owen Roberts to a policy of great deference to legislative decisions. The 1930s Conflicts trilogy can best be seen as a harbinger of that doctrinal watershed, often referred to as "the switch in time that saved Nine." *Clapper* reflected the activist, conservative Court of the beginning of the decade that saw no reason to defer to legislative judgments. It also was a very formal opinion, with its concentration on abstract contractual rights—rights defining when employment began—rather than with providing constitutional accommodation for New Hampshire's strong interests in protecting workers injured in that state. *Alaska Packers* reveals a Court unsure of itself, whose members are heading in different directions. Finally, in 1939, after the Court had abandoned its doctrinaire activism in most other areas, it made clear in *Pacific Employers* that it would not impose constitutional orthodoxy in choice of law decision making. The opinion in *Pacific Employers* is also noticeably less structured and less formal than the earlier two; it provides more room for lower courts to consider and balance interests rather than forcing them to conduct an often purposeless search for the place where a contract might have been "made."

Intermezzo

In the decades following *Pacific Employers*, the Court made clear that *Clapper* was no longer good law. In Carroll v. Lanza (1955),[33] for example, the Court held that the forum, the place of injury, could apply its own law instead of the law of the place of contracting and the parties' common domicile. The Court noted that the state of injury had legitimate concerns over items such as payment for medical care; those concerns were sufficient to justify application of forum law even though the injury was the only connection that either party had with the forum. Obviously, full faith and credit no longer presented a major hurdle in choice of law decision making.

More recently, the Court in Nevada v. Hall (1979)[34] demonstrated the very long reach of its new approach. There, an employee of the University of Nevada, driving a state automobile on official business, severely injured California residents in an accident on a California highway. In the ensuing litigation in California state courts, Nevada contended that no award could exceed the $25,000 limit imposed by the statutory waiver of sovereign immunity under Nevada law. Nevada argued that the Full Faith and Credit Clause required California courts to recognize and apply the Nevada limit. The trial court, however, disagreed, and the jury eventually awarded plaintiffs $1,150,000.

The Supreme Court also rejected Nevada's sovereign immunity argument. Justice John Paul Stevens's masterful opinion first held that a state does not have a constitutional right to sovereign immunity in the courts of another state. He then turned to full faith and credit analysis and found that the case closely resembled *Pacific Employers*; in both, California had a "legitimate public policy" in protecting those injured within the state, either in a workplace accident or on the highway. To require it to act otherwise would be "obnoxious to its statutorily based policies of jurisdiction over nonresident motorists and full recovery. The Full Faith and Credit Clause does not require this result."[35] California, in other words, had a significant interest in liability for accidents on its highways; the interest of other states, no matter how strong, could not overcome the interest of California without that state's consent.

In an important footnote, Justice Stevens explained why the holding in Nevada v. Hall did not offend basic notions of federalism. "California's exercise of jurisdiction in this case poses no substantial threat to our constitutional system of cooperative federalism. Suits involving traffic accidents occurring outside of Nevada could hardly interfere with Nevada's capacity to fulfill its own sovereign responsibilities."[36] In other words, although Nevada could restrict its own liability within its own borders, once its employees traveled to another state, that is, entered into the territory of another sovereign, Nevada, through their authorized acts, had voluntarily submitted its treasury to actions by other states. Such volitional waiver did not raise full faith and credit concerns—it did not threaten "cooperative federalism"—even though the doctrine of sovereign immunity goes to the very heart of a state's interest and policies.

Questions still remained even after Nevada v. Hall, however. The first issue was whether there were any limits under the Full Faith and Credit Clause on the forum's application of its own law, or, indeed, any limits on the forum's application of any other state's law; second, if there are any such limits, what are they; and, third, where do those limits originate—in the Due Process Clause or the Full Faith and Credit Clause?

The 1980s Trilogy

The Supreme Court provided answers (of sorts) to those questions ultimately in another trilogy, this one decided during the 1980s. The first case delineated the basic constitutional rule, the second provided an example of the rule's violation, and the third demonstrated that the application of traditional choice of law principles nearly always would pass constitutional muster.

Allstate Ins. Co. v. Hague: The Key Decision

Allstate Ins. Co. v. Hague (1981),[37] the first case of the trilogy, is the most significant. The litigation began with the death of Ralph Hague, a passenger on a motorcycle that was hit by a car in Wisconsin near the Minnesota border. Ralph had worked in Minnesota, commuting there from his Wisconsin home, but the accident was not related to Ralph's employment.

Neither the driver of the motorcycle nor the driver of the car that hit him carried any liability insurance. Ralph, however, held an Allstate policy that covered three automobiles he owned. That policy contained a clause insuring him against loss suffered in accidents with uninsured motorists; the uninsured motorist coverage was limited to $15,000 for each car.

After the accident, Ralph's widow remarried and moved across the state border to Minnesota. She then sued Allstate in a Minneapolis court contending that the $15,000 uninsured motorist coverage on each of Ralph's three cars should be combined, or "stacked" to provide for a total of $45,000 coverage. Allstate defended on the ground that the "stacking" question should be answered under Wisconsin law; after all, the policy had been delivered to Ralph there, the accident had occurred there, and all persons involved were Wisconsin residents at the time of the accident. The Minnesota courts, however, eventually applied Minnesota law, which permitted stacking, rather than Wisconsin law, which did not. The Minnesota courts arrived at their decision purportedly using Robert Leflar's choice influencing considerations.

The Supreme Court split three ways. Four justices joined in a plurality opinion written by Justice William Brennan. Justice Stevens wrote a separate concurring opinion, and the other three justices dissented in an opinion authored by Justice Lewis Powell. Despite that seeming divergence of views, there was a good deal of consensus among seven members of the Court (that is, between the plurality and dissenting opinions). In fact, seven of the eight sitting justices agreed on two fundamental points: the relationship between the Due Process and Full Faith and Credit Clauses in choice of law cases, and the test to be employed in evaluating a choice of law question under either provision. They split, however, on the proper application of that test to the facts at bar. Justice Stevens was the only member of the Court who argued that different tests should be applied to the full faith and credit and due process questions.

The Allstate Test

The plurality announced a deceptively simple test in Allstate: For a state's law to be applied, "that State must have a significant contact or significant aggregation of contacts, creating state interests, such that choice of its law is neither arbitrary nor fundamentally unfair."[38] That test, of course, calls only for minimal scrutiny and means that the decision to apply a particular law will be free from serious constitutional review. That test satisfies two salutary purposes: First, it is easy to apply and supervise, and second, it brings full faith and credit analysis in line with mainstream constitutional law.

Ease of Application

There can be no doubt that the minimal scrutiny test adopted by the majority has the virtue of simplicity. The plurality's application of the minimal scrutiny test to the facts in *Allstate* confirms this conclusion. Justice Brennan's opinion found only three "significant" contacts between Minnesota and the dispute: First, Ralph had worked in Minnesota for fifteen years before his death; second, Allstate did business in Minnesota; and third, the plaintiff, Ralph's widow, had moved to Minnesota after his death.

Each of these three contacts, however, is of questionable significance. First, the Minnesota employment clearly would have mattered if the choice of law issue in the case had had anything to do with employment. In fact, however, the accident did not occur during Ralph's commute to work; the issue was simply the quantum of the death benefit for a plaintiff widowed by a Wisconsin accident that killed her Wisconsin-domiciled husband. How that issue relates to Ralph's employment in Minnesota is difficult to see and not explained by the Court.

Second, the fact that Allstate was doing business in Minnesota was important, according to Justice Brennan, because it showed that the insurer could "hardly claim unfamiliarity with [Minnesota's] laws," or "surprise that [its] . . . courts might apply forum law to litigation in which the company is involved."[39] Once again, however, the relevance of the connection is constitutionally dubious. Allstate's business operations in Minnesota were completely unconnected with the policy it had sold to Ralph in Wisconsin. Further, Allstate (not surprisingly, in light of its name) did business in every state, so Justice Brennan's opinion reasoning on this point arguably would permit any state to apply forum law in any case involving the company; at the least the second contact greatly increases the vulnerability of a company to litigation everywhere that it does business.

The third contact with the case was the plaintiff's post-accident acquisition of a Minnesota domicile. That, Justice Brennan argued, gave Minnesota an interest in her complete compensation in order to keep her off Minnesota welfare rolls. Here he hedged somewhat, noting carefully that a postoccurrence move standing alone would be insufficient to produce legislative jurisdiction, but that it otherwise might be part of an adequate aggregation of contacts. As the preceding sentence indicates, this is the most dubious contact of all. To be sure, the contact with Minnesota was real, but minimal; worse, counting the move as a relevant contact provides strong encouragement for plaintiffs to forum shop by changing their domiciles to states with plaintiff-friendly substantive law rules and choice of law regimes.

Because the Court upheld Minnesota's exercise of legislative jurisdiction on the basis of just those three dubious contacts, it seems clear that any plausible, nontrivial assertion of prescriptive jurisdiction will be constitutional. A test so easily satisfied is correspondingly easy to apply. And ease of application brings an additional virtue. It means that the Court will find it straightforward to supervise the lower courts' use of the test. Those two virtues must have weighed heavily in the Court's thinking when it adopted the minimal scrutiny test.

Consider the alternative. In the years before *Allstate*, and in the commentary that followed that decision, a number of scholars had contended that the Supreme Court should adopt a test that required some kind of accommodation, or balancing, of the competing state laws. Some wanted the Court to establish a framework or even a code to control judicial decision making in choice of law cases.

The Court was obviously reluctant to take such a huge step. First, such a framework or code would have required significant federal judicial intervention in what traditionally had been a state matter. And the history of the Court's previous attempt at just such an intervention—the 1930s trilogy discussed above—was instructive; the Court had not been able to formulate a standard that led to predictable and efficient decision making.

The world of choice of law was far different in 1980 when *Allstate* was decided, than it had been in the 1930s. Nonetheless, the Court's agnosticism concerning its ability to rationalize state choice of law decisions is readily apparent in *Allstate*. The task was too distasteful to undertake; choice of law is not the sexiest of topics. Moreover, doing so would have required the reversal of a strong trend in favor of leaving state courts alone. Finally, the Court would have had to pick a winner among the competing choice of law methodologies described earlier in this chapter. It is difficult to see that happening on a badly divided Court. In any event, if it were to adopt some variant of the most popular of those, the Second Conflicts Restatement's "most significant relationship" test, it is difficult to see how that test—a very malleable one—could have furthered predictability.

Even if the Court had felt up to the task of devising an appropriate framework for choice of law, another powerful consideration weighed in favor of not attempting the task. A framework or code requires supervision, and that task necessarily would have fallen to the Supreme Court.[40] And a daunting task it would have been, given the hundreds of choice of law opinions American courts issue every year. Discretion, the better part of valor, counseled restraint. And so those who had wanted the Supreme Court to impose effective constitutional limits on states' choice of law decisions were disappointed. Minimal scrutiny and minimal supervision go hand in hand.

Mainstreaming Full Faith and Credit

The *Allstate* test also brought full faith and credit law into harmony with the mainstream of constitutional law. When *Allstate* was decided, it was quite clear that minimal scrutiny—in practice, virtually no scrutiny—was the prevailing test in most areas where state legislation was subject to constitutional challenge.[41] By making minimal scrutiny the standard for choice of law cases, the *Allstate* Court ensured that state decisions in that area would be subject to the same deference given to state decisions in other areas. In other words, the Supreme Court decided that it was time to let state and lower federal courts make choice of law decisions with only the barest of guidance from the Supreme Court.

Was Justice Stevens Right? Is There a "Difference" between the Two Clauses?

The plurality opinion relegated to a footnote its discussion of the relationship between full faith and credit and due process analysis in choice of law cases. The treatment by the plurality was perfunctory:

> This Court has taken a similar approach in deciding choice of law cases under both the Due Process Clause and the Full Faith and Credit Clause. In each instance, the Court has examined the relevant contacts and resulting interests of the State whose law was applied.[42]

The three dissenters joined in this part of the plurality opinion. Thus, only Justice Stevens argued that analysis of the choice of law problems under the two provisions should be approached differently.[43]

Justice Stevens based his argument on his belief that the two clauses serve different ends. First, he observed that the Due Process Clause was designed to protect *individuals* from unreasonable governmental behavior; it has little or nothing to do with the protection of state interests. The Due Process Clause would be violated, therefore, if a choice of law decision were

> totally arbitrary or if it were fundamentally unfair to either litigant. The Full Faith and Credit Clause, on the other hand, fulfills a completely different purpose in choice of law cases, where it ensures that each state has a "valid interest in the litigation."[44]

Thus, Stevens concluded, "the Clause should not invalidate a state court's choice of forum law unless that choice threatens the federal interest in national unity by unjustifiably infringing upon the legitimate interests of another State."[45]

Justice Stevens is surely correct in separating the Due Process and Full Faith and Credit Clauses for purposes of analysis. The essence of the former provision, of course, is fairness to the individual, while the heart of full faith and credit is ensuring that each state respects the rights of other states. The two concerns do overlap somewhat, of course; an individual's involvement with a particular state so that due process is satisfied, for example, certainly can affect the analysis under the Full Faith and Credit Clause by giving the forum a legitimate reason to apply its own law. Indeed, the analysis often will be identical under either clause. That does not mean, however, that the analysis always will be identical; after all, the two clauses protect two theoretically separate interests.

Why then was Justice Stevens the lone wolf on this issue? As noted, the rest of the Court gave no answer to his analysis. It is possible to guess, however, that the court avoided the issue primarily because it did not matter. If choice of law issues really were going to be decided by minimal scrutiny—the way most everything else in constitutional law is decided—the separate tests and analysis really are unnecessary. Professors might have liked the Court to be more honest and to have elaborated its reasoning more fully, but judges and lawyers are no doubt happy enough with a unified, workable standard.

Phillips Petroleum Co. v. Shutts: The State That Went Too Far

In the middle case of the 1980s trilogy, Phillips Petroleum Co. v. Shutts (1985),[46] the Supreme Court struck down a state's choice of law for the first time since 1947. *Shutts* involved a class action brought in Kansas state court by royalty owners of gas wells located throughout the United States; the owners sought to recover interest due but not paid on certain royalty payments. The choice of law problem related to the applicable interest rate, which differed in the several states involved in the litigation. In holding for the class members, the Kansas court applied its own law (i.e., its own interest rate) to all of the contracts at issue. The losing defendants took the case to the Supreme Court.

The Supreme Court held that the ruling violated both the Full Faith and Credit and Due Process Clauses. Justice William Rehnquist's opinion for a seven-justice majority began by affirming the *Allstate* minimal scrutiny test; a state could apply its own law to a dispute if the state had "a significant contact or significant aggregation of contacts, creating state interests, such that choice of its law is neither arbitrary nor fundamentally unfair."[47] In so doing, the Court noted that over 99 percent of the gas leases, and 97 percent of the class members, had no apparent connection with the state of Kansas. That state, therefore, lacked an interest in the claims that were unrelated to Kansas and could not apply its own law to them where Kansas law materially conflicted with the law of other jurisdictions. (Justice Stevens dissented on whether there was in fact such a conflict.)

In reaching its conclusion, the Court discounted several purported contacts and interests that the Kansas courts had relied on. Kansas's strong interest in the business of oil and gas extraction certainly could support the application of Kansas law to claims that had some connection with Kansas, but it was not relevant to choice of law for those claims that had no such connection. The Kansas courts had relied on the notion that the entire amount of interest owed to the class of plaintiffs was analogous to a common fund located in Kansas, but the Court dismissed that notion as the obvious fiction that it was; there was, in fact, no common fund.

Justice Rehnquist also easily dismissed the argument that the plaintiffs, by failing to opt out of the class, had shown their desire to be governed by Kansas law. Accepting for argument's sake that the plaintiffs had "consented" to the application of Kansas law, he pointed out that the plaintiff's desire for forum law cannot be given controlling weight against the defendants' wishes or else the invitation to forum shop would be irresistible. In other words, the plaintiffs cannot control applicable law by their choice of a forum.

Finally, the Kansas Supreme Court had relied in part on litigational convenience, expressing the view that it had much greater latitude to apply forum law because the case was a nationwide class action; performing the choice of law calculation for each of hundreds of individual claims would be a massive burden on the court. Justice Rehnquist's response was that convenience cannot trump the constitutional restrictions on state court choice of law decisions:

> the constitutional . . . calculus is not altered by the fact that that it may be more difficult or more burdensome to comply with the constitutional limitations because of the large number of transactions which the State proposes to adjudicate and which have little connection with the forum.[48]

The *Shutts* opinion thus presents a substantial obstacle to the efficient resolution of complex litigation, including state class actions. The application of forum law to such a case would mean that choice of law would not prove a difficult burden. After *Shutts*, however, choice of law became a serious matter in complex cases, making it much harder to resolve those cases quickly and efficiently. The result is certainly ironic because a different part of the *Shutts* decision had upheld jurisdiction in a state class action over nonresident members of the class who had not affirmatively withdrawn from the class. Thus, although it had become easier after *Shutts* to bring class actions, it had become harder to resolve them. The lawyers, of course, were the clear winners.

Shutts shows that a state can, in fact as well as in theory, go too far in applying its own law. The holding caused speculation that the time-honored practice of routinely applying forum law to traditional "procedural" issues—evidence and pleading, for example—might be unconstitutional. Doing so, it could be argued, would violate the *Shutts* holding because Kansas, the forum state, lacked a sufficient nexus with the litigation to apply, say, its own hearsay or limitations rule. In other words, if it violated full faith and credit for Kansas to apply its own interest rate to a multistate substantive problem having no real connection with Kansas, full faith and credit (as well as due process) also would be violated by a Kansas decision to apply its own statue of limitations to the same situation. This conclusion was congenial to interest analysis choice of law scholars, who had argued that routine application of forum law on many "procedural" issues (statute of limitations, especially) made no sense because doing so served no purpose of the forum.[49] The scholars were to be disappointed.

Sun Oil Co. v. Wortman: The Safe Harbor

Just three years after *Shutts*, the Court rejected an invitation to invalidate what it called the "traditional" substance/procedure dichotomy. Ironically, it did so in the very same class action that had been involved in *Shutts* itself. In Sun Oil Co. v. Wortman (1988),[50] the Court held that a forum's

> interest in regulating the work load of its courts and determining when a claim is too stale to be adjudicated certainly suffices to give it legislative jurisdiction to control the remedies available in its courts by imposing statutes of limitations.[51]

In other words, a state apparently would always be justified in applying its own limitations law (a procedural law, in other words), regardless of an absence of contacts with the problem. By extension, the holding would apply to most, if not all, procedural issues.

The conflict between *Shutts* and *Wortman* is real; no essential difference between limitation periods and interest rates can possibly justify the difference in outcomes. There is a functional difference, however, one highlighted by the *Wortman* Court's reference to the forum's "interest in regulating the work load of its courts." That quotation recognizes the difficulty, if not impossibility, that would arise if a forum were required to apply foreign law to the myriad of problems that must be resolved during litigation. Read as broadly as possible, *Shutts* would require that a forum lacking a substantial interest in the litigation must apply the law of another state (or maybe more than one other state) to such problems as pleading, evidence, remedies, burden of proof, and so forth. That task would be an impossible one given the constraints of contemporary litigation, hence the *Wortman* Court's reference to "work load" and its upholding of the "traditional" substance/procedure distinction.[52]

There was, however, another reason why the distinction was read into the Constitution. At the time *Wortman* was decided, the Supreme Court was engaged in a lengthy internal debate over the relevance of history in constitutional interpretation. More specifically, the Court was considering whether a practice accepted at the time of the ratification of the Constitution in 1789 (or of the Fourteenth Amendment in 1868) could ever be held invalid even though later precedents had pointed to just such a result. (The best expression of this debate among the justices can be found in the several opinions in Michael D. v. Gerald H. (1989)).[53] The emphasis on "traditional" procedure reflects the willingness of the Supreme Court to defer to time-honored methods of conducting litigation. When that deference to tradition is coupled with workload consideration, it is easy to see why the substance/procedure dichotomy survived the state interest test enunciated in *Allstate* and *Shutts*.[54]

Easy to see, perhaps, but still troubling. The opinion in *Wortman* readily could be read to guarantee the per se constitutionality of any choice of law decision based on one of the traditional *lex loci* rules of the First Restatement of Conflicts. That would be an unfortunate reading of the law. Suppose contracts for the sale of police radar detection devices are valid in Montana but invalid as against public policy in Massachusetts and New York. Assume further that the Buyer in Massachusetts and the Seller in New York conduct telephone negotiations for the sale of some of the devices, and Buyer, while on vacation in Montana, telephones his acceptance of Seller's last telephone offer. According to the traditional *lex loci* rule (place of making of the contract), the contract would be valid, even though Montana does not have a significant contact creating state interests so that the application of its law would be neither arbitrary nor unfair. Meanwhile, the only two states that do have an interest—Massachusetts and New York—cannot enforce their strongly held public policy. The hypothetical shows that *Wortman*'s holding of per se constitutionality for traditional rules eventually will run afoul of the *Allstate* test. Then the Court will have to choose.

The 2003 Reaffirmance

Very recently, the Court reaffirmed its position on minimal scrutiny of state choice of law decisions. It did so, in a case, Franchise Tax Board of California

v. Hyatt (2003),[55] which is only remarkable in that it involved the states of California and Nevada, the same states that were involved in Nevada v. Hall (1979), discussed earlier in this Chapter, where the Court permitted California to apply its own law and ignore Nevada's claim of sovereign immunity. *Hyatt* was the mirror image of *Hall*. This time, however, it was California trying to interpose its own law of sovereign immunity as a defense to a lawsuit in a Nevada court. (The attorneys for California must have loved the irony of their state's change of position on the issue.)

The Supreme Court upheld Nevada's application of its own law denying the immunity asserted by California. Justice Sandra Day O'Connor's opinion looked to precedent to reject California's attempt to limit the holding of *Hall*: "Our past experience with appraising and balancing state interests under the Full Faith and Credit Clause counsels against adopting [the] proposed new rule."[56] Once again, as it had done earlier in *Allstate* and *Alaska Packers*, the Court rejected the siren song of balancing for the comfort of minimal scrutiny.

Full Faith and Credit and Choice of Law Today: A Summary

It is relatively easy to set forth the contours of constitutional limits on a state's choice of law decisions:

1. The analysis is the same under both the Due Process and Full Faith and Credit Clauses.
2. A state must have enough contact with the litigation to provide a minimal state "interest" to have its law applied. Moreover, mere post-occurrence-residence in the forum state is not sufficient.
3. "Traditional procedural" concerns—evidence, pleading, limitations—virtually always will supply that minimal interest and justify the forum's application of its own law.
4. It is possible, but not certain, that any choice made according to a traditional *lex loci* rule will be per se constitutional.

With a test so general, of course, the devil is in the details. But the devil, if there be one, is one solely of state law; the federal constitutional limits on choice of law are few and rarely enforced, at least for the time being.

FULL FAITH AND CREDIT AND "DOOR-CLOSING" STATUTES

At one time, a number of states had statutes that prevented their courts from hearing actions based on another state's laws. These so-called door-closing laws, now unconstitutional, were typically directed at specific types of laws, especially workers' compensation and wrongful death statutes. Their effect was to keep out of court causes of action arising from the sister state laws that the forum legislature did not like.

The Case Law

The leading case is Hughes v. Fetter (1951),[57] which involved a wrongful death claim brought in Wisconsin under the Illinois law of wrongful death; although all of the parties were Wisconsin domiciliaries, the accident had taken place in Illinois. The Wisconsin court held that the action must be dismissed because the Wisconsin wrongful death statute precluded recovery for accidents that had occurred outside of the state. As a result, suit for deaths outside Wisconsin could not be brought in Wisconsin under either its own law, or the wrongful death law of any other state.

The Supreme Court of the United States reversed, holding that the Illinois wrongful death statue was a public act within the meaning of the Full Faith and Credit Clause. Wisconsin, therefore, must recognize that law by enforcing it in Wisconsin courts. Justice Hugo Black's opinion for the Court observed that because Wisconsin enforced wrongful death claims under its own laws, it had no public policy that would be offended by enforcing the Illinois claim; in other words, enforcement of wrongful death claims was not "obnoxious" to Wisconsin. In a footnote, Justice Black made clear that Wisconsin, once it entertained plaintiff's litigation, could choose to use its own law, rather than that of Illinois, "to measure the substantive rights of the parties." Thus, the *Hughes* decision does not affect a state's choice of law options; rather, it establishes a constitutional right to sue on transitory causes of action (that is, any action not involving real property), in any court that has personal jurisdiction over the defendant. *Hughes*, however, does not dictate what law must be applied in such an action.

The door-opening focus of *Hughes* was not revolutionary. Almost twenty years earlier, for example, in Broderick v. Rosner (1935),[58] the Court had held that New Jersey courts must enforce a New York statute that levied assessments on the stockholders of an insolvent bank. The Court ruled that the imposition by New Jersey courts of what the court styled "impossible" procedural obstacles to enforcing the New York law, violated full faith and credit.

The *Hughes* principle is subject to three important limitations. First, the opinion in *Hughes* expressly reserves to the forum court the right to refuse to hear litigation based on foreign law on grounds of *forum non conveniens* (a doctrine permitting a court to dispose of a case because it could be tried more conveniently elsewhere). Nothing in the full faith and credit clause compels a state to expend judicial resources on an inconvenient trial of a dispute that has nothing to do with the forum.

Second, by noting in *Hughes* that Wisconsin had "no real feeling of antagonism" toward wrongful death actions, Justice Black allowed for an indeterminate exception to the *Hughes* rule. What would happen when the forum did have a strong antipathy to the foreign claim? The standard answer has been that a court may refuse to apply foreign law that violates its fundamental public policy. Sometimes courts exercise that option by dismissing the case upon jurisdictional grounds; in other cases, the court simply applies its own law, incorporating its own policy, on the contested issue. That second option is available only if the forum state has the contacts and interests required by the *Allstate* rule. It is interesting to note the difference between this situation and the one where the sister-state claim has been reduced to a sister-state judgment. There, of course, a rigid rule of full faith and credit requires the forum to enforce the foreign judgment even though the underlying claim offends the forum's basic public policy.

The final limitation on the *Hughes* rule involves the forum's power to apply its own statute of limitations. In Wells v. Simonds Abrasive Co. (1953),[59] the Court held in a brief opinion by Chief Justice Fred Vinson that the forum could apply its own statute of limitations, even though it was shorter than the limitations period of the state where the claim arose. There was no conflict with *Hughes*, according to the Court, because *Hughes* had involved discrimination against actions based on foreign law; *Wells*, by contrast, involved no discrimination because the forum's short limitations period was applied to all claims, both those originating at home and those originating abroad. Thus, the Court in *Wortman*, discussed earlier in this Chapter, strongly confirmed the *Wells* exception.

A different kind of door-closing law attempts to keep litigation at home. This has long been unconstitutional. Tennessee Coal, Iron & Railroad Co. v. George (1914)[60] is the key case. There, an Alabama employee injured in that state brought suit in a Georgia court under the Alabama workers' compensation law. That law expressly provided, however, that all actions brought under it could be brought *only* in an Alabama court "and not elsewhere." The Court held that a "transitory" cause of action such as the one at bar can be sued on anywhere. (A "transitory" cause of action, generally speaking, is one that does not involve real property.) The Court held that, "it would be a deprivation of a fixed right if the plaintiff could not sue the defendant in Alabama because he had left the state.[61] Litigation, in short, cannot be kept at home because doing so might deny a "fixed right." The plaintiff's rights under the Alabama law, in other words, had "vested" when he was injured in Alabama; he could sue on that vested right in any state where he could serve the defendant.

This somewhat circular vested rights type rationale was later extended in Crider v. Zurich Insurance Co. (1965).[62] There, the Court held that an Alabama court could entertain an action under the Georgia workers' compensation statute (thus, *Crider* presented the exact converse of the situation in *George*, involving the same two states) even though the Georgia law expressly gave exclusive enforcement jurisdiction to a Georgia administrative agency, a forum obviously unavailable in the Alabama litigation. In short, a state cannot keep litigation at home even if a special tribunal has been set up to deal with claims arising under the statutory law of that state.

An Assessment of Door-Closing Law

Hughes has been the subject of some criticism on the ground that modern notions of long-arm jurisdiction and *forum non conveniens* render the decision unnecessary. A defendant, so the argument goes, generally will be amenable to long-arm jurisdiction in the state where it caused an injury; and courts will apply the doctrine of *forum non conveniens* to insure that the case will be heard by the "proper" court if more than one state has jurisdiction. Nevertheless, *Hughes* and *Broderick* reach the right result. It is difficult to understand how a state can justify its refusal to hear a properly filed claim over which it has proper jurisdiction simply because the claim arose under the law of another state. The purpose of the Full Faith and Credit Clause—to ensure extraterritorial recognition of each state's laws in order to restrict friction among the states—compels that conclusion. Wisconsin, after all, does not have to follow Illinois law, but it cannot refuse to consider applying it.

No doubt Wisconsin in the *Hughes* case could, and, indeed, must, refuse to recognize the Illinois law if that law violates the federal constitution, but that would not lead to the kind of interstate friction that Article IV was designed to prevent; instead, that holding would create a wholly different kind of friction, one between the federal and state governments, a friction dealt with by the Supremacy Clause, not by the Full Faith and Credit Clause. Cases like *Hughes* and the others discussed in this section help make certain that friction among states—the kind of problem that Article IV was designed to prevent—is kept to a minimum.[63]

Other Sources of Relevant Law

The Analysis up to this point has examined how the Full Faith and Credit Clause has operated in the realm of public acts. There are several other constitutional provisions and one statute that also have a potential role in federal regulation of state choice of law decisions. We discuss those briefly, beginning with the full faith and credit implementing statute, 28 U.S.C. § 1738.

The Full Faith and Credit Implementing Statute

The original implementing statute, adopted in 1790, did not mention "public acts" among the items it covers, although the Full Faith and Credit Clause itself does. When the statute was revised in 1948 as part of a general recodification of the Federal Judicial Code, it was amended to include "public acts" expressly. The possible significance of that change has been explored only once, and that briefly, by the Supreme Court.

In Hughes v. Fetter (1951), the Court observed in a footnote that two earlier cases had suggested that full faith and credit law:

> might make a distinction between statutes and judgments of sister states because of Congress' failure to prescribe the extra-state effect to be accorded public acts. Subsequent to these decisions the Judicial Code was revised so as to provide: "Such acts [of the legislature of any state] . . . and judicial proceedings . . . shall have the same full faith and credit in every court within the United States . . . as they have . . . in the courts of such State . . . from which they are taken."[64]

The *Hughes* Court, however, found that it was "unnecessary" to consider whether that change in § 1738 had any significance. Apart from a remark made a few years later by Justice Felix Frankfurter dissenting in Carroll v. Lanza (1955)[65] (he said that the change in § 1738 "cannot be disregarded"),[66] the addition of "public acts" to the full faith and credit statute has received no play in the Supreme Court. But should it have?

Good arguments can be made on either side. First, it is a standard contention in statutory construction that when the legislature changes a well-known statute, it likely does so because it has some substantive goal in mind. Here, the goal of the change would be to equate "acts" and "proceedings." That argument is strengthened by the immediate linkage of "acts" and "proceedings" with the word "same." Surely, the inclusion together with the linkage make clear the congressional goal: to require the same full faith and credit be given to both statutes and judgment.

On the other hand, the 1948 revision of the Judicial Code (Title 28, U.S.C.A.) was designed to clarify the nation's procedural law, rather than to change it. More important, perhaps, the 1948 revisers knew (or, at least, should have known) that the Supreme Court had *never* given the "same effect" to public acts and to judicial proceedings. Moreover, ever since the *Clapper* decision, the divergence between the full faith and credit due a judicial decision and that which was due a state's law had become even more marked. It is highly unlikely that the 1948 revisers intended to make such a dramatic sea change in the law while working on a project that had been designed to be merely revisory, rather than controversial. And even if that had been the revisers' intention, nothing indicates that any member of Congress or, indeed, anyone else shared that intention, or even had knowledge of it.

The conclusion, therefore, must be that the change in language was not meant to produce a change in substance. That conclusion still leaves a troublesome question: Why, then, was the language of § 1738 changed? To that question, a scholar can only say that she has no answer. But she can be fairly confident that the Supreme Court will not change the settled law.

Other Possibly Relevant Constitutional Provisions

Several other parts of the Constitution have something to say about the respect that one state should give to the laws of another state. Article IV itself contains the Privileges and Immunities Clause, which provides that, "The Citizens of each State shall be entitled to all Privileges and Immunities of Citizens in the several States."[67] The clause has been used only infrequently in choice of law cases, most notably in Supreme Court of New Hampshire v. Austin (1985).[68] There the Court struck down a New Hampshire law that prevented persons who were not New Hampshire residents from becoming members of the New Hampshire bar even though they had passed that state's bar exam and intended to practice in that state. *Austin*'s prohibition of state discrimination against nonresidents has an obvious relevance to the modern choice of law methods which emphasize the domicile of the various parties. The Supreme Court, however, has so rarely referred to the Privileges and Immunities Clause of Article IV that it does not seem likely that the clause will find much use in the area of choice of law, absent blatant discrimination. More generally, the whole area of Article IV Privileges and Immunities rights has been quiescent for many, many years.

The Equal Protection Clause of the Fourteenth Amendment has long been a favorite of commentators thinking to branch out beyond traditional full faith and credit analysis. The allure is apparent. When a state treats a resident differently from a nonresident, without justification, then the latter has been denied equal protection. This scenario, of course, is quite common in all modern choice of law models, with their penchant for favoring forum residents. The rub, of course, is that the Supreme Court apparently believes that state residence or domicile alone provides adequate explanation for the disparity. In any event, the Court has never decided a choice of law case on equal protection grounds, and it is quite likely that it never will.

Another constitutional provision which might be used in reviewing state choice of law decisions is the Due Process Clause of the Fourteenth Amendment. Earlier we explained how, ever since *Allstate* (1980), the Supreme Court has treated the Due Process Clause and the Full Faith and Credit Clause as in *pari materia* for choice of law purposes.

Occasionally, however, there might be a separate use for due process review. Punitive damages provide an example. In recent years, the Supreme Court has been struggling with the problems posed by massive trial court awards of punitive damages. The Court has subjected those awards to due process analysis based on a test that focused on the degree of defendant's "reprehensibility." The choice of law problem arose when the forum sought to measure the reprehensibility of defendant's conduct by activities in other states, activities that were legal in those other states, although illegal in the forum.

This proved too much for the Supreme Court's patience. In State Farm Mutual Automobile Ins. Co. v. Campbell (2003),[69] the Court struck down a punitive damage award of $145 million even though the plaintiffs did "not dispute that much of the out-of-state conduct was lawful where it occurred."[70] Relying in part on the old decision of Huntington v. Attrill (1892), involving the enforcement of penal laws, Justice Anthony Kennedy wrote that, "States cannot punish a defendant for conduct that may have been lawful where it occurred."[71] In full faith and credit terms, a state can only punish conduct in which it has a legitimate interest.

Finally, there is the "Dormant" Commerce Clause. This unwritten, but vigorous, constitutional "clause" prohibits a state from discriminating against trade from other states. The Court uses the Dormant Commerce Clause to strike down protectionist legislation and legislation which interferes with the free flow of commerce. Although the Dormant Commerce Clause has been used to invalidate many state laws, those decisions have not usually involved choice of law as we usually define the area. There is one kind of case, however, where the Dormant Commerce Clause has been deployed in true choice of law situations. This area is the "internal affairs" doctrine of corporate law, an area where the Court has established a kind of per se rule to prevent inconsistent and disabling state regulation.

Here is the problem: What state regulates the activities of General Motors or of McDonald's or of Microsoft? Each company is a vast enterprise with significant activities in nearly every state and many foreign countries. It has long been understood that a state may protect its citizens and property by imposing its own laws involving safety or the environment or products liability. Most corporate activity, therefore, is subject to regulation by more than one state. A problem arises, however, when it comes to corporate governance—issues such as when shareholders can elect a new board or the duty of the board of directors when someone offers to buy the company. What law, in other words, regulates what has become known as the "internal affairs" of a corporation?

There are a number of possible regulators, including the state of incorporation, the state where the company has its headquarters, the state where the most employees work, and the state where the most shareholders live. It is easy to see that inconsistent regulations could spell disaster. For example, one state might require a company that receives a hostile takeover bid to submit it directly to the shareholders; another might require a decision to be made solely in the exercise of the discretion of the board of directors. But both rules could not apply at the same time, making all actions of the board illegal, a senseless result.

Long ago, states developed the "internal affairs" doctrine to avoid this mess. ("Internal affairs" generally speaking, are those corporate activities which fall under the rubric of "governance.") The internal affairs doctrine is simple: Only the state of incorporation can regulate the internal affairs of a corporation, a rule that met with near universal acceptance. That acceptance changed, however, in the 1980s when a wave of hostile merger attempts motivated some states to adopt antitakeover legislation designed to protect local interests even when the corporations whose internal affairs were being regulated were not chartered in that state.

The problem eventually was resolved (sort of) by the Supreme Court in CTS Corp. v. Dynamics Corp. of America (1987).[72] The lower courts in that case had struck down an Indiana antitakeover law which applied only to corporations chartered in Indiana. On review, the Supreme Court first discussed Commerce Clause precedent that had invalidated state laws in order to avoid the possibility of "inconsistent regulation." Then, in an opinion by Justice Powell, the Court observed that:

> This Court's recent Commerce Clause cases also have invalidated statutes that may adversely affect interstate commerce by subjecting activities to inconsistent regulations. The Indiana Act poses no such problem. So long as each State regulates voting rights only in the corporations it has created, each corporation will be subject to the law of only one State. No principle of corporation law and practice is more firmly established than a State's authority to regulate domestic corporations, including the authority to define the voting rights of shareholders.[73]

In other words, by placing regulation in one easily and objectively defined state, the internal affairs doctrine avoids the great economic harm that can be caused by inconsistent regulation. The *CTS* Court did not refer to the Full Faith and Credit Clause, although there were precedents suggesting that it could have been used. There were probably two reasons for that lacuna. First, the Full Faith and Credit Clause is about interstate harmony, while avoiding economic harm caused by state regulation is the purpose behind the Dormant Commerce Clause. Thus, the latter provision fits the problem better. Moreover, if the Full Faith and Credit Clause had been used, the court would have been forced to justify a choice between competing state laws, something that it had spent the previous decade declining to do.

To be sure, *CTS* does not hold that *only* the state of incorporation can regulate internal affairs, but the dictum and its explanation of the reasons behind the internal affairs doctrine are clear. Any state that wishes to regulate internal affairs of a corporation chartered elsewhere is going to have a very difficult time doing so.

In short, there are parts of the Constitution other than the Full Faith and Credit Clause that can have an occasional impact on choice of law decisions, but it is unlikely that they will play a significant role in our jurisprudence. Rather, it is clear that the Full Faith and Credit Clause, and the policies that it furthers, is far and away the most important provision dealing with interstate government, in contemporary life and law.

NOTES

1. Sun Oil Co. v. Wortman, 486 U.S. 717, 722 (1988).

2. The current status of the First Restatement is more complicated than a simple percentage figure can convey. States that use the First Restatement as their dominant choice of law methodology routinely depart from it in selected areas, such as workers' compensation. Furthermore, states that have rejected it still use it in other selected areas, such as real property. William M. Richman and David Riley, *The First Restatement of Conflict of Laws on the Twenty-fifth Anniversary of Its Successor: Contemporary Practice in Traditional Courts*, 56 Maryland L. Rev. 1196 (1997).

3. David Cavers, The Choice-of-Law Process 9 (1965).

4. Louise Weinberg, *Methodological Interventions and the Slavery Cases; Or, Night-Thoughts of a Legal Realist*, 56 Maryland L. Rev. 1316 (1997).

5. Intercontinental Hotels Corp. (Puerto Rico) v. Golden, 15 N.Y.2d 9, 13, 254 N.Y.S.2d 27, 203 N.E.2d 210 (N.Y. 1964).

6. For a general description of the interest analysis method, *see* William M. Richman, *Diagramming Conflicts: A Graphic Understanding of Interest Analysis*, 43 Ohio State L.J. 317 (1982).

7. Brainerd Currie, *Notes on Methods and Objectives in the Conflict of Laws*, Duke L.J. 171, 176 (1959).

8. Cavers, *supra* note 3; Aaron D. Twerski, *Enlightened Territorialism and Professor Cavers—The Pennsylvania Method*, 9 Duquesne L. Rev. 373 (1971).

9. William F. Baxter, *Choice of Law and the Federal System*, 16 Stanford L. Rev. 1 (1963). *See also* Herma Hill Kay, *The Use of Comparative Impairment to Resolve True Conflicts: An Evaluation of the California Experience*, 68 California L. Rev. 577 (1980).

10. Erwin v. Thomas, 264 Or. 454, 506 P.2d 494 (Or. 1973), is an example of such a case.

11. *See generally* Robert A. Leflar, Luther L. McDougal, and Robert L. Felix, American Conflicts Law 102–108 (4th ed., 1986). A collection of scholarly comments on Prof. Leflar's method appears in Symposium, "Leflar on Conflicts," 31 South Carolina L. Rev. 409 (1980). The Leflar methodology has been adopted in five states.

12. Restatement (Second) of Contracts §§ 145,188.

13. *Id.*

14. Patrick J. Borchers, *Courts and the Second Conflicts Restatement: Some Observations and an Empirical Note*, 56 Maryland L. Rev. 1232, 1247–1249 (1997).

15. Nationwide Mutual Ins. Co. v. Black, 656 N.E.2d 1352 (Ohio Ct. App. 1995).

16. Allstate Ins. Co. v. Hague, 449 U.S. 302, 313 (1981).

17. Lochner v. New York, 198 U.S. 45 (1905) held that legislation regulating the hours that bakers can work violated the Due Process Clause.

18. *Allstate*, 449 U.S. 302 (1981).

19. *Sun Oil*, 486 U.S. 717 (1988).

20. *See* Phillips Petroleum v. Shutts, 472 U.S. 797 (1985).

21. *Id.* at 726.

22. *Id.* at 728–29.

23. Just such a case is Phillips Petroleum v. Shutts (472 U.S. 797, 1985), in which the Court struck down the decision of the Kansas Supreme Court to apply its own law, principally for reasons of administrative convenience, to all claims in a multistate class action. *Shutts* is treated more fully *infra*.

24. Caroll v. Lanza, 349 U.S. 408 (1955).

25. Smithsonian Institution v. St. John, 214 U.S. 19 (1909).

26. Magnolia Petroleum Co. v. Hunt, 320 U.S. 430 (1943).

27. Allgeyer v. State of Louisiana, 165 U.S. 578 (1897).

28. This was part of the development of what has become known as the "*lex loci*" rules, so-called because they referred the problem to the law of some particular place (the "*lex locus*"). Thus, the choice of law rule for torts was the *lex locus delicti* ("the law of the place of wrong"), for contracts the *lex locus contractus* ("the law of the place of contracting"), and for property the *lex sitae* ("the law of the place when the property is located").

29. "Substantive" due process theory argued that certain "substantive" rights could not be "denied" by the State consistent with the protection of "liberty" guaranteed by the Due Process Clause of the Fourteenth Amendment. Substantive due process closely resembled the vested rights theory of choice of law in that both suggested that a person's rights were not infinitely malleable by judges. Both theories also proved hospitable to business interests, although that did not necessarily have to be the case with either theory.

30. Bradford Electric Light Co. v. Clapper, 286 U.S. 145 (1932).

31. Pacific Employers Insurance Co. v. Industrial Accident Commission, 306 U.S. 493 (1939).

32. *Id.* at 501, 504–05 (1934).

33. *Carroll*, 349 U.S. 408 (1955).

34. Nevada v. Hall, 440 U.S. 410 (1979).

35. *Id.* at 424.

36. *Id.* at 424 n.24.

37. Allstate Ins. Co. v. Hague, 449 U.S. 302 (1981).

38. *Id.* at 313.

39. *Id.* at 317–18.

40. The various United States Courts of Appeals could not be given the job of reviewing state choice of law decisions because of the *Rooker-Feldman* doctrine, which holds that appeals from state court decisions cannot be heard by the federal circuit courts. *See* Rooker v. Fidelity Trust Co., 263 U.S. 413 (1923); District of Columbia Court of Appeals v. Feldman, 460 U.S. 462 (1983). Thus, the Supreme Court was the only judicial body that could have supervised the myriad state court decisions on choice of law. That was a task it clearly did not want to undertake.

41. Exceptions include cases involving the exercise of fundamental rights (e.g., free speech) or discrimination against suspect classes (e.g., discrimination based on race or religion).

42. Allstate, 449 U.S. 308 n.10.

43. *Id.* at 644 (Stevens, J., concurring).

44. *Id.* at 643.

45. *Id.*

46. Phillips Petroleum Co. v. Shutts, 472 U.S. 797 (1985).

47. *Id.* at 801.

48. *Id.* at 821.

49. *See, e.g.*, William M. Richman and William L. Reynolds, Understanding Conflict of Laws § 93[a] (3d ed., 2002); Louise Weinberg, *Choosing Law: The Limitations Debates*, University of Illinois L. Rev. 683 (1991); Margaret Rosso Grossman, *Statutes of Limitations and the Conflict of Laws: Modern Analysis*, Arizona State L.J. 1 (1980).

50. *Wortman*, 486 U.S. 717 (1988).

51. *Id.* at 730.

52. *Id.* at 731.

53. Michael D.V. Gerald H., 491 U.S. 110 (1989). *Michael D.* involved a constitutional challenge to California's adoption laws. Both Justice Scalia and Justice Brennan wrote at length and with some heat about the role that history should play in constitutional interpretation.

54. Indeed, only two years after *Wortman*, the Court held that in-state personal service on a defendant was sufficient to obtain constitutionally satisfactory personal jurisdiction over him precisely because that was a common method of doing so in 1868 when the Fourteenth Amendment was adopted. Burnham v. Superior Court of California, 495 U.S. 604 (1990).

55. Franchise Tax Board of California v. Hyatt, 538 U.S. 488 (2003).

56. *Id.* at 498.

57. Hughes v. Fetter, 341 U.S. 609 (1951).

58. Broderick v. Rosner, 294 U.S. 629 (1935).

59. *Wells v. Simonds Abrasive Co.*, 345 U.S. 514 (1953).

60. Tennessee Coal, Iron, & Railroad Co. v. George, 233 U.S. 354 (1914).

61. *Id.* at 359.

62. Crider v. Zurich Insurance Co., 380 U.S. 39 (1965).

63. Arguably, the public policy exception to the *Hughes* rule also helps reduce interstate friction. *But see* Larry Kramer, *Same-Sex Marriage, Conflict of Laws, and the Unconstitutional Public Policy Exception*, 106 Yale L.J. 1965 (1997) (arguing that states should not be able to use the public policy escape route in order to refuse to apply sister-state marriage laws).

64. *Hughes*, 341 U.S. 609, 613–14, n. 16 (1951).

65. *Carroll*, 349 U.S. 408 (1955).
66. *Id.* at 422, n. 4 (1957) (Frankfurter, J., dissenting).
67. U.S. Constitution Article IV, § 1.
68. Supreme Court of New Hampshire v. Austin, 470 U.S. 274 (1985).
69. State Farm Mutual Automobile Ins. Co. v. Campbell, 538 U.S. 408 (2003).
70. *Id.* at 422.
71. *Id.*
72. CTS Corp. v. Dynamics Corp. of America, 481 U.S. 69 (1987).
73. *Id.* at 88.

4

Judicial Proceedings: The Basic Rule

The third prong of the Full Faith and Credit Clause applies to "judicial proceedings." In this chapter, we examine the meaning of that term and the scope of its application. Because the effect of the judicial proceedings provision has been to make each state's law of preclusion part of the Constitution, we then examine briefly the basic outline of the law of preclusion. The final section examines the basic rule of full faith and credit—that the states must enforce each others' judgments.

WHAT ARE "JUDICIAL PROCEEDINGS"?

The full faith and credit mandate applies most forcefully to "judicial proceedings." The term is neither defined nor self-defining, and over the years it has created some problems. Some applications are obvious, some less so.

Obvious Cases

The Constitution does not define the term "judicial proceeding" but there are some very obvious examples of what falls within that category.

All civil cases in law and equity are "judicial proceedings" within the meaning of the Full Faith and Credit Clause and thus are entitled to full preclusive effect in the courts of other states. Criminal cases are treated differently, as we shall explain. For constitutional purposes, the specific type of resolution in the initial proceeding does not matter; thus, judgments resulting from full contested litigation, default judgments, consent judgments between private litigants and governmental entities, and judgments based upon settlement agreements between private parties are all within the purview of the constitutional recognition requirement. The only limitation here is that some types of resolutions do not have full preclusive effect according to the law of the rendering court, and thus are not entitled to full preclusive effect in other state and federal courts.

Arbitration Proceedings

In this country, arbitration is almost exclusively a creature of statute. Laws concerning arbitration typically provide for a great deal of judicial deference to arbitral awards; usually, they can be set aside only for want of jurisdiction, if the problem for decision involves an area of great public concern, or if the award was procured by fraud or corruption. Nevertheless, arbitral proceedings are not "judicial proceedings" for purposes of the Full Faith and Credit Clause. The result differs, of course, if a court of general jurisdiction confirms the arbitration award or otherwise orders its enforcement. In that event, the judicial confirmation or order of enforcement is itself a "judicial proceeding," constitutionally worthy of full faith and credit.

A fortiori, international arbitral awards are not *constitutionally* entitled to recognition. However, such awards are controlled by the 1958 United Nations Convention (generally known as the "New York Convention"), implemented in this country in 1970. Under the convention, a signatory state, such as the United States, must enforce *agreements* to arbitrate, a provision the Supreme Court enforces with a vengeance. In Mitsubishi Motors Corp. v. Soler Chrysler-Plymouth, Inc. (1985),[1] for example, the Court enforced an agreement to arbitrate international antitrust claims even though Congress has provided exclusive federal jurisdiction for antitrust claims. In addition, the convention requires American courts to recognize foreign arbitral awards.

Administrative Proceedings

Administrative agency adjudications are not judicial proceedings and thus do not fall within the constitutional or statutory requirements for full faith and credit. As with arbitration awards, however, courts often uphold on appeal the decisions of administrative agencies, and, unlike the administrative determination itself, the resulting judicial judgment falls within the constitutional mandate.

Constitutional law aside, the trend in state and federal statutory and decisional law is to provide that administrative adjudicatory determinations (as opposed to rule-making decisions) should receive full preclusive effect in subsequent judicial proceedings. Thus, in University of Tennessee v. Elliott (1986),[2] the Court fashioned a rule of federal common law according preclusive effect to decisions of administrative agencies.

The trend makes sense. After all, the decision has been rendered by an impartial tribunal according basic due process rights to litigants in an adversary proceeding. Not surprisingly, therefore, many states and the United States Supreme Court treat agency decisions as having as much preclusive effect as do judicial decisions. That also is the view of the American Law Institute.[3]

"EVERY OTHER STATE"

The Full Faith and Credit Clause requires recognition in every state of the judicial proceedings of "every other state." The last phrase obviously includes all states admitted to the Union, but does not extend, in express terms, to judicial proceedings in United States territories and possessions, federal courts, or foreign nations. The full faith and credit implementing statute, 28 U.S.C. § 1738, remedied the omission in part by extending the requirement of recognition to judicial proceedings in courts of American territories and possessions. The statute also exceeds the clause in requiring that *federal courts* give full faith and credit to the judicial proceedings of state and territorial courts.[4]

On the other hand, neither the Constitution nor the statute explicitly requires that state or federal courts recognize the judicial proceedings of American federal courts; nevertheless, the Supreme Court consistently has held that federal court judicial proceedings must receive full faith and credit in subsequent federal and state court proceedings. Any other result would be bizarre, indeed.

Tribal Courts

The Supreme Court has never squarely addressed the full faith and credit effect that is due judgments from Indian tribal courts. Are those judgments to be treated as judicial proceedings from other states or as proceedings from other nations? In a dictum in Santa Clara Pueblo v. Martinez (1978), the Court, however, did observe: "Judgments of tribal courts, as to matters properly within their jurisdiction, have been regarded in some circumstances as entitled to full faith and credit in other courts."[5] That dictum, however, hardly clears up the issue.

International Judgments

Neither the Constitution nor the full faith and credit statute requires American courts to recognize or enforce judgments entered in the courts of other nations. At one time in American courts such judgments were only prima facie evidence of the validity of the underlying claim. Thus in the suit on the judgment the defendant could raise any defenses that would have been available to him in the original claim.[6] Today, however, those courts recognize foreign-nation judgments based on the principle of comity—the "recognition which one nation allows within its territory to the legislative, executive or judicial acts of another nation" Hilton v. Guyot (1895).[7] Comity is not a principle of constitutional law; rather, it is a matter of common law, and the courts of the states are free to apply their own understanding of it.

In *Hilton*, the Supreme Court adopted an unfortunate interpretation of the principle, distinguishing among foreign-nation judgments based on the parties to the action. Such judgments would have conclusive effect in cases where (1) both parties are citizens of the foreign state, or (2) the defendant is a citizen of the foreign state, but the plaintiff is not, or (3) the plaintiff is a citizen of the foreign state, and the victorious defendant is not. However, in cases where the foreign citizen recovers a judgment against a noncitizen, the American court would recognize the foreign judgment only if the courts of the rendering state would give preclusive effect to an American judgment.

This additional requirement—known as the reciprocity rule—has little to recommend it; why penalize a foreign plaintiff for the acts of her country's courts? The general policies that stand behind the finality doctrines—fairness, judicial economy, respect for the foreign state's courts and the parties' reliance—should determine the preclusive effect of the foreign judgment instead.

Fortunately, *Hilton* has had only minor precedential effect. As an interpretation of federal common law, rather than the Constitution or federal legislation, it does not bind state courts, and many have rejected it.[8] Moreover, federal courts, under the *Erie* decision are required to apply state rather than federal law on the issue in diversity cases.[9]

Most American state courts reject the reciprocity requirement and give foreign nations' judgments almost the same respect that they accord the judgments of sister states. There are caveats, however. First, American courts will not give preclusive effect to a foreign judgment that resulted from a proceeding that was fundamentally unfair because the foreign court was corrupt, prejudiced, or otherwise unable to render a fair verdict.[10] The foreign court's procedures need not mirror the technical requirements of American due process law; they need only be fair in the sense that they would be so recognized by the great number of civilized jurisdictions throughout the world. Second, even if the proceeding was basically fair, if the foreign judgment is based on a claim that is morally offensive to American sensibilities, such as slavery or *de jure* racism, the judgment will not be recognized.[11]

Unfortunately, American courts do not always deal with such clear-cut situations. Foreign libel judgments provide an example. Consider Telnikoff v. Matusevitch (1997).[12] The Maryland court in that case refused to enforce a British libel judgment. The libel had been published in a London newspaper, and both parties were British residents. The defamation concerned a British topic. The court did not enforce the judgment because British law did not provide the same level of protection for speech as American law. That result seems dubious given the lack of any Maryland or American interest in the matter, and it shows how the policy exception can undermine the basic principles of finality and respect due to other courts.

An even more fundamental difficulty with the *Hilton* regime is that it leaves the issue of foreign judgment recognition to state law. That aspect of *Hilton* holding contrasts starkly with other strong rulings of the Supreme Court that make it very clear that foreign policy is the exclusive preserve of the federal government.[13] There are several reasons for that exclusivity. The first reason is uniformity, because the United States must speak with a single voice on foreign affairs. The *Hilton* rule of state control can and does lead to uncertainty and confusion concerning enforcement. More important, however, judgment recognition decisions can create serious foreign-policy problems. It is, after all, an affront to another sovereign to tell it that we do not like its policy; or, worse, that its courts are so debased that they cannot satisfy even a minimalist fairness inquiry, and that justice in that country is apparently for sale in the marketplace. If such a ruling is in fact necessary, it should be handed down by a court in a system entrusted with responsibilities across the entire country.

Moreover, some foreign countries also require a finding of reciprocity before they will enforce an American judgment; a national—as opposed to state—standard certainly would facilitate that inquiry by the foreign court. That, in turn, is likely to make American judgments as a whole more enforceable.

Even with the *Hilton* rule of state control of enforcement decisions, it would still be possible to generate national uniformity on the issue of foreign judgment recognition. The most straightforward approach would be to negotiate mutual recognition treaties with our most important trading partners. That has been the approach on the European continent, the members of the European Economic Community and of the European Free Trade Association having concluded mutual recognition agreements,[14] that provide nearly all of Europe with the practical equivalent of a full faith and credit clause.

The prospects that the United States will adopt a similar strategy are poor. After extensive negotiations between the United States and the United Kingdom from 1974 to 1976, for example, the parties initialed a draft convention, but Britain eventually balked based on its unwillingness to recognize "excessive" American tort damage awards and treble-damage antitrust judgments. In 1980, the negotiations were suspended indefinitely.

In 1992 the United States proposed that the Hague Conference on Private International Law prepare a convention on the recognition of judgments in civil and commercial matters. The conference produced a draft convention in 1999, but American ratification does not seem likely.

Another possibility is the adoption by the states of uniform legislation recognizing foreign judgments. The Conference of Commissioners on Uniform State Laws proposed the Uniform Foreign Money Judgments Recognition Act, and it has been adopted in thirty-one states.[15] The most obvious way to produce uniformity and national control in this area would be for Congress to enact a statute specifying the extent to which American courts must recognize foreign-nation judgments. The American Law Institute has proposed such a statute, but it does not seem to be near the top of anyone's legislative agenda.

FULL FAITH AND CREDIT AND THE PRECLUSION DOCTRINES

Exactly what does it mean to give "full faith and credit" to judicial proceedings? Because that question is inextricably bound up with the law of preclusion, in older terminology, res judicata, a brief discussion of that topic is necessary here. Preliminarily, it is worth considering the precise relationship between the common-law preclusion doctrines on the one hand and the constitutional and statutory full faith and credit mandates on the other. Full faith and credit law involves the effect of a judgment rendered in one state on proceedings in a second state, and the decisions of the Supreme Court have made that decision turn on the effect that the judgment would have on proceedings in the rendering state. That domestic effect in turn depends upon the law of preclusion of the rendering state.

Preclusion is an ancient concept, although the term itself is quite modern (dating to the Second Restatement of Judgments, published in 1981). Historically, judges and lawyers referred to preclusion by the terms "res judicata" and "collateral estoppel," but, regardless of the terminology, the policies behind the law are ancient and clear. Finality in litigation is an important goal for the litigants and for society. The litigants need a resolution of their dispute that they can rely on so that they can order their future affairs sensibly. Further, because litigation is so expensive for the parties, repeated resolution of a single dispute can be prohibitively expensive. Society also benefits from finality because it can allocate only limited resources to dispute resolution. Given the resources available to the judiciary, litigating one dispute twice makes it more likely that some other dispute cannot be resolved at all.

Preclusion, however, is not an absolute rule. The major policy limiting the use of preclusion is justice, defined broadly. Judges have created various ways to avoid the apparently harsh impact of preclusion law in particular cases because it seems to them that the first litigation may have reached results that can be seen in retrospect as plainly wrong. The urge to step in and right those wrongs must be almost irresistible. The tendency increases as courts recognize broad rules of preclusion, like other procedural rules, can deprive a litigant of her rights because she failed to assert them properly and seasonably. Judges like to do justice, and that deprivation can be particularly tempting for them to rectify. In short, the tension between finality and justice has always been active in the development of the law of preclusion.

The Law of Preclusion

Preclusion law divides into two branches. Claim preclusion, or, as it once was called, res judicata, prohibits a second suit based upon the claim or cause of action that was asserted in a prior suit. Issue preclusion, or collateral estoppel, prohibits relitigation of issues actually decided in the prior proceeding regardless of whether the two suits are based upon the same claim or cause of action.[16] So, for instance, if the plaintiff's and the defendant's automobiles collide, claim preclusion will prohibit the plaintiff from bringing one suit to recover for the damage to his car and a second suit to recover for injuries to his person. Because the two suits are based upon the same claim or cause of action, the second action is precluded entirely.

Issue preclusion works differently. Suppose there are two collisions between the same plaintiff and defendant. Claim preclusion will not prohibit two different lawsuits because each collision represents a single cause of action, but issue preclusion may prohibit relitigation of factual issues actually decided in the first proceeding. Thus, if the defendant claims a charitable immunity in the first action, and the court rules that the defendant is not a charity, the defendant will be precluded from raising that same defense in the second suit even though the two suits are based upon different claims or causes of action.

Variations in Preclusion Law

Preclusion law varies from state to state, and although the variations are technical, understanding them is crucial for comprehension of the extent of the states' constitutional obligations under the Full Faith and Credit Clause. Because a complete treatment of the variations in preclusion law is well beyond the scope of this book, a few examples will suffice.

The scope of claim preclusion is a prominent example. Recall that if two suits are based upon the same claim or cause of action, the second suit is precluded entirely; if, instead, the two suits are based upon different claims or causes of action, only issues actually litigated and decided in the first lawsuit are precluded in the second. Thus it is crucial to determine when two suits are based upon the same claim or cause of action: What, in other words, are the dimensions of the single claim or cause of action? An expansive definition of what constitutes a single claim will produce a large scope of operation for the doctrine of claim preclusion, and by contrast, a restrictive definition will produce a much smaller scope of operation.

Although there are many possible definitions of claim or cause of action, two predominate in the case law. The primary right theory posits that a claim consists of the violation of a single primary right; thus the victim in a single name-calling/pushing-and-shoving altercation might have two claims, one for defamation and another for battery. The theory produces this result because the law gives a person a primary right to recover for damage to her reputation and another to recover for harmful or offensive contact to her person. The result is that the victim could bring one lawsuit for defamation and a second lawsuit for battery.

In this same example, the transactional theory of claim or cause of action would find only a single claim because it defines a claim to include all rights emerging from a single transaction or occurrence.[17] Since both the defamation and the battery occurred in the same incident, they constitute a single claim or cause of action; thus, if the victim sued once for defamation only, a second lawsuit for battery would be precluded.

Another variation in preclusion law concerns the universe of people affected by the decision: Who is bound by and who may use the result in subsequent litigation? On the first question there can be no deviation because the federal due process clauses of the Fifth and Fourteenth Amendments prohibit using the result of a litigation against a person who was not a party to or in privity with a party to the lawsuit. (Privity is a term of art that applies principally to persons representing the same legal interest as a party or successors in interest to a party.) A stranger to the first lawsuit would have had no opportunity to address the decision maker or otherwise affect the outcome of the litigation, so binding him to the result would be fundamentally unfair.

Consider, for instance, an automobile accident in which the defendant injures two potential plaintiffs. If the first plaintiff sues the defendant and loses because she is unable to prove the defendant's negligence, that result can have no effect on the second plaintiff in a second lawsuit. Due process prohibits depriving the second plaintiff of his claim without affording him the opportunity to prove the defendant's negligence to the finder of fact.

On the second question—who may use the results from the first lawsuit—there is constitutional room for variety, and the courts, both state and federal, have produced a range of different answers. The common-law answer was the mutuality rule, which provided that a stranger to the first lawsuit could not use its results against a party to that lawsuit in subsequent litigation. Reconsider the example of the automobile accident involving a single defendant and two potential plaintiffs, but this time assume that the first plaintiff succeeds in proving that defendant's negligence in the first lawsuit. The common-law mutuality rule would prohibit the second plaintiff from using the result against the defendant in subsequent litigation.

Beginning in the middle of the twentieth century, however, some courts began to reject the mutuality rule and thus began to permit strangers to the first lawsuit to use its results against parties to that action. Today federal and state courts use a variety of different approaches, some adhering to the common-law mutuality rule, some permitting a stranger to use the result from the first lawsuit but only defensively (as a defendant in the second lawsuit), and others permitting the stranger to use the result either offensively or defensively. The question is one of state or federal common law, and the Constitution leaves room for the courts to disagree.

Whose Law of Preclusion?

The variations in preclusion law raise a fascinating question of full faith and credit: Clearly the clause requires the recognizing state (F-2) to give full faith and credit to a judgment of the rendering state (F-1), but the amount of faith and credit given to a judgment is determined by the law of preclusion and that law varies from state to state. Therefore, the question is: Whose law of preclusion must the F-2 court apply when the F-1 judgment is presented for recognition in F-2? One possibility—that might be termed the nondiscrimination principle—would require the F-2 court to treat the F-1 judgment as it would treat one of its own judgments. That solution would at least prevent state courts from discriminating against judgments from other states, one of the goals of the Full Faith and Credit Clause.

The Supreme Court, however, not satisfied with that minimal reading of the Full Faith and Credit Clause, has required more of the recognizing state. By and large, the Court has held that the obligation of the recognizing state to give full faith and credit to a judgment of the rendering state means that it must give the judgment the same effect that a court in the rendering state would give it. That it can do, however, only if it applies the preclusion law of the rendering state.

Preclusion law permits two possible permutations of this rule: the law of F-2 might be less preclusive than that of F-1, or it might be more preclusive. Considering each of these possibilities in turn provides added texture to the Supreme Court's interpretation of the Full Faith and Credit Clause. Suppose first that the law of F-2 is less preclusive than that of F-1: This could occur, for instance, if F-2 has adopted the primary right theory of cause of action while F-1 has opted for the transactional theory, or if F-2 has retained the mutuality rule while F-1 has abandoned it.

The policy behind the Full Faith and Credit Clause suggests that F-2 should not be able to apply its own less preclusive law. An attempt to do so, although consistent with the nondiscrimination principle, would give the F-1 judgment *less* effect than it would get in F-1. Certainly it would result in giving the F-1 judgment some faith and credit, but it would be hard to argue that the "faith and credit" awarded was "full."

The Court's statements on the issue have been clear and fully consistent with full faith and credit policy. Relying on the "plain meaning" of the Full Faith and Credit Clause and the full faith and credit statute, 28 U.S.C. § 1738, which provides that an F-1 judgment, presented in F-2, receive "the same faith and credit . . . as they have . . . in the courts of such state . . . from which they are taken," the Court has held that an F-2 court must give the F-1 judgment "at least the res judicata effect . . . [that] would be accorded in the state which rendered it" (Durfee v. Duke, 1963).[18] Thus, the result of this permutation is clear: An F-2 court presented with an F-1 judgment must measure its preclusive effect according to the law of F-1 when that law is more preclusive than its own.

When the law of F-2 is more preclusive than the law of F-1, the situation is more complex. The law of F-2 might be more preclusive than that of F-1 if F-2 used the transactional definition of cause of action instead of F-1's less preclusive primary right theory, or if F-2 had abandoned the mutuality rule while F-1 retained it.[19] In both cases if F-2 applied its own preclusion law, the result would be more preclusive effect for the F-1 judgment than that judgment would receive in F-1.

In this permutation, there is a strong argument for permitting F-2 to apply its own, more preclusive, law. Arguably the result should not be offensive to F-1, nor should it be inconsistent with the policy of national unity that stands behind both the Full Faith and Credit Clause and statute. The goal of both provisions is to prevent the lack of respect to F-1's judicial process that would be shown by underrecognition of the F-1 judgment. No similar disrespect accompanies overrecognition of that judgment. Moreover, why should the less preclusive law of F-1 force the courts of F-2 to expend judicial resources to relitigate claims or issues that the finality policies of F-2 regard as settled? Does not the strong interest of F-2 in judicial economy permit it to spare its courts what, according to its law, is needless effort?[20]

There are, however, contrary arguments. For one thing, giving more preclusive effect to the F-1 judgment might be seriously unfair to the losing litigant in F-1. That litigant might well have chosen the theories of recovery to present in its complaint or the amount of effort to expend in the proceeding based upon the relatively unambitious preclusion law of F-1. Applying the more preclusive law of F-2 would frustrate those justified expectations. (The same arguments can be made by F-1 defendants.) A second argument is based on the language of the full faith and credit statute, 28 U.S.C. § 1738, which requires that the judgment receive the "*same* faith and credit" in F-2 that it would receive in F-1 (emphasis added). Arguably, that phrase prohibits overrecognition as well as underrecognition, "the same" signifying "at least as much *and* no more."[21]

These arguments may have only academic interest after the Supreme Court's decision in Marrese v. American Academy of Orthopaedic Surgeons (1985),[22] which held that 28 U.S.C. § 1738 prohibits a federal court from giving a state court judgment more preclusive effect than it would receive in a court of the state that rendered it. It is possible that the court intended *Marrese* to apply only to federal courts, but nothing in the language of the full faith statute suggests such a result; its mandate applies to "every court within the United States," which includes state as well as federal courts. Finally, the policy arguments against overrecognition are the same, regardless of whether F-2 is a federal or state court.

An Important Exception

There is one long-standing and uncontroversial exception to the law-of-the-rendering-state rule. The law of the enforcing state determines the methods for enforcing a judgment of the rendering state.[23] The exception embraces such issues as whether a new action must be brought in the enforcing state or whether the original judgment simply can be registered, whether a summary judgment procedure is available in the enforcement action, how an equity order (e.g., an injunction) can be enforced, and whether certain enforcement mechanisms are available at all.[24]

By and large the issues embraced by the exception deal with mechanics that do not substantially affect the ability to obtain relief at all. The one notable contrary example is limitations. Every state has a statute of limitations on actions brought to enforce judgments, and the exception means that the statute of the enforcing state can cut off the right to enforce a judgment even though the law of the rendering state would not. The enforcing state cannot, of course, apply a discriminatory limitations period against foreign judgments.

Methods of Enforcement

By far, the most commonly litigated application of the Full Faith and Credit Clause is the enforcement in one state of a money judgment obtained in a sister state.[25] Not only was this function of the clause an important tool of the Constitution's Framers for making a united nation out of a set of independence states, but it also facilitated the movement of eastern capital to western and southern states to develop the natural resources there. An eastern creditor would be quite reluctant to lend money to a southern or western debtor if a judgment obtained in the creditor's state could not be enforced against assets of the debtor in his home state.

But exactly how does sister-state enforcement of a judgment occur? One way to begin answering the question is to consider how a state court judgment is enforced at home. The usual device is a writ of execution, an order to a sheriff or other judicial official to seize some of the defendant's property, sell it at auction, and apply the proceeds to the plaintiff's judgment. One might expect the enforcement of a sister state's judgment to proceed in similar fashion, with the plaintiff presenting a writ of execution from the rendering state to the sheriff in the enforcing state, and that official seizing some of the defendant's property there.

In fact, however such a simple and direct method for enforcement has never been required by the Full Faith and Credit Clause. Rather, the usual process is for the plaintiff to bring an action in the enforcing state based on the judgment debt created by the judgment issued in the rendering state. The plaintiff would then enforce this second judgment via a writ of execution presented to the enforcing state sheriff, who would then seize some of the defendant's local property and conduct a judicial sale.

This traditional procedure is slow and clumsy; the plaintiff in the enforcement action, having already won a lawsuit in the rendering state, must file a second lawsuit in the enforcing state and serve the defendant with process; the defendant usually will answer and may assert defenses; and even a disposition by a summary judgment might take months. As a result, commentators have condemned the traditional procedure[26] leading federal and state legislators and rule drafters to seek alternatives.

In 1948, Congress legislated just such an alternative, albeit only for federal courts. This law permitted a judgment from one federal district court to be registered in any other district.[27] According to the statute, a "judgment so registered shall have the same effect as a judgment of the district court of the district where registered and may be enforced in like manner." Thus the registered judgment becomes essentially a judgment of the enforcing district, which like any other such judgment, can be enforced by writ of execution against any of the defendant's property in that district. The plaintiff need not bring a separate lawsuit, nor need the judgment debtor be notified.

The Full Faith and Credit Clause would probably permit Congress to enact a similar registration statute for state court judgments, but so far Congress has not done so. Stepping into the breach was the Conference of Commissioners on Uniform State Laws, which proposed a procedure analogous to the federal act. Under the Uniform Enforcement of Foreign Judgments Act (UEFJA),[28] the plaintiff can "file" a judgment from the rendering state in the enforcing state court, and a judgment "so filed has the same effect and is subject to the same procedures, defenses and proceedings for reopening, vacating, or staying as a judgment of . . . [the enforcing state] and may be enforced or satisfied in like manner."[29]

Although the federal statute and the Uniform Act differ on important technical questions, the motivating policy and effect of the two are the same, the salutary modernization of the procedures for enforcing sister-state judgments. The federal act applies throughout the federal district court system and the Uniform Act has been adopted in forty-one states.

Summary

The law of full faith and credit is based in large part on the law of preclusion. Motivated by the needs of both the litigants and the judicial system for finality, preclusion law consists of two primary components, claim preclusion and issue preclusion. Claim preclusion prohibits a second lawsuit based on single claim or cause of action that proceeded to judgment on the merits in a prior action; issue preclusion prohibits relitigation of factual issues actually decided in the prior action regardless of whether the two suits are based upon the same claim or cause of action. The law of preclusion varies from state to state, with some courts willing to give greater scope to the doctrines of claim and issue preclusion than others. In the interstate, or full faith and credit context, that variation raises the question whether F-2 can apply its own law of preclusion to an F-1 judgment or whether, on the contrary, the Full Faith and Credit Clause and statute require it to apply the preclusion law of F-1. The Supreme Court has stated clearly that an F-2 court must apply the law of F-1 when that law is more preclusive than its own; although not as certain, it is likely that the Supreme Court would hold that F-2 also must apply the law of F-1 when it is less preclusive than its own preclusion law. The only settled and uncontroversial exception to the law of the rendering state rule concerns methods of enforcement, which are controlled by the law of the enforcing state.

FULL FAITH AND CREDIT AND JUDICIAL JURISDICTION

Although a full treatment of jurisdiction is well beyond the scope of this book, the concepts of jurisdiction and full faith and credit are so intertwined that a summary discussion is required. The reason that the concepts are so closely connected is the basic principle that a judgment rendered by a court that lacks territorial jurisdiction constitutes a violation of the due process clause and, therefore, is not entitled to full faith and credit.

The Traditional Taxonomy

In our legal system a state cannot exercise judicial jurisdiction over the person or property of the defendant without some sort of connection or relationship to that defendant or to the property. Further, the type of relationship or connection determines the kind of jurisdiction that the state may exercise. Traditionally, American courts have exercised jurisdiction in four principal ways: personal (in personam) jurisdiction, in rem and quasi in rem jurisdiction, and attachment jurisdiction. The category of jurisdiction the court exercises controls two principal variables, the kind of contact required with the defendant or her property, and the kind of judgment the court can issue.

A court with personal jurisdiction over the defendant can issue a personal judgment against the defendant for money or any other kind of legal, equitable, or declaratory relief permitted under the substantive law. A plaintiff with a money judgment then can enforce it against any of the defendant's property within the forum state and, by operation of the Full Faith and Credit Clause, against any of the defendant's property in other states. If, instead, the plaintiff seeks equitable relief, the court, with the threat of contempt, can order the defendant to do or refrain from doing any act.

The requirement for exercising the plenary power of personal jurisdiction, articulated by the Supreme Court in International Shoe Co. v. Washington (1945), is that the defendant must have "certain minimum contacts with [the state] such that the maintenance of the suit does not offend 'traditional notions of fair play and substantial justice.' "[30] The Supreme Court in World-Wide Volkswagen Corp. v. Woodson (1980)[31] read that formula to require a two-part test.[32]

First, the defendant must have purposefully established prelitigation connections with the state. The defendant satisfies the contacts requirement by "purposefully avail[ing] itself of the privilege of conducting activities within the forum State, thus invoking the benefits and protections of its laws."[33] The defendant's activity must be such "that it could reasonably anticipate being haled into court in the forum."[34] In a products liability case, it is probably sufficient that the defendant placed its product into the stream of commerce with the knowledge that the stream would take it into the forum state.[35] With intentional torts, such as defamation, intentional action geographically targeting the plaintiff in the forum is enough to make the defendant amenable there.[36] In contract cases, a defendant who enters a transaction that has a significant connection with the state is likely to satisfy the contacts portion of the due process requirement.[37]

The second branch of the test requires the court to determine that the exercise of jurisdiction is fair or reasonable, taking into account the interests of the defendant, the plaintiff, and the forum state, as well as litigational convenience.[38]

A court exercising in rem, quasi in rem, or attachment jurisdiction can affect the defendant only in a very limited way. It exercises power over property, which is attached at the commencement of the action, and its authority is limited to creating and destroying interests in the property.[39] In an in rem action, the court litigates the preexisting claims of title in the thing of everyone in the world. Justified primarily by necessity, in rem jurisdiction is concentrated in a few narrow areas—such as forfeiture, eminent domain, admiralty and probate—where it is essential that the court be able to create unassailable title in the thing in one person and destroy the interests of everyone else.

Quasi in rem jurisdiction is similar to in rem jurisdiction in that the underlying dispute involves preexisting claims of ownership in the thing but differs in that the court exercises jurisdiction over the named parties only, not the whole world.[40] Attachment jurisdiction is fundamentally different from the other two because the underlying dispute does not involve rival claims of title to the attached property; rather the plaintiff has a personal claim (contract or tort, for example) against the defendant, and, unable to obtain personal jurisdiction over the defendant, uses a piece of his local property as a hostage, compelling him either to appear and defend or default and forfeit the property.

The due process requirement for in rem or quasi in rem jurisdiction is satisfied simply by the presence of the property within the territory of the state; there is no requirement that the defendant have "minimum contacts" with the forum.[41] The same was also true of attachment jurisdiction until the Supreme Court's decision in Shaffer v. Heitner (1977). In that landmark decision, the Supreme Court held that except in cases where attachment jurisdiction is used to secure or enforce a personal judgment, the contacts and fairness standard of *International Shoe* applies to attachment actions as well as lawsuits based on personal jurisdiction.

The Relationship of the Taxonomy to Full Faith and Credit

The faith and credit that F-2 owes to an F-1 judgment depends upon the type of jurisdiction the F-1 court exercises. If the F-1 court validly exercises personal jurisdiction and issues a personal judgment against the defendant, the obligation of the F-2 tribunal is quite clear. In a lawsuit in its courts based upon the F-1 judgment, the F-2 court must recognize the validity of the F-1 judgment and make available to the plaintiff the same enforcement procedures that would be available to a litigant who had procured an F-2 judgment.

The full faith and credit obligation to recognize and enforce any form of in rem (in rem, quasi in rem, or attachment) judgment is a more complicated question.[42] A useful place to begin is with the generalization that an in rem judgment is entitled to full faith and credit. To assess the import of that generalization, however, it is crucial to remember the very limited effect that an in rem judgment has. All that an F-1 court with in rem jurisdiction can do is to create and destroy interests in the attached property, so an F-2 court's obligation under the Full Faith and Credit Clause is simply to recognize those interests.

The most straightforward example is an action in F-1 to probate a testator's will. If the F-1 court admits the will to probate, and the will gives the testator's automobile to his niece, the F-1 court's judgment will establish the niece's title in the car and extinguish the rival claims of everyone else in the world. Thus, if the niece drives the car into F-2, and the testator's son sues her for the car, the F-2 court must rule in favor of the niece even if the F-1 court lacked personal jurisdiction over the testator's son. The F-1 court had in rem jurisdiction over the automobile simply because it was within the territory of F-1; thus, it had authority to award it to the niece and extinguish the claim of the son. The obligation of the F-2 court, then, is simply to recognize the interests created and destroyed in the F-1 proceeding; that is, it must recognize that the car belongs to the niece, and not the son.[43]

If an F-1 court with only in rem jurisdiction acts beyond its limited powers and purports to issue a personal judgment, that judgment will not be entitled to full faith and credit in F-2. A fairly typical example involves a mortgage foreclosure, where the creditor has lent money to the debtor and received in return a mortgage on the debtor's land in F-1. Upon the debtor's default, the creditor sues the debtor in an F-1 court seeking to foreclose the mortgage, relief that the court can grant simply because the land is within the territory of F-1. If, however, the proceeds from the sale of the property are insufficient to cover the full amount of the debt, the court cannot issue a deficiency judgment for the remainder without having personal jurisdiction over the debtor. Any such judgment will be invalid and thus not entitled to full faith and credit in F-2.[44] In other words, if the creditor sues the debtor on the judgment in an F-2 court, it will not recognize the F-1 deficiency judgment; if the creditor wants to be able to execute against the defendant's property in F-2, it will have to bring a new lawsuit based upon the original debt, rather than one based upon the F-1 judgment.

So far the discussion has focused upon the claim preclusive effects of the F-1 proceedings, but there may be issue preclusion effects as well. The leading case is Harnischfeger Sales Corp. v. Sternberg Dredging Co. (1939).[45] The debtor there purchased a dredge from the creditor and gave the creditor a promissory note for the purchase price and a chattel mortgage on the dredge. When the debtor defaulted, the creditor sued in Louisiana seeking to foreclose the mortgage on the dredge and also to obtain a personal judgment. (The debtor was subject to personal jurisdiction in Mississippi, but not in Louisiana.) The parties appeared in the Louisiana court and fully litigated the debtor's defense that the dredge would not handle a "two-yard bucket," as the creditor had warranted. After the court resolved this issue in favor of the creditor, it foreclosed the chattel mortgage, ordered the sale of the dredge, and issued a personal judgment against the debtor for the remainder of the purchase price. The Louisiana Supreme Court, however, upheld on appeal only the mortgage foreclosure, reversing the in personam judgment because the trial court had lacked personal jurisdiction over the debtor.

When the creditor next sued the debtor in Mississippi for the portion of the debt not realized in the sale of the dredge, the debtor again pleaded in defense the creditor's breach of the two-yard bucket warranty. The Mississippi Supreme Court held that the warranty defense was precluded by the findings on that issue in the Louisiana court. It did not matter that the personal judgment issued by the Louisiana trial court was invalid for lack of personal jurisdiction. The Mississippi action was not a suit to enforce that invalid judgment, nor was it a suit to enforce the in rem portion of the Louisiana judgment, which already had been satisfied, of course, by the sale of the dredge. Rather, because the creditor's Mississippi lawsuit was based upon the original debt, the only effect of the Louisiana proceeding would be to preclude the two-yard bucket warranty defense. The lesson from *Harnischfeger* is that the Full Faith and Credit Clause requires an F-2 court not only to give claim preclusion effect to the judgments of the F-1 court but also to give issue preclusion effect to that court's findings, even when they are made in an in rem action.

Evaluation of the *Harnischfeger* rule requires considering the circumstances when it usually applies—when the defendant has made a limited appearance in the F-1 proceeding. The limited appearance is a device designed to mitigate the unfairness to the defendant inherent in an action where jurisdiction is based only upon the presence of property in the state.[46] Traditionally, such a defendant faced an unattractive choice: It could default and forfeit its interest in the attached property, or it could appear and by doing so consent to the court's personal jurisdiction. The limited appearance device gave the defendant an additional option by permitting it to appear to litigate the merits of the controversy without consenting to the court's personal jurisdiction.

One effect of the limited appearance is to raise the *Harnischfeger* issue: Without that device, no factual issues can be actually litigated and decided in a property-based jurisdiction action, because the defendant would have to appear and consent to personal jurisdiction in order to litigate those questions. Thus, the issue of preclusion would never arise.

There is some controversy about the *Harnischfeger* principle. The argument against the principle is that it minimizes the value to the defendant of the limited appearance—the purpose of which is to allow the defendant to defend its interest in the property without requiring it to submit to personal jurisdiction. The *Harnischfeger* principle, by giving preclusive effect to the F-1 court's findings, produces a result for the defendant that is nearly as damaging as the personal judgment would be.

The counterargument is based on preclusion principles and judicial economy. In the F-1 action there was a full and fair litigation and determination of the issues, which taxed the court's and the parties' limited resources. It would be wasteful to relitigate those issues and expend more of the court's and the parties' time and resources in litigation in F-2.

Ultimately, the *Harnischfeger* principle seems correct, especially after the Court's decision in *Shaffer*, which removed much of the possibility of unfairness to the defendant of an attachment action. After *Shaffer*, the limited appearance no longer seems so crucial to assure fairness to the defendant; thus, any diminution in its value caused by *Harnischfeger* preclusion principle is more than compensated for by gains in judicial economy and finality.

THE IRON LAW OF FULL FAITH AND CREDIT

The long common-law development of the Full Faith and Credit Clause has worked quite well, which probably explains why there has been so little legislative activity concerning its "effect." That is not surprising, for the clause really is all about litigation and its effects, and those kinds of question are best handled by judges and lawyers in the crucible of real cases. Both the basic rule and its exceptions have long been established. The heart of the Full Faith and Credit Clause is what we have elsewhere styled the "Iron Law of Full Faith and Credit."[47] This Iron Law is majestic in its simplicity: A judgment rendered by one American court (state or federal) and presented for recognition in another American court shall have at least the same preclusive effect in the recognizing court as it would have in the rendering court. The Iron Law serves two basic and complementary purposes. First, it removes much of the friction that might otherwise arise in the daily dealings of states, and their citizens, with one another. Second, by avoiding the relitigation of issues and facts that have already been decided, the Clause produces immense savings of time and resources for both the courts and the litigants.

Because we are dealing with a legal principle, there are, of course, a number of qualifications and exceptions; the most important arises when there is a lack of personal jurisdiction in the rendering state. Because the full faith and credit rule relating to judgments truly is an "Iron Law," however, the exceptions are few and subject to relatively little fudging by the courts.

This section begins with an examination of the Iron Law of Full Faith and Credit: what it is, where it comes from, and its status today. It then proceeds to consider the special application of the rule to inconsistent judgments. The next chapter treats three types of qualifications or exceptions to the Iron Law.

The Basic Rule

The Iron Law is a rule of complete preclusion: Any judgment of an American court is entitled (at least) to the preclusive effect that it would have enjoyed in the state of rendition. This rule of preclusion has a long history, dating back to John Marshall's Supreme Court and received its most famous enunciation in Fauntleroy v. Lum (1908).

On the surface, *Fauntleroy* was an easy enough case. The parties had entered into a "futures" contract in Mississippi for the sale of cotton (that is, a contract for cotton to be delivered sometime in the future). After a purported breach, the controversy went to arbitration, and the winner of the arbitration then sued the defendant in Missouri to enforce the arbitration award. In that litigation, the defendant raised the defense of illegality for the first time, contending that the future's contract was a gambling transaction under Mississippi law and, therefore, void. The Missouri court, however, held for the plaintiff, who then took the Missouri judgment to Mississippi, and sought to enforce it there. When the Mississippi Supreme Court denied enforcement to the Missouri judgment, the case made it to the Supreme Court of the United States.

That Court reversed. Writing for a five-member majority, Justice Oliver Wendell Holmes treated the problem as a routine application of well-settled law. Justice Holmes relied on a case decided almost a century earlier, Hampton v. McConnel (1818). There, Chief Justice Marshall had opined that

> the judgment of a state court should have the same credit, validity and effect, in every other court in the United States, which it had in the state where it was pronounced, and that whatever pleas would be good to a suit thereon in such state, and none others, could be pleased in any other court in the United States.[48]

In the closest the *Fauntleroy* opinion came to a policy argument, Justice Holmes dealt with the possibility that the Missouri court might have made a "rare" mistake:

> If it was mistaken, it made a natural mistake. The validity of its judgment, even in Mississippi, is . . . not a matter to arouse the susceptibilities of the states, all of which are equally concerned in the question and equally on both sides.[49]

In other words, (a) No court will cheat on its constitutional obligations, although a court of course might be mistaken; and (b) there is an internal political check in that all states benefit equally from having their judgments recognized. Expressed somewhat differently, each state recognizes that its best interests will be served by unquestioning recognition of the judgments of every other state.

Justice Holmes concluded definitively: "[T]he judgment cannot be impeached in Mississippi even if it went upon a misapprehension of the Mississippi law."[50] Thus, the Iron Law of Full Faith and Credit can be traced, through Justice Holmes, directly back to Chief Justice Marshall, an awesome lineage of revered judges. At the end of his typically laconic opinion, Justice Holmes duly noted that "[o]f course, a want of jurisdiction over either the person or the subject-matter might be shown."[51]

The *Fauntleroy* dissent was written by Justice Edward White. It began with a sophisticated states' rights argument: Because different conditions may prevail in different states, there will be variations in the exercise of the police power among the states, and each state, naturally enough, will wish to enforce its law in its own territory. According to the dissent, however, the ruling in *Fauntleroy* "endow[s] each state with authority to overthrow the public policy and criminal statutes of the others, thereby depriving all of their lawful authority."[52] Justice White then argued that the Full Faith and Credit Clause surely could not have been intended to reach that result. Rather, it was meant to embody an enforceable version of the "rules of comity"; those rules were not designed to deny the state's regulatory authority over a contract between citizens of Mississippi, made in that state and to be performed there.

The choices presented by the two *Fauntleroy* opinions are clear. Justice Holmes's functional approach is easy to apply and eases friction among the states. The deferential, states' rights policy approach of the dissent certainly enhances state policy interests but at the cost of predictability. That loss, however, surely would *increase* interstate friction, something the Full Faith and Credit Clause was designed to prevent. The role, if any, of public policy in interstate enforcement of judgment will be revisited *infra*, Chapter 5.

The importance of *Fauntleroy* cannot be overstated. The majority ordered that the Missouri judgment be enforced even though that judgment was illegal under Mississippi law—the law of the state that surely was the one most concerned with the transaction. In other words, the F-1 judgment trumps the policy interest of any other state that the judgment might offend, thus making the Iron Law of Full Faith and Credit a very potent weapon of enforcement.

A Special Application: Inconsistent Judgments

Consider the problem presented when a court in Delaware refuses to enforce a judgment rendered by a New Jersey court on the ground that the New Jersey court lacked jurisdiction over the defendant. The plaintiff, following her disappointment in Delaware, then asks a court in Florida to enforce the New Jersey judgment. What should the Florida court do? Which of the earlier (and inconsistent) two judgments should it follow? Or should it make its own independent determination of the question of whether the New Jersey court had personal jurisdiction over the defendant?

Fortunately, the Supreme Court provided a definitive answer to those questions in Treinies v. Sunshine Mining Co. (1939).[53] The case involved a dispute between S and D over the ownership of stock. First, S won a judgment from a state court in Washington. Then he tried to use the judgment in litigation in Idaho between the same two parties. That court refused to enforce the earlier judgment because it found that the Washington court had lacked subject matter jurisdiction and its decree, therefore, was void. A third round of litigation then began in federal court, and wound up in the Supreme Court of the United States. The Court adopted a "last-in-time" rule, which states that the last decision in a line of inconsistent judgments must be recognized for purposes of full faith and credit. A party unhappy with a decision by one court, therefore, must appeal that decision to a superior court within that system, and finally, to the Supreme Court if necessary.

Treinies, therefore, is faithful to the theme of Fauntleroy v. Lum: The correct way to attack "wrong" decisions is to appeal them to a superior court, rather than wait to mount a collateral attack in a separate court system. The lesson to the losing party is an easy one: Always appeal the case to the next level or risk losing your rights. The *Treinies* rule also has the great advantage of ease of application: No messy state interest balancing is necessary to apply it. All that the third court must do is enforce the last decision; of course, that decision must have been rendered by a court with jurisdiction over the defendant.

The last in time rule of *Treinies* does suffer from a possible drawback, for it depends on the good faith of the enforcing court. But if that be a defect, it is one that it shares with Fauntleroy v. Lum; and, indeed, with the federal system itself, for a basic premise underlying that system is that each state will treat the other states with respect. And, after all, that is what Article IV is all about.

In any event, the rule seems to have caused little trouble in practice. Its most problematic application occurs when F-3 is also F-1. The best known example is Colby v. Colby (1962).[54] There, a Maryland court had refused to recognize a Nevada divorce decree on the ground that the Nevada court lacked subject matter jurisdiction (the petitioner, the court found, had not been domiciled in Nevada at the time of the divorce). The Maryland court issued its own inconsistent decree, which was presented for enforcement in Nevada. The Nevada court, however, refused enforcement.

Under *Treinies* and *Fauntleroy*, that refusal was wrong. The latter decision makes that result quite clear; in *Fauntleroy*, F-2 could not refuse to recognize a judgment even though that judgment apparently led to the enforcement of a contract that violated F-2 law. When that decision is combined with the "last-in-time" rule of *Treinies*, it is difficult, if not impossible, to argue in support of the *Colby* decision.

NOTES

1. Mitsubishi Motors Corp. v. Soler Chrysler-Plymouth, Inc. 473 U.S. 614 (1985).

2. University of Tennessee v. Elliott, 478 U.S. 788 (1986).

3. *See* American Law Institute, *Restatement of the Law, Second, Judgments* § 83 (St. Paul: American Law Institute Publishers, 1982); American Law Institute, *Restatement of the Law, Second: Conflict of Laws* § 92, comment a (American Law Institute Pub., 1971).

4. *Id.*

5. Santa Clara Pueblo v. Martinez, 436 U.S. 49 at 66 n. 21 (1978).

6. Some courts continued to follow this view until well into the twentieth century. *See, e.g.*, Svenska Handelsbanken v. Carlson, 258 F. Supp. 448 (D. Mass 1966), a 150-year-old Massachusetts case law that required that only prima facie effect be given to a Swedish judgment. For a discussion of the early cases, see Courtland H. Peterson, *Foreign Country Judgments and the Second Restatement of Conflict of Laws*, 72 Columbia L. Rev. 220, 224–27 (1972).

7. Hilton v. Guyot, 159 U.S. 113 (1895).

8. *See, e.g.*, Johnston v. Compagnie Generale Transatlantique, 242 N.Y. 381, 152 N.E. 121 (1926).

9. *See, e.g.*, Somportex, Ltd. v. Philadelphia Chewing Gum Corp., 453 F.2d 435 (3d Cir. 1971).

10. The Restatement (Second) of Conflict of Laws § 98 limits recognition to judgments resulting from "contested proceedings," which seems to disqualify default judgments, but the comments suggest that a default judgment should be recognized provided that the court had personal jurisdiction over the defendant and the defendant received adequate notice and an opportunity to be heard.

11. The Restatement (Third) of Foreign Relations Law of the United States 482(1)(a), (2)(d), requires nonrecognition if the foreign judicial system does not provide impartial tribunals or fair procedures, and permits nonrecognition of a judgment based on a cause of action "repugnant to the public policy" of an American jurisdiction.

12. Telnikoff v. Matusevitch, 347 Md. 561, 702 A.2d 230 (1997).

13. *See, e.g.*, Crosby v. National Foreign Trade Council, 120 S. Ct. 2288 (2000), which

held unconstitutional a Massachusetts law designed to punish companies doing business in Burma.

14. The Brussels Convention on Jurisdiction and the Enforcement of Judgments in Civil and Commercial Matters, September 27, 1968, applies to the European Economic Community, and the parallel Lugano Convention on Jurisdiction and Enforcement of Judgments in Civil and Commercial Matters, September 16, 1988, includes the six additional nations of the European Free Trade Association.

15. 13 U.L.A. 261 (2000 Supp.).

16. *See* Cromwell v. County of Sac, 94 U.S. 351 (1876).

17. The example is based on Rush v. City of Maple Heights, 167 Ohio St. 221, 147 N.E.2d 599, *cert. denied.*, 358 U.S. 814 (1958).

18. Durfee v. Duke, 375 U.S. 106, 109 (1963).

19. The leading case is Hart v. American Airlines, Inc., 61 Misc.2d 41, 304 N.Y.S.2d 810 (N.Y. Sup. Ct. 1969).

20. This issue is examined in Sanford N. Caust-Ellenbogen, *False Conflicts and Interstate Preclusion: Moving Beyond a Wooden Reading of the Full Faith and Credit Statute*, 58 Fordham L. Rev. 593 (1990); Robert C. Casad, *Intersystem Issue Preclusion and the Restatement (Second) of Judgments*, 66 Cornell L. Rev. 510, 523 (1981); Jeffrey E. Lewis, *Mutuality in Conflict—Flexibility and Full Faith and Credit*, 23 Drake L. Rev. 364 (1974).

21. Barbara Ann Atwood, *State Court Judgments in Federal Litigation: Mapping the Contours of Full Faith and Credit*, 58 Indiana L.J. 59, 70, n. 54 (1982).

22. Marrese v. American Academy of Orthopaedic Surgeons, 470 U.S. 373 (1985).

23. ALI, Restatement (Second) of Conflict of Laws § 99.

24. *Id.*, comment b. Some states and the federal court system provide for the registration or filing of the original judgment in the enforcing state and do not require a separate enforcing action to be filed. *See, e.g.*, 28 U.S.C. § 1963; the Uniform Enforcement of Foreign Judgments Act, 13 U.L.A. 149 (1964).

25. The procedures for enforcing non-money judgments are different. Some, such as a decree of divorce or adoption, are self-executing in the sense that they do not require initiating a judicial proceeding in the recognizing state. Others, ordering equitable relief, such as an injunction or specific performance, are enforced by the court's contempt power. Presumably if the defendant escaped the rendering state before it could exercise that power over him, the plaintiff would have to sue the defendant in the state of his refuge, seeking recognition for the rendering state judgment there. Via that mechanism, the plaintiff could obtain an injunction from the second state, which then would enforce it with its own contempt power. *See* Baker v. General Motors, 522 U.S. 222 (1998) (Scalia, J., concurring).

26. *See, e.g.*, Brainerd Currie, *Full Faith and Credit, Chiefly to Judgments: A Role for Congress*, Supreme Court Rev. 89 (1964); Robert H. Jackson, *Full, Faith and Credit—The Lawyer's Clause of the Constitution*, 45 Columbia L. Rev. 1 (1945).

27. 28 U.S.C. § 1963.

28. 13 Uniform Laws Annotated 149 (1964).

29. The Uniform Reciprocal Enforcement of Support Act (URESA), 9B Uniform Laws Annotated 381 (1968) provided for a similar enforcement process for sister-state child and spousal support orders, as did its successor, the Revised Uniform Reciprocal Enforcement of Support Act (RURESA). 9C Uniform Laws Annotated 273 (2001). The Uniform Interstate Family Support Act (UIFSA), 9 Uniform Laws Annotated (Part IB) 235 (1999), retains the registration option of its predecessors and also provides several mechanisms for more direct enforcement of a support order in a sister state.

30. International Shoe Co. v. Washington, 326 U.S. 310, 316 (1945).
31. World-Wide Volkswagen Corp. v. Woodson, 444 U.S. 286 (1980).
32. Burger King Corp. v. Rudzewicz, 471 U.S. 462, 472 (1985).
33. Hanson v. Denckla, 357 U.S. 235, 253 (1958).
34. World-Wide Volkswagen Corp. v. Woodson, 444 U.S. 286 (1980).
35. *Id.*
36. Calder v. Jones, 465 U.S. 783 (1984).
37. Burger King Corp. v. Rudzewicz, 471 U.S. 472 (1985); McGee v. International Life Ins. Co., 355 U.S. 220 (1957).
38. Asahi Metal Industry Co., Ltd. v. Superior Court, 480 U.S. 102 (1987).
39. See William M. Richman and William L. Reynolds, *Understanding Conflict of Laws* §§ 11, 111 (3d ed., LexisNexis, 2002).
40. ALI, Restatement (Second) of Judgments § 6, comment a.
41. *Id.* § 6, comment e.
42. See generally Richman & Reynolds, *supra* note 39 at § 111.
43. ALI, Restatement (Second) of Judgments § 30 (1).
44. *Id.*, § 30 (2). The example follows Combs v. Combs, 249 Ky. 155, 60 S.W.2d 368 (1933).
45. For commentary on the *Harnischfeger* decision, see Charles W. Taintor II, *Foreign Judgments in Rem: Full Faith and Credit v. Res Judicata in Personam*, 8 Pittsburgh L. Rev. 223 (1942).
46. 189 Miss. 73, 191 So. 94 (1939). The limited appearance differs from a similar sounding device, the special appearance, in two important respects. First, the limited appearance occurs only in an action where the court's jurisdiction is based upon the presence of property in the state; a defendant can make a special appearance in any type of action, in personam or in rem. Second the function of the special appearance is only to allow the defendant to litigate the court's jurisdiction without the appearance constituting a consent to that jurisdiction. Unlike the limited appearance, the special appearance does not permit the defendant to litigate the merits of the claim.
47. Richman & Reynolds, *supra* note 39, at §§ 114–16.
48. Hampton v. McConnel, 16 U.S. (3 Wheat.) 234, 235 (1818).
49. *Id.* at 238.
50. Fauntleroy v. Lum 210 U.S. 230 at 237 (1908).
51. *Id.*
52. *Id.* at 239. (White, J., dissenting). As the Mississippi Supreme Court had noted in refusing to enforce the Missouri judgment, "If this be law, all that is necessary to free the most corrupt transaction from all objection is to obtain service on a party, and get judgment in another state." Lum v. Fauntleroy, 80 Miss. 757, 32 So. 290, 291 (1902).
53. Other fundamental cases are in accord. E.g., Baldwin v. Iowa State Men's Traveling Ass'n., 283 U.S. 522 (1931) (holding that a judgment rendered after a finding of personal jurisdiction in F-1 cannot be attached in F-2. The leading article is Ruth B. Ginsburg, "Judgments in Search of Full Faith and Credit: The Last-in-Time Rule for Conflicting Judgments," 82 *Harvard L. Rev.* (1969) 798; at the time she wrote the article, Justice Ginsburg was still a law professor.
54. Colby v. Colby, 78 Nev. 150, 369 P.2d 1019, *cert. denied*, 371 U.S. 888 (1962).

5

Exceptions and Qualifications to the Rule of Finality

EXCEPTIONS I: JUDGMENT NOT PRECLUSIVE UNDER F-1 LAW

The previous chapter discussed the basic law of preclusion: The enforcing state must give the same preclusive effect to a judgment as would the rendering state. This chapter discusses the exceptions. There are three types of cases where an F-2 court need not give preclusive effect to an F-1 judgment. The first of these does not represent an exception to the Iron Law of Full Faith and Credit because it is made up of cases where the judgment is not entitled to preclusive effect according to the law of F-1 itself. Examples are when the F-1 judgment is not final, when it is not on the merits, when it is modifiable, or when it was procured by fraud. In these cases, the mandate that the earlier decree be given as much preclusive effect in the enforcing jurisdiction as it would in the rendering state is not violated because the rendering state would not treat its own judgment as preclusive.

The second class of cases that might be considered to be exceptions to the Iron Law turn out, on analysis, not really to be true exceptions to the full faith and credit mandate. These are cases where the F-1 judgment violates federal constitutional law; an example would be an effort to enforce a judgment where the F-1 court lacked personal jurisdiction over the defendant.

The final class of cases, however, does consist of true exceptions to the Iron Law. This class is made up of cases that are due preclusive effect according to the law of F-1 and do not violate the federal Constitution, yet they still lack preclusive effect in F-2 because they impinge too greatly on the interests of F-2. The first category of exceptions and exclusions is treated in this section; the second and third in the following sections.

JUDGMENTS NOT PRECLUSIVE WHERE RENDERED

Nonfinal Judgments

Preclusive effect usually attaches to a judgment only after it has become final. As a corollary, nonfinal decisions need not be given full faith and credit. The definition of finality under the Iron Rule, of course, depends on the preclusion law of the rendering state. State treatment of finality is not uniform; a few states, for example, give some judgments preclusion effect when they become final at the *trial* level, even if they are still on appeal. In other words, there is no federal definition of "finality" and the moment when a judgment becomes "final" can be determined only by looking to the law of the state that entered the judgment.

Generally speaking, however, a judgment becomes entitled to recognition when the losing party can no longer "appeal" the decision. Here, the word "appeal" is used in a limited sense to mean a review within the judicial system that the party is entitled to pursue as a matter of right (that is the technical definition of the word "appeal"), rather than a review that is committed to the discretion of the reviewing court (this is usually, but not always, referred to as "certiorari" review). To illustrate: Consider a case tried in federal court resulting in a jury verdict for defendant. If the plaintiff does not appeal within the proper time, the judgment is final and must be recognized in all other American courts. If the plaintiff does appeal, however, the trial verdict is *not* final and, therefore, has no preclusive effect. It is only when the appellate court renders its *final* decision (in the federal system, that occurs when the "mandate" issues thirty days after the decision has been made public), that the judgment has preclusive effect. That is so, even if the losing party were to file a petition for certiorari review in the Supreme Court. That filing does not delay the preclusive effect of the judgment because the grant of the petition is discretionary; that is, the Supreme Court does not have to grant review (and, in fact, it does so in very few cases). Because the decision by the Supreme Court is discretionary, preclusive effect takes place earlier, at the time when the mandate issues from the Circuit Court.

Judgments Not on the Merits

An F-1 judgment that is not on the merits will not have claim preclusive effect in F-2. This is simply a corollary of the general rule that F-2 need grant the F-1 judgment only as much faith and credit as that judgment would have in F-1. Since a judgment that is not on the merits generally would not have claim preclusive effect in the rendering state, it is not entitled to that effect in the recognizing state.

An F-2 court considering an F-1 judgment must use the same definition of "on the merits" that the F-1 court would use, and the law on that question differs somewhat from state to state. Nevertheless, a few points are clear. When the judgment rests upon the soundness of the parties' claims and defenses under substantive law, usually it is said to be "on the merits." By contrast, some types of judgments nearly always are held not to be on the merits. Federal Rule of Civil Procedure 41 (b) is typical in that that it limits dismissals lacking preclusive effect to a few instances; among them are judgments based upon lack of personal jurisdiction, improper venue, or misjoinder or nonjoinder of parties. The reason is that judgments in such cases suggest that the plaintiff sued in the wrong court or committed some other procedural error, not that the plaintiff's claim lacked substantive validity. Also, a dismissal on limitations grounds usually is not on the merits; in other words, if the plaintiff's claim is time-barred in F-1, it might not be so barred in F-2, which is then free to apply its longer limitations period.[1]

More ambiguous are judgments based on a demurrer or motion to dismiss for failure to state a claim. If the dismissal results merely from a pleading error, it may not be considered to be "on the merits." If instead the complaint is dismissed because of some irreparable defect, the dismissal should be accorded claim preclusive effect in subsequent litigation at home or in a sister state.[2]

Judgments Procured by Fraud

Historically, fraud in obtaining a judgment has been a ground for collateral attack upon that judgment both in the rendering forum and elsewhere. As in other areas, F-2 can permit collateral attack based on fraud if the fraud is the type that would justify a collateral attack in F-1. This follows from the general principle that F-2 must give the F-1 judgment the same preclusive effect that it would receive in the courts of F-1.

While the states differ somewhat on the kinds of fraud that will sustain a collateral attack, a distinction drawn between intrinsic and extrinsic fraud explains many of the cases. An intrinsic fraud is one that the rendering court had the chance to rule on and accept or reject before delivering its decision. Examples include perjured testimony or forged documents. Historically, allegations of intrinsic fraud would not support a collateral attack on a judgment; because the rendering tribunal had the chance to determine whether the evidence was fraudulent or not, its determination of that issue had issue preclusion effect and thus prohibited relitigation of the issue in a collateral attack.[3]

By contrast, extrinsic fraud could not have been passed upon by the rendering tribunal because the nature of the fraud was to prevent the F-1 litigant from presenting the truth to that tribunal. An example of this sort of fraud involves cases where the plaintiff, in settlement negotiations, induces the defendant to default by promising to dismiss the action and then instead pursues it, receiving a default judgment when the defendant fails to show up for trial. Other examples include those cases where the plaintiff insures that the defendant will not learn of the commencement of the lawsuit by failing to serve process and then falsifying the return of process.[4] The key ingredient in these cases is that the defendant had no opportunity to bring the fraud to the attention of the rendering tribunal, and thus the issue of fraud could not have been litigated and determined there. Permitting a collateral attack, therefore, does not violate the principle against relitigation.

More recently, many courts have discarded the intrinsic and extrinsic fraud distinction in favor of a functional determination. On this approach, fraud denominated heretofore as intrinsic might yet support a collateral attack if the defrauded litigant had no opportunity to learn the truth of the matter. The argument in support of this position is that if the defrauded party could not have learned of the perjured testimony or the forging of documentary evidence before the trial was over, it had no opportunity to reveal the fraud and litigate it before the F-1 tribunal and so should be able to do so in a collateral attack. The Restatement (Second) of Judgments and the Federal Rules of Civil Procedure have adopted this position and permit collateral attack based on fraud "whether heretofore denominated intrinsic or extrinsic"[5] if the defrauded party "made a reasonable effort . . . to ascertain the truth of the matter."[6]

Modifiable Judgments

An F-1 judgment that is modifiable does not have preclusive effect in subsequent litigation in F-1. Rather, the F-1 tribunal in the second action will consider whether the judgment should be modified based on changed conditions or for any other reason recognized by its own law. Modifiable judgments occur most frequently in the area of family law cases, especially in the areas of support and child custody.

Support decrees offer an additional wrinkle to the problem because the states differ with regard to prospective and retrospective modification of support orders. Thus, until recently, in some states spousal and child support orders were modifiable only prospectively, that is, with respect to payments that have not yet accrued; in others, again until recently, awards were also modifiable retrospectively; that is, with respect to payments that already had accrued as well as to future payments.

In the full faith and credit context, modifiable judgments operate according to the orthodox law of preclusion; F-2 must give the F-1 judgment the same preclusive effect that it would get in F-1. F-2 courts achieve that result here, as elsewhere, by applying, under constitutional mandate, the modifiability law of F-1. In other words, if the F-1 decree was subject to retroactive modification in F-1, it could be modified wholesale in F-2. The unsuitability of such a rule for child custody matters should be readily apparent. Nowadays, the entire topic is considerably less interesting because congressional and uniform state statutes, which this book treats in detail in chapter 6, *infra*, have dealt with the issue.

Equity Decrees

Until quite recently, equity decrees provided a major exception to the Iron Law of preclusion. Nowadays courts are more willing to recognize that there is no functional reason to distinguish between the preclusive effect of final equity decrees and judgments at law. Language in Baker v. General Motors Corp. (1998)[7] said as much: "The Court has never placed equity decrees outside the full faith and credit domain."[8] This trend probably does not mean that an equity order from an F-1 court must be enforced directly in F-2 by the contempt power of the F-2 court. Rather, as Justice Scalia pointed out in his concurring opinion in *Baker*, an F-1 injunction, like an F-1 money judgment, must be enforced by way of an F-2 action seeking full faith and credit. If the F-2 court determines that the F-1 injunction is entitled to full faith and credit, it would issue an injunction of its own, which it could enforce by use of its own contempt powers.

The most troublesome application of the issue historically has been the antisuit injunction. Consider the leading case of James v. Grand Trunk Western Railroad Co. (1958).[9] In that case, a wrongful death action had been brought in Illinois. The defendant employer then obtained an ex parte injunction from a Michigan court, ordering the Illinois plaintiff not to proceed with the case there. That led to an Illinois injunction against the employer ordering it not to proceed with the Michigan suit. Thus, each party had been ordered by a court in a different state not to proceed with the action in the other state. The result, of course, was a judicial standoff.

One way out of the imbroglio would be to give full faith and credit to the most recent injunction under the last in time rule for inconsistent judgments. That has not been the practice, however. Typically, F-2 courts have not granted full faith and credit to F-1 antisuit injunctions, not because they are equity decrees, but because they involve an attempt by F-1 to control the judicial machinery of F-2, an unjustified intrusion by one state into the governmental affairs of another.

The Supreme Court has never faced this issue squarely. The closest it has come is in *Baker*, which it decided on another rationale, the completely uncontroversial principle that a judgment cannot bind persons who were not before the court. Nevertheless, there is dictum in *Baker* that suggests that antisuit injunctions are not entitled to full faith and credit:

> [A]ntisuit injunctions regarding litigation elsewhere . . . in fact have not controlled the second state's actions with regard to litigation in that court. . . . Sanctions for violations of an injunction, in any event, are generally administered by the court that issued the injunction.[10]

EXCEPTIONS II: UNCONSTITUTIONAL JUDGMENTS

A judgment rendered in violation of the federal Constitution does not have preclusive effect in F-2, or for that matter in F-1. The typical reason why a judgment violates federal constitutional provisions is that the court that rendered it lacked jurisdiction over the person of the defendant, the property that is the subject of an in rem action, or subject matter jurisdiction (competence) over the case.

Lack of Personal Jurisdiction

A court has personal jurisdiction over a defendant when it properly exercises power over the "person" of the defendant. That is, the court has power to enter a judgment which can be enforced against the person (or property) of the defendant. (Such jurisdiction *in personam* should be contrasted with jurisdiction in rem where the court adjudicates interests in a "res" or piece of property.)

The Due Process Clauses of the Fifth and Fourteenth Amendments prohibit the enforcement of any judgment that was entered by a court lacking proper jurisdiction over the defendant's person;[11] the protections of the Due Process Clause, in other words, trump the mandate of the Full Faith and Credit Clause. This aspect of the Due Process Clause protects a liberty interest—the liberty to be free of the judicial compulsion of the courts of a state with which the defendant has no contacts, ties, or relations. Litigants should not be forced to travel to distant and inconvenient courts in order to protect their rights. Nor should they be subject to the substantive law regime of a state with which they have had no contact or connection.[12]

For a court to have constitutionally sufficient personal jurisdiction over a defendant, it must satisfy two requirements: There must be an adequate *jurisdictional basis*, and the defendant must receive *adequate notice* of the proceedings and an opportunity to offer a defense. The jurisdictional basis requirement, in turn, incorporates two separate tests. First, the defendant must have certain minimum contacts with the state such that the maintenance of the action satisfies traditional notions of fair play and substantial justice. Second, the exercise of jurisdiction must be fair or reasonable taking into account the interests of the parties, the forum state, and factors relevant to litigational convenience (International Shoe Co. v. Washington, 1945).[13]

The notice portion of the due process requirement mandates a procedure that is reasonably likely to inform the defendant of the action, or, if such notice is impossible, a procedure that is as likely to inform the defendant as any other method the court reasonably could adopt.

There are complexities, of course. How does the enforcing state know, for example, that the rendering state lacked personal jurisdiction? That issue arises when an action is brought in F-2 to enforce the F-1 judgment. The F-2 defendant will assert in the F-2 court that F-1 lacked personal jurisdiction over her. If the defendant is right, then the F-1 judgment cannot be enforced. If the result were otherwise, then the Full Faith and Credit Clause would require F-2 to enforce a judgment from F-1 that violates the Due Process Clause.

The full faith and credit obligation of F-2 depends in part on whether the defendant defaulted in F-1 or instead appeared there to assert her jurisdictional objection. The defendant's options in response to the F-1 action raise two important questions. First, may the defendant suffer a default judgment in F-1 and then raise the question of lack of jurisdiction for the first time when enforcement is sought in F-2? Second, what happens if the defendant litigates the question of personal jurisdiction in F-1 and loses; may she raise the same question later when enforcement is sought in F-2? The answers to both questions are relatively straight-forward.

Default and Collateral Attack

Consider the plight of the Texan who never has been outside of that state in her life, but one day receives in the mail a summons to appear as a defendant in an action in New York, a state with which she has never had any contacts. Must she go to New York to defend the litigation or can she choose to suffer a default judgment there and raise the jurisdictional issue later, when enforcement is sought in Texas? Clearly, default and collateral attack must be an option available to the defendant. Were it not, the value of the defendant's Due Process rights would be reduced considerably; for then she would have to travel to New York to defend her interests, subjecting her to the very unfairness that the Due Process Clause was designed to prevent.

The Texan, however, ignores the New York summons at her peril because default and collateral attack is a risky strategy. If the defendant chooses to defend the lawsuit in New York, the court there will rule first on the jurisdictional objection, and then, if it finds the defendant amenable to jurisdiction, she will have the opportunity to defend against the merits of the plaintiff's claim. If she chooses default and collateral attack instead, the Texas court will rule on the New York court's jurisdiction; if it determines that the New York court had jurisdiction, she will not be able to present her defense to the merits of the claim in Texas. The Texas court will be faced with a sister state judgment that it has found to be constitutionally valid because it was rendered by a court with personal jurisdiction. Thus, it will be obliged by the Full Faith and Credit Clause to enforce the New York judgment without any further inquiry into the merits of the claim. In other words, defending the action in F-1 guarantees the defendant a chance to litigate both issues (personal jurisdiction and the merits), while choosing to default and raise the jurisdiction question by way of collateral attack risks the loss of the opportunity to defend on the merits.

Why then would the defendant ever choose the default and collateral attack option? The answer involves litigation strategy; under some circumstances, the default choice makes sense. If, for example, the defendant's case on jurisdiction is very strong, she can be reasonably certain that the Texas court will find the New York default judgment invalid, and she will be able to litigate both jurisdiction and merits in Texas. Furthermore, if her defense on the merits is very weak, risking the opportunity to assert it represents no great cost. The cost of litigation also may favor default and collateral attack, especially if the relative cost of defending the action in New York, as opposed to Texas, is high, and the amount that the plaintiff demands is relatively low. Finally, choice of law might play a role. If the substantive law of New York is so unfavorable to the defendant that the opportunity to litigate the merits there is useless, it will make sense for the defendant to risk everything on the Texas court's jurisdictional ruling in hopes of being able to defend the merits under the more favorable Texas substantive law.

Defending in F-1: Jurisdictional Preclusion

What happens when the Texan *does* travel to New York, raises the issue of lack of personal jurisdiction there and loses on both that issue and on the merits. May she resist enforcement of the subsequent New York judgment in Texas? The answer is no, and it flows ineluctably from the rationale of the basic Iron Rule of preclusion. A final judgment in New York, of course, is entitled to recognition in Texas as to all issues that would receive preclusive effect in a New York court. Because the jurisdictional issue was put at issue in New York by the voluntary act of the defendant (that is, by her appearance in New York) there is no due process reason not to apply the normal rules of Full Faith and Credit. The losing litigant in those circumstances cannot retry the jurisdictional issue because the New York court's finding precludes that issue, and she cannot litigate the merits because that issue is merged into a valid New York judgment. Her only hope is to appeal the case within the New York judicial system. That requirement serves all three purposes of the Full Faith and Credit Clause: preserving interstate harmony, protecting individual rights, and conserving always scarce judicial resources.

Lack of In Rem Jurisdiction: The Land Taboo

The common law has long distinguished between matters involving land (usually called "real property") and everything else. The reasons for this distinction are historical and, as we will explain, today have no functional basis. Nevertheless, the distinction still plays a role in our law in a number of areas. In full faith and credit, the distinction is important in whether a court must hear an action because it is "transitory," and whether the forum must enforce a foreign judgment concerning land located in the forum. That is the topic discussed in this section.

The rule has long been said to be that a court cannot enter a judgment concerning land in another state. Indeed, that rule has been thought so strong that it has acquired an emphatic sobriquet: "The Land Taboo."[14] The key Supreme Court decision is Fall v. Eastin (1909). In *Fall*, a Washington divorce court had awarded title of the husband's real property located in Nebraska to the wife. Later, the Washington court ordered a deed to the land executed in the wife's favor. Then, in a quiet title action in Nebraska, the Nebraska court refused to honor either the original award or the deed.

The Supreme Court affirmed, holding that the courts of one state cannot directly affect title to land located elsewhere. Before considering arguments for or against the rule, it is helpful to consider its very narrow scope. It is clear that the Supreme Court has no objection to a decree from an F-1 court that has an indirect effect on the land in F-2. In *Fall*, for instance, if the Washington court had threatened the husband with contempt, and, under that duress, he had executed a deed conveying the Nebraska land to his wife, the deed would have been valid, and the Nebraska court would have recognized it. Further, if the wife had merely asked for a different remedy in Nebraska, she may have been successful. If instead of suing on the deed prepared at the order of the Washington court, she had sought recognition in Nebraska for the Washington decree ordering her husband to convey the land to her, the Nebraska court probably would have granted full faith and credit to that decree and issued its own order compelling the husband to execute the deed.[15] The two hypothetical cases show that the *Fall* rule is very limited. It permits an F-2 court to ignore an F-1 decree only if it directly affects title to land in F-2. It does not, however, prevent an F-1 court from acting indirectly in ways that ultimately will control title to land in F-2.

But is the situs rule justified, even in such a limited form? One argument for it relies on the need for the situs to maintain reliable land records, records that might be muddled by foreign decrees to the disadvantage of subsequent innocent purchasers. In other words, a foreign decree affecting title to land located in the situs might not properly be reflected in the land records in the situs and, therefore, would interfere with a proper search of the title. If that were to happen, the marketability (and, therefore, the value) of situs land, which depends on the quality of its title, would necessarily diminish. That would not be a good thing.

The response to that argument is that the situs could easily protect its land records without discriminating against foreign judgments. It could do so by simply requiring one who claimed under a foreign decree to file that decree in the land records. Once filed, the decree would warn subsequent purchasers and mortgagees just as would any other document in the chain of title.

Another argument in favor of the *Fall* deference to the courts of the situs is that the situs has the greatest interest in its land, and, thus, questions involving ownership should be decided in a way that is consistent with the situs state's policies. But that premise often will be false. The situs may indeed have the greatest interest in its land if the question involves, for example, environmental protection or marketability of title. But the facts in *Fall* show that on many other issues another state will have a greater interest in the ownership of the land. Why would Nebraska care about the property distribution accompanying the divorce of a married couple domiciled in Washington? It certainly seems as though Washington has the greater interest in the question. Nor is distribution of real property assets upon divorce the only example. Consider the administration of the estate of a decedent in F-1, who owns a valuable piece of land in F-2. If all the contestants are domiciled in F-1, it certainly seems that F-1 would have a greater interest in the resolution of the dispute than F-2. If so, why should its courts be unable to act directly to enforce that interest?

Based on arguments of this sort, some F-2 states have chosen to ignore their prerogative under the *Fall* rule to ignore F-1 judgments directly affecting land within F-2.[16] That result seems more consistent with the rule of Fauntleroy v. Lum (1908), which requires F-2 to recognize and enforce an F-1 judgment even though that judgment runs counter to the public policy of F-2. If the land records of the situs are not imperiled, and the substantive issue does not affect the situs's interest in the stewardship of its land, the basic law of preclusion probably should control.

Lack of Subject Matter Jurisdiction

Every first-year law student learns that a judgment rendered by a court without jurisdiction over the subject matter is "void." Because the judgment is void, there is, quite literally, nothing to enforce. Thus, when a court in F-2 is asked to enforce a void judgment from an F-1 court, it will refuse. The Full Faith and Credit Clause, in other words, does not compel a state to enforce a void judgment of a sister state. It has long been the law, therefore, that the Full Faith and Credit Clause did not require the recognition of a judgment entered by a court lacking subject matter jurisdiction.

It is easy to understand why tradition attaches the label "void" to a judgment entered by a court lacking jurisdiction over the subject matter of the complaint.[17] An inquiry into the presence *vel non* of subject matter jurisdiction is a shorthand way of asking whether the court has the constitutional authority[18] to enter a judgment in the dispute before it. This is perhaps easiest to illustrate by looking to the federal court system. There are two ways for a federal court to acquire subject matter jurisdiction: by the presence of a federal question or by the parties' diversity of citizenship. If neither of these bases is present, the federal court, as a matter of basic constitutional authority, lacks the *power* to decide the issue brought to it for resolution.

All of the above is simple, hornbook law. Like all apparently straightforward legal rules, however, the "void for want of subject matter jurisdiction" rule is subject to an important qualification known in this context as "The Bootstrap Principle."[19] This principle is simple: Every court has jurisdiction to determine whether it has subject matter jurisdiction. Thus, once a court has determined that it has subject matter jurisdiction, that finding has issue preclusion effect and must be respected by other courts, even if it is wrong. The leading example is Durfee v. Duke (1963).

There were two questions in *Durfee*: First, who owned land located on the border between Nebraska and Missouri, land that had been created by the meanderings of the Missouri river; and, second, which state's courts had jurisdiction to decide the issue? The jurisdictional issue was really a question of geography; after all, a state's courts have jurisdiction only over land within its territory. So, was the land in Nebraska or Missouri? The answer to that question depended upon whether a shift in the course of the river had been the result of avulsion (a sudden shift) or accretion (a gradual shift). The Nebraskan sued first in a federal court in Nebraska, and the parties there fully litigated the jurisdictional/hydrological issue. The court found that it had jurisdiction because the land was located in Nebraska, and it awarded title to the land to the Nebraska claimant. The disappointed Missouri litigant then brought suit in her home state hoping that a Missouri court would reach a contrary holding.

The primary question there, however, was whether the Nebraska judgment was entitled to full faith and credit in Missouri. The Missourian argued that it was not; because the land really was located in Missouri, the Nebraska court had lacked subject matter jurisdiction and, therefore, it could not enter a valid judgment. The problem with that argument was that the parties had already litigated that question in the Nebraska court, and that court had decided that indeed it did have jurisdiction. Was that decision entitled to issue preclusive effect in the Missouri courts, or was the issue of the Nebraska court's jurisdiction open for relitigation?

The Supreme Court eventually decided in favor of preclusion, announcing, in an opinion written by Justice Potter Stewart, the rule that would come to be styled the "Bootstrap Principle." After reviewing the precedents, Justice Stewart wrote:

> From these decisions there emerges the general rule that a judgment is entitled to full faith and credit—even as to questions of jurisdiction—when the second court's inquiry discloses that those questions have been fully and fairly litigated and finally decided in the court which rendered the original judgment.[20]

The Bootstrap Principle—issues concerning subject matter jurisdiction of the F-1 court are precluded from being retried in F-2 if they were fully litigated and decided in F-1—has much to recommend it. It is clear and provides an answer in cases where there is a collision between two of the most fundamental principles in our law. On the one hand, the validity principle holds that courts cannot act beyond the subject matter competence allotted to them by their constituting authority. On the other hand, the finality principle decrees that issues once decided may not be relitigated. Both cannot prevail all the time, and it makes sense to privilege the finality rule because otherwise repetitive contradictory determinations of subject matter jurisdiction could occur.[21]

The Supreme Court has pushed the Bootstrap Principle very hard on occasion; in Des Moines Navigation and Railroad Co. v. Iowa Homestead Co. (1887),[22] for example, it forbade collateral attack on a federal diversity judgment even though (1) the face of the complaint revealed the lack of subject matter jurisdiction, and (2) the jurisdictional issue had never been litigated.

The Supreme Court's pronouncements on the issue, however, have not been completely consistent with the Bootstrap Principle. In a dictum in Kalb v. Feuerstein (1940), the Court suggested that a litigant could base a collateral attack on lack of subject matter jurisdiction even though the issue had been fully litigated in F-1. In *Kalb*, the state court had reached the wrong conclusion that it had jurisdiction over a matter that Congress had restricted to the federal courts by the Frasier-Lemke Act, a Depression-era bankruptcy statute designed to aid desperate farm families. The Supreme Court inferred from the statute a congressional intent to preempt any possible state interference in bankruptcy matters; thus, "considerations as to whether the issue of jurisdiction was actually contested in the County Court, or whether it could have been contested, are not applicable where the plenary power of Congress over bankruptcy has been exercised as in this Act."[23] The Court determined, apparently, that the federal policy was sufficiently urgent and the possibility of interference by creditor-friendly state courts was sufficiently great as to warrant displacing the usual Bootstrap Principle that a court has jurisdiction to determine if it has jurisdiction.

Other pronouncements of the Court are also apparently inconsistent with the Bootstrap Rule, but in the opposite direction. In both Sherrer v. Sherrer (1948) and Chicot County Drainage District v. Baxter State Bank (1940)[24] the Court held that lack of subject matter jurisdiction could not furnish a ground for collateral attack even though there had been little or no litigation of the issue in the F-1 court. In both cases, the Court relied on the fact that the defendants had not chosen to default and, therefore, had had an opportunity to litigate those issues in F-1.

It may be expecting too much for the Court to adhere to a clear, universal solution when values as fundamental as the validity and finality principles collide. Both the Supreme Court and the American Law Institute[25] have come to the conclusion that the Bootstrap Principle cannot serve as the entire answer. Rather, there is room to balance the two policies of validity and finality, policies that may differ in importance depending on the litigation context. It seems fair to conclude that the finality policy is likely to prevail in most cases, but that the validity policy may trump it when the Court concludes that the jurisdictional restriction was designed by the legislature to protect some especially strong federal, or perhaps state, policy.

Finally, it is worth noting that the Bootstrap Principle involves a question of federal or state common law of preclusion. Thus, the states are free to adopt their own solutions when the question arises between two courts of a single state. In such cases, of course the Full Faith and Credit Clause does not apply, so unless a state's solution to the problem is so unfair as to implicate due process, federal law has no role to play.

EXCEPTIONS III: REFUSING RECOGNITION TO A VALID, PRECLUSIVE F-1 JUDGMENT

In the preceding discussion, the justification for denying preclusive effect to a sister-state judgment was that there was some defect in the judgment itself, that it would not be given preclusive effect under the law of the rendering state, or that it violated the federal constitution. In this section the focus shifts to the more controversial question whether F-2 can deny preclusive effect to a perfectly constitutional F-1 judgment that would have preclusive effect under the law of F-1. Despite the Iron Law, there are a few cases where F-2 can deny recognition; some of these cases are not controversial and others are quite the contrary.

Lack of a Competent Court

The Full Faith and Credit Clause does not require the states to furnish courts with jurisdiction over every type of claim that might arise nor does it require them to issue every type of remedy known in the law. Thus, in a desire to conserve judicial resources, a state could set a lower limit on the jurisdictional amount of cases heard in its courts; or in a desire to avoid rendering advisory opinions, it could forbid its courts from issuing declaratory judgments. That raises the following questions: Can F-2 use its plenary authority over its own courts to deny full faith and credit to judgments from other states by simply drafting its jurisdictional statutes to withdraw from its courts subject matter jurisdiction to hear the action to enforce the F-1 judgment? (Remember that the Iron Law of full faith and credit prohibits F-2 from refusing recognition to an F-1 judgment because that judgment was based on a claim not recognized under the law of F-2, or because the underlying claim violates the public policy of F-2.)

Illinois attempted that strategy in Kenney v. Supreme Lodge (1920), but the Supreme Court reversed. The Illinois court had held that it lacked jurisdiction to enforce an Alabama judgment based on an Alabama wrongful death statute because an Illinois law denied its courts jurisdiction to hear an action based on the underlying claim, that is, a claim based on an out-of-state death. Justice Holmes, echoing his opinion in *Fauntleroy* fourteen years earlier, dealt with that strategy succinctly:

> [T]he Constitution does not require the State to furnish a court. But it also is true that there are limits to the power of exclusion and to the power to consider the nature of the cause of action before the foreign judgment based upon it is given effect.
>
> . . . [I]t is plain that a State cannot escape its constitutional obligations by the simple device of denying jurisdiction in such cases to Courts otherwise competent.[26]

This holding is of course consistent with Hughes v. Fetter and the Door-Closing Cases, discussed at the end of chapter 3.

There are two clear limitations on the *Kenney* doctrine. First, the judgment creditor must seek a type of relief that forum courts are able to supply. Usually that limitation presents no problem; a judgment creditor typically seeks a money judgment, and all states provide such a mechanism for the collection of a debt. The Constitution, however, does not require a state to provide procedures for enforcement not available in domestic actions. Second, the judgment creditor must bring the enforcement action within the limitations period that the forum typically applies to its own judgment enforcement actions. This requirement is one of the few exceptions to the general rule the F-2 must apply the preclusion law of F-1 in the enforcement action.

A third limitation on *Kenney* is less clear. It may be that F-2 can refuse enforcement of an F-1 judgment if the enforcement action is brought by someone who lacks capacity to sue under F-2 law. Seventeen years before *Kenney*, and three years before *Fauntleroy*, the Court held in Anglo-American Provision Co. v. Davis Provision Co. (1903) that a state could decline to hear an action between foreign corporations based on a foreign judgment. It is not clear whether that holding survives *Kenney* and a much more benevolent view of foreign corporations (once regarded in many places as akin to the Devil's whelp) in today's courts. The opinion in Milwaukee County v. M. E. White Co. (1935) contains dicta suggesting that *Anglo-American* might retain some potency. In any event, *Anglo-American* should *not* be good law today for it is inconsistent not only with more recent cases but, of more importance, with the spirit of comity that animates the Full Faith and Credit Clause.

"Penal" Laws

Another class of valid judgments ordinarily entitled to preclusive effect which may not subject to the Iron Law of Full Faith and Credit are those that are in some sense "penal." The concept extends back to the early days of the Republic when Chief Justice Marshall, writing in *The Antelope* (1825), created a penal law exception to the Full Faith and Credit Clause. The case involved an effort by the United States government to determine "ownership" of persons (in a captured vessel) asserted to be slaves under Spanish and Portugese law. Because the case involved the potential application of the laws of other nations, the Full Faith and Credit Clause, by its express terms, did not apply. Nonetheless, the great Chief Justice opined: "The Courts of no country execute the penal laws of another."[27]

This statement, however authoritative it may sound, rested on a shaky foundation. At the time of the decision in *The Antelope*, the common law arguably was to the contrary—historically, English courts *did* enforce some "penal" laws of other countries. Although it is true that in at least two cases English courts had refused to recognize the laws of other nations, that nonrecognition occurred at a time when those other nations were at war with England and were confiscating the property of English nationals. Otherwise, English law favored enforcement.

Despite its weakness historically, and perhaps because it was written by the great Chief Justice Marshall, the *Antelope* dictum has exerted great influence in American law over the long period since it was decided. It also has been the source of a great deal of controversy, which continues to the present day. The biggest problem involves litigation where the goal is to obtain some form of relief other than monetary compensation. Thus, this section examines the effect of the Full Faith and Credit Clause on criminal, quasi-criminal, tax, and punitive damages laws and judgments—all of which have been thought of at one time as penal. In reading this section, it is important to remember that the modern Supreme Court has not required that a particular choice of law rule be adopted by any state. Expressed differently, a state may apply the *law* of any state to a problem if that state has either a minimal relation with the problem, or if the problem might be styled "procedural." On the other hand, the Iron Law of Full Faith and Credit requires that, with certain limited exceptions, a *judgment* entered by one state must be enforced in other states. In short, the "penal" exception raises two different kinds of full faith and credit problems: choice of law and judgment recognition. We explore the problem in three different areas: criminal law, tax law, and punitive damages.

Criminal Law

When Chief Justice Marshall used the term "penal" in *The Antelope*, he was using it almost surely as a synonym for "criminal." That remains true in the United States today, for nothing has happened since the decision in *The Antelope* to suggest that the Constitution requires enforcement of another state's criminal laws. Thus, if an Ohio criminal defendant flees to Indiana, that state will not prosecute and punish the fugitive. Instead Indiana's obligation is found under the Extradition Clause of Article IV of the United States Constitution, another provision of the Interstate Comity Article. That obligation is clear: The state must return the fugitive to Ohio when presented with a proper application from the governor of that state. Thus, the Extradition Clause is complementary to the Full Faith and Credit Clause; civil laws may need to be enforced in other states, but criminal laws must be enforced at home.

Strong policy reasons support this result. A criminal offense lies at the very heart of sovereignty; a criminal offense is a violation of the rights of all. The offended sovereign can only redress the harm that it along with everyone in the jurisdiction has suffered if it is the one that conducts the prosecution. Further, a criminal prosecution involves a considerable exercise of discretion—by the prosecutor in determining whether to investigate and proceed, and by the judge in determining the sentence. The prosecutors and judges of the offended sovereign are in the best position to make the required discretionary calculations and balances. Finally, as a practical matter, no state wants to undertake the financial burden of caring for the prisoners of another state.

Criminal Judgments

The rule of *The Antelope* vitiates the need for F-2 to enforce the criminal law of F-1. But what about the criminal judgments issued by F-1's courts? Does *The Antelope's* dictum that "no court executes the penal laws of another" mean that a criminal conviction in one state can have no full faith and credit consequences in another state? Answering that question requires extensive analysis, more than might be thought necessary.

The traditional rule has long been that a criminal conviction does not have claim preclusive effect in another state. Thus if a Maryland court tries and convicts an offender and sentences him to a fine, a Virginia court need not enforce the judgment (that is, the fine). Nevertheless, the judgment may have other collateral effects in Virginia. If, for example, Virginia has heightened penalties for recidivist criminal offenders (e.g., a three strikes and you're out statute), the Maryland conviction may be used to show a required element of the Virginia penalty, a prior conviction. The same holds true for certain crimes, such as possession of a firearm by a convicted felon.

The question of issue preclusion effect for findings made in a criminal prosecution is more complicated. First, it is clear that an acquitted defendant cannot use issue preclusion in subsequent civil litigation because of the different standards of proof in the two proceedings. The acquittal, for example, shows only that the prosecution was not able to prove the defendant's guilt beyond a reasonable doubt; it does not mean that a subsequent civil litigant will be unable to prove the defendant's fault by a preponderance of the evidence.[28]

The issue is more controversial when a defendant is convicted in the criminal case and later sued civilly. Will the subsequent civil plaintiff be able to use the findings from the criminal trial to establish some element of her claim? The older rule, stated in both Wigmore's great treatise on evidence and Freedman's work on judgments, was that there should be no issue preclusion, but the modern position is the opposite.[29] The justification for the modern position lies in the higher standard of proof in criminal trials. As long as the issues are the same in the criminal and civil trials, a showing of defendant's guilt beyond a reasonable doubt logically entails his civil liability by a mere preponderance of the evidence. Because preponderance of the evidence is a less exacting standard than is proof beyond a reasonable doubt, proof of the latter necessarily encompasses proof of the former. As for the old rule advocated by Wigmore and Freedman, it is likely that it was the result of the courts simply overgeneralizing from the acquittal cases to conclude that criminal to civil preclusion was inappropriate in all cases.

Some policy reasons for the old rule have been offered over the years, but all are spurious. A number of authorities have cited the difference in standards of proof, but that difference explains only why an *acquittal* should have no issue preclusion effect in subsequent civil litigation; the distinction should cut the other way in the case of a *conviction*. The prosecution has a much higher burden than a civil litigant so a criminal conviction should be even more reliable than a civil judgment and, *a fortiori*, should be given preclusive effect in a later civil action.

The second rationale emphasizes the greater importance of the issues involved in criminal cases. No doubt that disparity may exist, but it is hard to see how it can justify the traditional rule; if anything it suggests that a criminal conviction is *more* worthy of preclusive effect because of the enhanced care that presumably was taken at trial to insure reliable fact finding. Moreover, some civil cases do involve extremely important interests—school desegregation comes readily to mind. Should the importance of such issues mean that they deserve less preclusive effect than garden-variety negligence findings?

The third justification involves the highly technical doctrine of mutuality of estoppel. The old mutuality rule permitted preclusion only when the first litigation involved identical parties (or their privies). That, of course, would be unusual in the criminal to civil preclusion context, where the prosecution (the Government) has been replaced in the second suit by a private citizen seeking to vindicate her own interests. (If the Government sues civilly in the second action, of course mutuality is much less of a problem.) The argument based on the substitution of parties at least has the virtue of apparent fairness; after all, why should a stranger to the earlier proceedings, a person who would not have been bound by an acquittal, be able to take advantage of a conviction? Recent decades, however, have seen a serious erosion of the mutuality rule as courts have concentrated on saving judicial time and energy; the waning of the mutuality rule considerably diminishes the force of the third justification for the non-preclusion rule.

A variation on the previous two arguments relies on differing motives for the defendant in the criminal and the civil proceedings. If the stakes are low in the criminal action, the defendant is tempted to cut his losses and plead guilty; if those stakes are raised significantly because of the judgment's impact in a related civil proceeding, the incentive to plead is removed. That can have serious consequences.

As an example, consider a driver who gets a speeding ticket in connection with a minor accident. Most drivers do not contest such tickets and end up with a default verdict of guilty, which is a criminal conviction in most states. Later, if that driver is sued by someone who claims to have been injured in the accident in a state that gives criminal convictions preclusive effect, the guilty verdict becomes prima facie evidence of negligence (under a doctrine known as negligence per se), and the defendant starts the civil litigation in serious trouble. The defendant, therefore, would have every incentive to actively contest the speeding ticket; if many drivers did so, the traffic courts could become very clogged. In order to get the crowded criminal dockets to work, therefore, a state may wish to limit the preclusive effect of guilty pleas.

Differential litigation incentives, moreover, are not limited to criminal judgments. They can also arises in civil litigation, often in cases involving mass disasters such as plane crashes or train wrecks. If the first plaintiff has minimal damages, the defendant might not defend vigorously; then, if the jurisdiction permits offensive nonmutual preclusion, subsequent plaintiffs with much higher damages can cash in on the initial, minimally contested finding of fault. Thus, the differential incentives phenomenon is not unique to criminal-to-civil preclusion, but rather is an inherent problem with nonmutual preclusion—one that courts can deal with by using the same safeguards that they use in ordinary civil preclusion cases.

That leaves the fourth, and strangest, justification for the old rule found in the literature. Convictions, it has been argued, cannot be given preclusive effect in later litigation because they constitute inadmissible "hearsay." As the Supreme Court of Minnesota opined, "[T]he judgment in a criminal case is nothing more than the opinion of 12 jurors and, consequently, hearsay" (Travelers Ins. Co. v. Thompson, 1968). This argument is silly. First, if believed, it would also deny preclusive effect to any *civil* judgment rendered by a jury; in both situations, "hearsay" would be involved. Further, the hearsay rule is based on unreliability, but a criminal conviction, because of the high standard of proof, is as reliable as anything in litigation can be, as is shown by the inclusion in the Federal Rules of Evidence of a hearsay exception for criminal convictions, but not one for civil judgments.[30] Thus, while a jury verdict may be "hearsay" in some very strict, technical sense, that technicality should not rob the verdict of its preclusive effect.

Tax Judgments and Claims

For a very long time, tax *laws* were considered to be in the same class as penal laws; as a result, tax *judgments* generally were unenforceable in other states. The pernicious consequence of the rule was to make life easier for the tax evader, who could avoid the enforcement of a New York tax judgment, for example, by the simple expedient of shifting her assets to Georgia. There, under the rule of *The Antelope* (as applied to tax matters), the transported assets were safe from execution; after all, "no state executes the penal laws of another." The result cannot be justified under any conceivable policy ground. The only possible justifications for the refusal are that the enforcement might offend the other sovereign or that the enforcing state does not understand the tax laws of the rendering state. These cannot be real problems. After all, by bringing the enforcement action, New York has asked Georgia for help in enforcing its judgment and thus has decided that its interests as a sovereign will not be offended when Georgia complies. Further, the Georgia court does not have the burdensome task of analyzing the tax laws of another state. All that the court need do is recognize a valid liquidated judgment rendered elsewhere and use it to execute upon the assets of the debtor. Remember that the issue before the Georgia court is simply the enforcement of a judgment debt, not the tax liability that occasioned it.

The Supreme Court agrees. Milwaukee County v. M.E. White Co. (1935) involved a suit brought against a taxpayer by a county in federal court. The opinion by Justice Harlan Fiske Stone, a noted Conflicts jurist, gave short shrift to the idea that tax judgments are penal and, therefore, cannot be enforced in other jurisdictions. "[T]he obligation to pay taxes is not penal,"[31] he wrote. "It is a statutory liability, quasi contractual in nature, enforceable . . . in the civil courts by the common-law action of debt or indebitatus assumpsit."[32] As a result, "full faith and credit must be given the [tax] judgment."[33] Only those defenses normally available in an enforcement action are available to the judgment debtor in a tax action. Justice Stone also laid to rest the argument that a judgment was entitled to full faith and credit only if the enforcing court would have entertained the action in the first place. Relying on *Fauntleroy*, the court concluded, "that a judgment is not to be denied full faith and credit . . . merely because it is for taxes."[34] So much for interstate tax evaders!

A tax claim not liquidated by an F-1 judgment raises different considerations. Tax laws are notoriously difficult to apply, and applying another jurisdiction's revenue laws—necessarily unfamiliar to the court—might be very hard. There is a substantial risk that injustice and/or bad precedent will result. Both problems can be ameliorated if the taxing state's courts will accept certified questions referred to it by the enforcing state. As for bad precedent, presumably the taxing state considered that possibility when it referred the matter for enforcement. In other words, the taxing state consented to the possibility that the enforcing state might get it wrong. Moreover, even if wrong, the precedential value of a Georgia court's one-time construction of a New York revenue statute is not likely to be very high.

Another argument against requiring the enforcement of another state's tax claims is that it imposes too great a burden on the enforcing state. Hearing another state's complicated tax cases may be onerous for the courts of the enforcing state, but the Full Faith and Credit Clause often forces onerous duties on the courts of recognizing states. Policy considerations aside, the state law on this question is becoming more settled in favor of enforcement.[35] The old rule that one state will not enforce the revenue laws of another largely has been abandoned.

It is unclear, however, whether enforcement is constitutionally required. A state tax claim that has not been reduced to judgment is not, of course, a judicial proceeding entitled to routine recognition elsewhere; that would be true only of a judgment based on that claim. Thus, any requirement for one state to enforce the tax claim of another, if grounded on full faith and credit at all, would be based on the enforcing state's obligation to give full faith and credit to the "public acts" of the taxing state. The Supreme Court explicitly left this question open in *Milwaukee County*. Another line of cases that might support an enforcing state's constitutional obligation is the Hughes v. Fetter line that forbids a state from closing the doors of its courts to litigation based upon sister-state statutes.

Also unclear is the current importance of the constitutional question. As indicated, most state courts are willing to hear sister-state tax claims without constitutional compulsion, and some states have entered into reciprocal enforcement of tax claim agreements.[36] Furthermore, even if the enforcing state is unwilling to hear the claim, and there is no constitutional obligation for it to do so, the taxing state has the easily available remedy of bringing suit in its own courts, which would ultimately produce a liquidated judgment that other states must enforce under constitutional compulsion. The only possible problem would be acquiring personal jurisdiction over the taxpayer, but if the taxpayer has enough contact with the state to justify imposition of the tax, it almost certainly will have sufficient contact to meet the minimum contacts[37] test for personal jurisdiction.

Judgments for Punitive Damages

Punitive damages are assessed to deter wrongful conduct rather than to compensate the victims (although there is, of course, a definite compensatory element to any award of punitive damages). The focus on deterrence—an effect which benefits society as a whole—means that an award of punitive damages might be considered "penal" and, therefore, within the scope of Chief Justice Marshall's dictum in *The Antelope*.

The Supreme Court first encountered the issue in Wisconsin v. Pelican Ins. Co. (1888). In that case, the plaintiff invoked the original jurisdiction of the Supreme Court to enforce a judgment rendered by a Wisconsin state court against a citizen of another state. The judgment was based on the failure of the defendant insurance company to file annual reports with the state of Wisconsin concerning its business there; that failure led to the judicial imposition of a statutory penalty of $500. Because the judgment was based on a "penal law," the Supreme Court refused to enforce it.

> The rule that the courts of no country execute the penal laws of another applies . . . to all suits in favor of the state for the recovery of pecuniary penalties. . . . If this were not so, all that would be necessary to give ubiquitous effect to a penal law would be to put the claim for a penalty into the shape of a judgment.[38]

Thus, the penal law exception to full faith and credit applied to "civil" as well as to "criminal" judgments.

In dictum, the *Pelican* Court tried to explain the relationship between the Full Faith and Credit Clause and the stated exception: "The cause of action was not any private injury, but solely the offense committed against the state by violating her law. The prosecution was in the name of the state, and the whole penalty, when recovered, would accrue to the state."[39] In other words, a judgment is penal if the action is brought by the state and any relief belongs to the state. The net effect of *Pelican*, therefore, is to limit the penal law exception to judgments that are penal in the "international" sense; that is, to limit the exception to judgments based upon the State's attempts to recover fines and penalties in its own name. But what about cases where the plaintiff is a private person who recovers punitive damages against a civil defendant?

In Huntington v. Attrill (1892), the Court had a chance to address the application of the penal law exception to a private action. The problem there involved a corporation that had filed a report, signed by Attrill (a corporate officer and director) that stated that the corporation's subscribed stock had been fully paid for. The report was false, however, and under New York law, Attrill was personally liable for any debt of the corporation. Huntington, who had loaned money to the corporation, sued Attrill in New York state court and won a monetary judgment.

Huntington then tried to enforce the New York judgment in a Maryland state court, which dismissed the enforcement action because it believed that the New York judgment was "penal" and fell within the exception to the Full Faith and Credit Clause. The Maryland court reasoned that the New York law was penal because it imposed liability without regard to fault.

The Supreme Court reversed. Although the Court discussed the penal law exception at some length, it is not clear how it defined the term. Perhaps the key passage is this:

> whether a statute . . . is a penal law, in the international sense, so that it cannot be enforced . . . depends upon the question whether its purpose is to punish an offense against the *public justice* of the state, or to afford a *private remedy* to a person injured by the wrongful act.[40]

Huntington's verdict was not a penal judgment because it had been rendered in an action brought to rectify a private wrong, and because his damages were "measured by the amount of his debt."[41] Thus, according to the opinion, even a private action might still be styled "penal" if the award was made to vindicate a public, rather than a private, wrong.

But the tide had turned. After *Huntington*, the penal law exception would receive only grudging recognition, at most, in later cases. In James-Dickinson Farm Mortgage Co. v. Harry (1927), for example, the Court held that a law providing for punitive damages up to twice actual damages was not penal and, therefore, was entitled to full faith and credit. Why did the Supreme Court begin to limit the reach of the penal exception? Although *James-Dickinson* itself does not really address the point, the Court must have been aware of the social and economic changes occurring at the end of the nineteenth century producing much legislation that provided remedies that were not strictly compensatory. To question the enforceability of the judgments based on those laws would have seriously undermined the efficacy of much reform legislation.

Finally, in *Milwaukee County*, discussed in detail in the preceding subsection, the Court expressed doubts about the penal law exception in general: "We intimate no opinion" the Court wrote, concerning whether there is such an exception at all. Our earlier conclusion about that case was that there simply is no reason for a state to deny enforcement to a creditor's claim that has been reduced to a monetary judgment.[42] That conclusion also holds when enforcement is sought of a judgment containing an award of punitive damages.

To be sure, punitive damages awards can be ruinously large. And the defendant who is about to be ruined may have a much stronger connection with the enforcing state than the rendering state. But that really is an argument that the rendering state must have a strong interest in the proceedings in order to apply its own law, an argument that the Supreme Court has rejected in the Allstate Ins. Co. v. Hague (1981), minimal scrutiny line of cases involving the constitutionality of choice of law decision making.[43] Thus, under the Iron Law of Full Faith and Credit, the enforcing state must bite the bullet and enforce the judgment.

There remains, however, a final problem with punitive damages. In some cases, states reserve for themselves a portion of any punitive damages awarded to private plaintiffs. Do those laws convert the state's portion of the judgment for punitive damages into "fines" within the penal law exception to full faith and credit and, therefore, render them unenforceable? The answer would seem to be that it does, a view adopted by at least one court.[44] Thus, to the extent that *The Antelope*'s "penal in the international sense" exception survives in the area of punitive damages it would seem to be limited, at most, to the unusual situation where a state receives part of the punitive damages award.

The Workers' Compensation Cases: A Separate Rule?

Another exception to the Iron Law of Full Faith and Credit can be found in a trilogy of cases involving the full faith and credit effect, if any, of a workers' compensation award. These cases present a confusing pattern: Two cases in the 1940s reached opposite results; a third case, decided in 1980, did not resolve the issue because the Supreme Court fractured badly in coming to a conclusion.

The problem arises this way. A worker, who lives in the District of Columbia, is injured on the job in Virginia and obtains a workers' compensation award in that state. Then, unhappy with the amount of the Virginia award, he sues for a larger sum in the District of Columbia. May that court increase the Virginia award, or does the full faith and credit owed to the Virginia decision preclude the District of Columbia court from doing so?

The Answer in the 1940s

The first case, Magnolia Petroleum Co. v. Hunt (1943), involved an accident in Texas injuring a Louisiana worker, who ordinarily worked in Louisiana. The worker then sought and received a workers' compensation award from the Texas Industrial Accident Board, and the employer began making the required payments. Subsequently the worker sought and received a higher workers' compensation award in Louisiana. The Louisiana courts rejected the employer's argument that the Texas award precluded the worker's claim, but the Supreme Court reversed on appeal, holding that it was improper for Louisiana to award a larger sum. The Court applied basic full faith and credit analysis:

> Respondent was free to pursue his remedy in either state but, having chosen to seek it in Texas, where the award was res judicata, the full faith and credit clause precludes him from again seeking a remedy in Louisiana upon the same grounds.[45]

Justices William Douglass and Black dissented separately, both arguing that the Texas award was not intended to bind the parties in Louisiana, and that if it were, the Full Faith and Credit Clause did not require Louisiana to cede control to Texas of matters so important to Louisiana's social policies and interests.

Four years later, however, in Industrial Comm'n of Wisconsin v. McCartin (1947), the Court reached a different result. An Illinois worker and his Illinois employer contracted in Illinois for the employee to work in Wisconsin, where he was injured on the job. The worker sought compensation in both states, but Illinois made the first award. It was based on a settlement agreement, which provided that it would "not affect any rights that applicant may have under the Workmen's Compensation Act of the State of Wisconsin." The Industrial Commission of Wisconsin awarded the worker a larger sum, but the Wisconsin courts, relying on the Supreme Court's recent decision in *Magnolia* reversed the Commission.

The Supreme Court reversed, relying in part on the language of the Illinois award, which would have sufficed to distinguish the case from *Magnolia*. But the Supreme Court, not content with such a narrow holding, added that even in the absence of a savings clause in the F-1 award, F-2 courts should seldom read such an award to preclude a higher recovery in F-2. It found "nothing in the [Illinois] statute . . . to indicate that it is designed to preclude any recovery . . . in another state."[46] Further the Court stated that it would be reluctant to "interpret such a statute so as to cut off an employee's right to sue under other legislation passed for his benefit. Only some unmistakable language by a state legislature or judiciary would warrant our accepting such a construction."[47]

In the fifty years since *McCartin*, few cases have found "unmistakable language" in workers' compensation statutes; state legislatures seldom consider the compensation schemes of other states or the preclusive effect of awards under their own statutes. As a result, *McCartin* has functioned for nearly half a century as a narrowly limited and, until 1980, relatively uncontroversial exception to the Iron Law.

The Answer in the 1980s

A third of a century elapsed before the Court was called upon to reconcile *Magnolia* and *McCartin*. The case, Thomas v. Washington Gas Light Co. (1980), involved the now-familiar pattern: A District of Columbia worker injured in Virginia, received an award in that state, and later sought and obtained a larger supplemental award from the District of Columbia. The question before the Court was whether the second award was valid. The Court held that it *was*, but it got to that result by a very strange path.

The Plurality Opinion

The Court split badly, writing three inconsistent opinions. Four Justices joined a plurality opinion written by Justice Stevens. The plurality rejected the "unmistakable language" solution of *McCartin*. A state, Justice Stevens wrote, can exercise indirect control over the full faith and credit due its judgments by prescribing their effect within the state. Once it has done so, however, by creating its own domestic preclusion law, it loses further control. The Supreme Court, applying the Iron Law of Full Faith and Credit, determines the judgment's preclusive effect in sister states. Thus, according to the plurality, the vice of the *McCartin* "unmistakable language" rule was its improper delegation to F-1 of a power properly exercised only by the Supreme Court. Once a state, via its preclusion law, has prescribed the domestic effect of its judgments, it cannot, by "unmistakable language" restrict the judgment's extraterritorial effect.

Justice Stevens next rejected *Magnolia*'s orthodox full preclusion rule for practical rather than theoretical reasons. Before *Magnolia*, the practice in most courts was not to give claim preclusive effect to workers' compensation awards. And after *McCartin*, only one state had chosen the "unmistakable language" option, to render its awards claim preclusive in sister states. Since the workers' compensation exception had existed before *Magnolia* and for thirty-some years after *McCartin*, Justice Stevens concluded that it was too well settled to abandon. What it needed was a fresh rationale.

The new rationale for the workers' compensation exception that it provided consisted of a balancing of state interests. The three relevant interests, according to the plurality, were the interest of Virginia in limiting the liability of employers and insurers, the interests of both jurisdictions in compensating the worker, and the interest of Virginia in the integrity of its administrative proceedings.

The plurality had no trouble discounting the first two interests. First, a supplemental award could not damage the common interest of the two jurisdictions in compensating the claimant. Second, Virginia's liability limiting interest would not be affected by a supplemental award because the employee had the initial choice to claim under either Virginia's or the District's compensation statute; the employer and the insurer, therefore, already had ample reason to calculate their potential liability according to the more generous of the two compensation schemes. Moreover, precluding a supplemental award would amplify the importance of the worker's initial choice of forum. That result would be undesirable in the workers' compensation context, where the worker typically begins proceedings informally and without the assistance of counsel.

In assessing Virginia's interest in the integrity of its quasi-judicial proceedings, the plurality distinguished between courts and administrative tribunals. The issue preclusive effects of factual findings should be the same for both, but the claim preclusive effects of the two types of proceedings should differ. A court in F-1 can consider whether the law of F-1 or F-2 should apply, thus factoring into its ultimate decision the state interests embodied in the laws of F-2. Administrative tribunals in F-1, on the other hand, cannot conduct a choice of law inquiry; their statutory authority is limited to application of the laws of F-1.

The plurality found this choice of law distinction crucial in determining the interstate claim preclusive effect of an F-1 administrative proceeding as opposed to an F-1 judicial proceeding. In making its choice of law decision, an F-1 court can consider the important interests of F-2, so F-2 cannot deny preclusive effect to the judgment based on those interests. On the other hand, because the F-1 administrative tribunal is unable to perform a choice of law calculation and thus consider the interests of F-2, the courts of F-2 can consider those interests in determining whether the F-1 compensation award should have full claim preclusive effect.

The Concurring Opinion

Justice White's concurrence, in which Chief Justice Warren Burger and Justice Powell joined, rejected the plurality's argument. That reasoning, the concurrence noted, could apply just as easily to an ordinary lawsuit in which a strong forum favoring choice of law rule required the F-1 court to apply F-1 law. If so, it would inject a whole new set of choice of law doubts into the hitherto straightforward Iron Law of Full Faith and Credit. The uncertainty was not worthwhile simply to justify an exception for workers' compensation cases. Thus Justice White favored retaining the *McCartin* rule, even though he agreed with the plurality that its rationale was questionable. Nevertheless he preferred it because it was more narrowly limited to workers' compensation cases and thus less likely to produce mischief elsewhere.

The Dissent

Only Justices Marshall and Rehnquist dissented, in an opinion written by the latter. (That unusual partnership alone suggests the real oddity of the other two opinions.) The dissent began with a devastating critique of the result produced by the plurality and concurring opinion.

> This is clearly a case where the whole is less than the sum of its parts. In choosing between two admittedly inconsistent precedents, . . . six of us agree that the latter decision,

McCartin, is analytically indefensible. The remaining three Members of the Court concede that it "rest[s] on questionable foundations." Nevertheless, when the smoke clears, it is *Magnolia* rather than *McCartin* that the plurality suggests should be overruled.[48]

The dissent then proceeded to attack, with some relish, the plurality opinion. The plurality had found that Virginia's interest in limiting the liability of its businesses could never outweigh the District's interest in protecting its residents. But that conclusion relied on two *choice of law* cases (*Alaska Packers* and *Pacific Employers*, discussed in Chapter 3), rather than cases involving the enforceability of judgments. The dissent observed that a strong distinction between the two lines of cases "makes perfect sense, since Virginia surely has a stronger interest in limiting an employer's liability to a fixed amount"[49] when that employer has reduced the employee's claim to judgment in a Virginia tribunal.

More generally, the dissent chided the plurality for "ignor[ing] any interest that Virginia might assert in the finality of its adjudications."[50] Virginia, after all, had expended its resources to resolve the workers' claim; if that resolution is not recognized as final, the Virginia court's "efforts and expense on an applicant's behalf are wasted when that applicant obtains a duplicative remedy in another State."[51]

Further, the dissent took issue with that part of the plurality's holding that focused on the statutory inability of the Virginia tribunal to consider any law other than Virginia's. The dissent found two defects in this argument. First, the worker had elected to seek relief from the Virginia tribunal. Second, the District of Columbia had no interest in forcing its residents to rely on District of Columbia law for relief.

Finally, the dissent disagreed with the practice of using "interest balancing" as a tool for interpreting the Full Faith and Credit Clause. While significant in the choice of law process, interest balancing should be irrelevant to the interstate recognition of judgments:

> The Full Faith and Credit Clause did not allot to this Court the task of "balancing" interests where the "public Acts, Records, and judicial Proceedings" of a State were involved. It simply directed that they be given . . . "Full Faith and Credit."[52]

Accordingly, the dissent would have followed the claim preclusive holding in *Magnolia*, "a rule whose analytical validity is, even yet, unchallenged."[53]

The Law Today

Today, the rule for workers' compensation cases is fairly clear: The Full Faith and Credit Clause does not prohibit a worker from seeking and obtaining a supplemental award in F-2 after receiving an initial award in F-1. The rationale for the rule, however, after *Thomas* is up in the air. The concurrence's choice of the *McCartin* solution probably makes the most sense. Although all nine justices of the *Thomas* court agreed that it rests upon foundations that are at least "questionable," it is still the last resolution ever to command a Supreme Court majority (the majority in *McCartin* itself). Further, its scope is obviously limited to workers' compensation cases, and thus it is easy to understand and, unlike the plurality opinion in *Thomas*, carries no risk of overgeneralization.[54] Further, unlike the dissent's full-preclusion solution, it does not require upsetting half a century of industry practice. The full faith and credit effect of workers' compensation awards is a narrow and circumscribed question, probably one that it is more important to settle than to settle correctly.

A General Public Policy Exception to Full Faith and Credit?

The criminal judgment and workers' compensation cases show that there are exceptions to a rigid rule of preclusion. Is it possible to generalize from those cases to a rule that a state may refuse to enforce the judgment of another state because it offends a deeply held policy of the forum? This section examines the support that can be mustered for that proposition including § 103 of the Restatement (Second) of Conflicts. In doing so, we revisit briefly some areas discussed in more detail earlier.

The Basic Rule

A state cannot refuse to enforce a judgment because it is based on a claim that the enforcing state finds repugnant to its own public policy. Although the Supreme Court has upheld that rule repeatedly, the issue will not stay buried; like the mythical Phoenix, the notion that there is a "public policy" exception to the Iron Law of Full Faith and Credit keeps trying to rise from the ashes.

The history recounted earlier in this book demonstrates that the basic unifying purpose behind the adoption of the clause would be sacrificed if a court could refuse to enforce a sister-state decision on the ground that the underlying claim violated some strongly held public policy of the enforcing state. Thus the earliest judicial decisions under the clause expressly rejected the "international rule," which permitted a general public policy exception, and adopted a strict rule of recognition.

That remains the law today. The key decision is Fauntleroy v. Lum (1908),[55] a dispute between two residents of Mississippi who had entered into a contract for the delivery of cotton in Mississippi at a future date. Mississippi law viewed futures contracts as a form of gambling and, therefore, held them to be illegal (and void). When a dispute arose concerning the contract, the parties went to arbitration, and the arbitrator made an award to the plaintiff. The plaintiff then brought suit in a Mississippi court to enforce the award, but the court dismissed the action because the contract was illegal. Plaintiff did not give up, however, and sued in a Missouri court, which held in favor of the plaintiff and enforced the arbitrator's award.

The plaintiff then sued in a Mississippi state court to enforce the Missouri judgment. The Mississippi courts, however, refused to give full faith and credit to the Missouri judgment, and the case eventually made it to the Supreme Court, which reversed.

Although he spoke for only a bare majority (5-4), Justice Holmes had no difficulty identifying the right result: "A judgment is conclusive as to all the *media concludendi*; and it needs no authority to show that it cannot be impeached either in or out of the state by showing that it was based upon a mistake of law."[56] Holmes traced the lineage of that rule back to Chief Justice Marshall's opinion in Hampton v. McConnel (1818):

> [T]he judgment of a state court should have the same credit, validity, and effect in every other court . . . which it had in the state where it was pronounced, and that whatever pleas would be good to a suit thereon in such state, and none others, could be pleaded in any other court in the United States.[57]

That both Marshall and Holmes took such a hard line is not surprising. Both were strong nationalists and knew from experience the dangers inherent in a system that let the states treat each other as foreign nations rather than as members of the same union.

For that was the position taken by the four dissenters in *Fauntleroy*. In an opinion written by Justice Joseph McKenna, they contended that the Full Faith and Credit Clause was not designed to replace the old international rule of comity, which should continue to define a state court's obligation to recognize a sister-state judgment. And, the dissent continued, comity never could require the forum to enforce a foreign court's mistaken interpretation of the forum's own law.

The majority surely has the better of the argument. First, that opinion was consistent with the desire of the Framers of the Full Faith and Credit Clause to keep the state courts from engaging in internecine warfare. Further, Justice Holmes's no-exception rule offered ease of application and thus served the ends of judicial economy and expediency.

In short, *Fauntleroy* was a strong endorsement of the rule of recognition precisely because its facts presented such a compelling case for an exception. The Court, after all, had forced Mississippi to recognize a Missouri judgment based on a Mississippi contract that violated the criminal law of Mississippi. A modern analogue shows how strongly the *Fauntleroy* rule subordinates states' rights to the full faith and credit policies. Suppose a Utah plaintiff obtained a Nevada judgment against a Utah defendant based on a prostitution contract made and performed in Utah. *Fauntleroy* would require Utah to enforce the judgment even though the underlying contract was invalid and indeed a felony under Utah law. The result is clear under *Fauntleroy*.

The Interests of F-2

But is there room, within the legal universe of *Fauntleroy* for a very limited exception to the rule of recognition? Suppose a Wyoming court obtained personal jurisdiction over the governor of New York and enjoined her from signing into law a bill passed by the New York legislature. Would the Supreme Court, following the *Fauntleroy* rule, compel the New York court to enforce the Wyoming judgment? The example is not quite as fanciful as it seems. No case has involved an F-1 court order purporting to control the executive function of the government of F-2, but there are several cases where F-1 courts have attempted to control judicial proceedings in F-2. These are the antisuit injunction cases, where an F-1 court enjoins a litigant from commencing judicial proceedings in F-2. The Supreme Court has never ruled on such a case, but the lower courts consistently have held that the F-2 court need not recognize the F-1 injunction.[58]

Supposing that there is an exception for the antisuit injunction cases, is it narrowly limited to those situations, or does it stand for a general principle that there comes a point beyond which states' rights need not yield to the Iron Law of Full Faith and Credit? The courts and commentators have found it difficult to resist the temptation to try to identify such a point.

The next time the issue attracted the attention of the Supreme Court was in Yarborough v. Yarborough (1933), a seemingly straightforward child-support case. A Georgia court had ordered the defendant-father to make a lump sum child support payment to his daughter. He made the payment, which, according to Georgia law, exhausted his support obligation to her. However, she later sued him in South Carolina, her domicile, for additional support for her education. The majority, speaking through Justice Louis Brandeis, had no trouble enforcing the Georgia order extinguishing the support obligation, according to the Iron Law; the order, preclusive in Georgia would be preclusive in South Carolina. Justice Stone, however, disagreed, viewing the case not as a simple application of the Iron Law principle, but rather as one where the interests of two states unavoidably collided. According to his view, the Court should resolve such cases not by a wooden application of the Full Faith and Credit Clause, but rather by attempting to accommodate the competing state interests:

> Between the prohibition of the due process clause, acting upon the courts of the state from which such proceedings may be taken, and the mandate of the full faith and credit clause, acting upon the state to which they may be taken, there is an area which federal authority has not occupied. . . . In the assertion of rights, defined by a judgment of one state, within the territory of another there is often an inescapable conflict of interest of the two states, and there comes a point beyond which the imposition of the will of one state beyond its own borders involves a forbidden infringement of some legitimate domestic interest of the other.[59]

To Justice Stone, in other words, there is a state's rights limit to the scope of full faith and credit (although he did not tell us how to find that limit).

The Workers' Compensation Cases

The public policy exception issue next surfaced only a few years later in a pair of workers' compensation cases, Magnolia Petroleum Co. v. Hunt (1943) and Industrial Comm'n of Wisconsin v. McCartin (1947). The issue in those cases was whether a compensation award in one state barred a later, higher award in a second state. The *Magnolia* Court had no trouble with the orthodox answer: Full faith and credit barred the second suit. Three years later in *McCartin*, however, a unanimous Court found a way to avoid giving full faith and credit to workers' compensation awards. The Court could have resolved the case easily because the F-1 compensation award stated explicitly that it "did not affect any rights that applicant may have under the Workman's Compensation Act of . . . [F-2]." However, the Court had bigger fish to fry; it wanted to establish a general workers' compensation exception to the Full Faith and Credit Clause—one that would extend to cases where the initial award did not contain a nonpreclusion clause. It grounded the exception in the language of the F-1 legislation:

> But there is nothing in the statute or in the decisions thereunder to indicate that it is completely exclusive, that it is designed to preclude any recovery by proceedings brought in another state for injuries received there in the course of an Illinois employment. . . . [W]e should not readily interpret such a statute so as to cut off an employee's right to sue under other legislation passed for his benefit. Only some unmistakable language by a state legislature or judiciary would warrant our accepting such a construction.[60]

McCartin's holding was consistent in part with the received learning under the Full Faith and Credit Clause. The F-1 statute was entitled to no more preclusive effect in F-2 than it was given by the F-1 lawmakers. However, the Court's nonpreclusive reading of the F-1 statute was not merely a matter of legislative intent because the Court also included the "[o]nly some unmistakable language" passage, which suggested that ordinary methods of statutory construction were to be ignored in favor of the Court's own presumption against the preclusivity of the first award. The Court made no attempt to justify its presumption, much less to ground it in the Constitution. That, of course, is not the way that courts should behave.

The Restatement (Second) of Conflict of Laws § 103

The next development in the search for a public policy exception to the Iron Law came not from the courts, but from the American Law Institute in the Restatement (Second) of Conflict of Laws, published in 1971. Section 103 of the Restatement permits nonrecognition of a sister-state judgment if enforcement "would involve improper interference with important interests" of the forum state. The inclusion of § 103 in the Restatement was highly controversial[61] and somewhat surprising given *Fauntleroy* and the unbroken line of cases since that decision denying the existence of a policy exception. Indeed, the drafters of the Restatement could rely only on the antisuit injunction cases, Justice Stone's dissent, the workers' compensation cases discussed earlier, and several decisions in family law.

The family law decisions can be distinguished easily. To be sure, each contains language that provides some support for § 103; however, they can be more readily explained on other grounds, principally the due process rights of the losing F-1 litigant.[62] The one exception, Williams v. State of North Carolina (1945, *Williams II*), does provide some support for the policy set forth in the section. (*See* Chapter 6, *supra*). There, the Court permitted the F-2 court to inquire into whether F-1 had made a proper finding that a spouse seeking a divorce in F-1 had been domiciled in that state at the time of divorce. That finding, which the Court labeled a "jurisdictional fact," necessarily had to be subject to collateral attack in F-2: "To permit the necessary finding of domicil[e] by one State to foreclose all States in the protection of their social institutions would be intolerable."[63] Although that language does support a policy exception, its precedential force is minimal; in the half century since it was handed down, the *Williams* decision has never been followed. In short, the family law cases provide little support for the proposition stated in § 103.

Nor are the workers' compensation cases much help for the proponents of § 103. All that those cases did was to announce a rule of construction: An injured worker could obtain a second, higher award in another state unless the first state's law, using "unmistakable language," precluded the second award. Further, if those cases do support a public policy exception, it is a narrow one, limited to worker's compensation cases, and based pragmatically on industry practice, rather than a general one based theoretically on states' rights. In short, the American Law Institute clearly exceeded the available Supreme Court precedent when it adopted § 103. Surprisingly, it took the Court thirty years to correct the Restatement's error.

It had missed an earlier chance to set the record straight in 1980 in Thomas v. Washington Gas Light Co. (1980). In *Thomas*, the Court attempted to rationalize the workers' compensation exception more satisfactorily than it had in *McCartin*. The claimant was a District of Columbia worker employed there by the defendant-employer. After being injured in Virginia in the course of his employment, he received a Virginia workers' compensation award and then later sought and obtained a larger supplemental award in the District of Columbia. The question before the Court was whether the second award violated the Full Faith and Credit Clause. The Court held that it did not, but it got to that result by a very strange path. Instead of affirming the settled and innocuous rationale of *McCartin*, it fractured badly, producing three opinions and no majority.

The interesting opinion, from the point of view of full faith and credit theory, was the four-justice plurality written by Justice Stevens. The plurality rejected both *McCartin* and *Magnolia*. The former, according to Justice Stevens, incorrectly allotted to the state the power to control the preclusive effect of its judgments by explicitly stating its intentions on the issue. Thus, according to *McCartin*, it could give its judgments one effect at home and a lesser effect in sister states. That, said Justice Stevens, was a violation of the most basic principle of full faith and credit. Justice Stevens also rejected the *Magnolia* solution because, prior to that decision, states had not given preclusive effect to workers' compensation judgments. Thus, *Magnolia* had overruled settled law (and had itself been partially overruled in *McCartin*). Returning to a rule of full preclusion for workers' compensation awards would thus upset industry practice settled for over thirty years. Unfortunately, the plurality then fashioned a new rule based on § 103 and its state-interest balancing test. The result not only rerationalized the workers' compensation exception to the Iron Law, but also threatened to create a more general policy exception of completely uncertain dimensions and contour.

A three-justice concurring opinion, authored by Justice White, wanted to retain the *McCartin* solution not for its analytical consistency, but because it was expressly limited to workers' compensation cases, and did not threaten the Iron Law with a broader ill-defined exception. Finally, dissenting Justice Rehnquist (joined by Justice Marshall), wanted to return to *Magnolia* and abolish the preclusion exception for workers' compensation cases. And there matters stood for some twenty years; the *McCartin* rule for workers' compensation cases persisted because no Supreme Court majority had overruled it, and the general state-interest balancing exception of § 103 remained in legal limbo.

Baker v. General Motors

In Baker v. General Motors Corp. (1998) the Supreme Court considerably restricted the range of any full faith and credit exception based on the public policy of the enforcing state and thus diminished the scope that the *Thomas* plurality had allowed to the § 103 theory. The facts in *Baker* are complex. In a Georgia product liability action that occurred before the *Baker* case, Elwell, an engineer employed by General Motors, had testified against GM, stating that the fuel system used in GM pickup trucks was less crashworthy than the ones employed in competing vehicles. When GM terminated Elwell's employment, he sued the company in Michigan for wrongful discharge, and GM counterclaimed for breach of fiduciary duty. GM and Elwell eventually entered into a settlement agreement, under which Elwell received a sum of money, and the parties stipulated to the entry of an injunction prohibiting Elwell from testifying against GM in future product liability actions. The settlement agreement contained an exception to the injunction, which held Elwell harmless for any testimony he gave pursuant to a court order.

Subsequently, the Bakers, survivors of a decedent killed in a Missouri highway accident and vehicle fire, sued GM in a Missouri court for wrongful death. GM removed the action to federal court, where the Bakers deposed Elwell and called him as a witness over GM's objection. The district court, which permitted the testimony, was reversed by the Eighth Circuit, which was reversed in turn by a unanimous Supreme Court.

The decision, though unanimous, produced three different opinions. Justice Ruth Bader Ginsburg, a well-known full faith and credit scholar in her previous academic career, wrote for a five-vote majority. She rejected the *Thomas* plurality's ambitious version of the public policy exception and reinforced the Iron Law of Full Faith and Credit.

> [O]ur decisions support no roving "public policy exception" to the full faith and credit due judgments. . . . We are "aware of [no] considerations of local policy or law which could rightly be deemed to impair the force and effect which the full faith and credit clause and the Act of Congress require to be given to [a money] judgment outside the state of its rendition."[64]

She also found no functional reason for the historical reluctance to give full faith and credit to injunctions or other equity decrees: "We see no reason why the preclusive effects of an adjudication . . . should differ depending solely upon the type of relief sought in a civil action."[65]

While the majority opinion disavowed a "roving public policy exception," it did rely on Fall v. Eastin (1909) and the state court antisuit injunction cases[66] as the grounds for a much narrower exception based on the themes in § 103.

> Orders commanding action or inaction have been denied enforcement in a sister State when they purported to accomplish an official act within the exclusive province of that other State or interfered with litigation over which the ordering State had no authority. Thus a sister State's decree concerning land ownership in another State has been held ineffective to transfer title. . . . And antisuit injunctions regarding litigation elsewhere, even if compatible with due process as a direction constraining parties to the decree, in fact have not controlled the second court's actions regarding litigation in that court.[67]

Even this minimal statement by the *Baker* majority of the public policy exception, however, may have limited precedential effect for it was but dictum in the case. The majority based its actual holding on a more fundamental, black letter preclusion principle: A court's judgment cannot bind persons who were not before it—persons over whom it had no jurisdiction and who were not parties to the action. Thus, without regard to any public policy exception, the majority held that the Bakers could not be precluded from using Elwell's testimony because they were strangers to the Michigan litigation between Elwell and GM.

Justice Scalia's concurring opinion[68] was the most satisfying analytically, relying on general well-accepted rules for the interstate enforcement of judgments. The Full Faith and Credit Clause, he noted, never has required F-2 to enforce an F-1 judgment directly. Thus an F-2 court need not issue execution upon an F-1 money judgment; rather the F-1 plaintiff must bring an enforcement action in F-2 based on the F-1 judgment debt. That enforcement action results in an F-2 judgment, which then can be executed against any of the defendant's property in F-2. Scalia reasoned that an analogous procedure should govern the enforcement of an F-1 injunction. In lieu of obtaining direct enforcement of the Michigan judgment, GM would need to sue Elwell in Missouri on the Michigan judgment. In that action GM could seek, and the court could issue, a Missouri injunction prohibiting Elwell from testifying. GM had not gone through this procedure, so

Scalia did not need to reach the §103 issue: whether a Michigan judgment, actuated by a *correct* enforcement procedure, could control the admissibility of evidence in a Missouri proceeding.

Justices Kennedy, O'Connor, and Clarence Thomas concurred in a separate opinion, authored by Justice Kennedy.[69] Concurring in the majority's rejection of a roving public policy exception to the Full Faith and Credit Clause, his opinion began with a strong statement of the basic rule of preclusion. He then went on to express reservations about even the majority's minimalist version of the § 103 exception. Preliminarily, he pointed out that some Supreme Court decisions had permitted courts in one state to affect title to land in another. Further, the Court had yet to face squarely whether the Full Faith and Credit Clause permitted an F-2 court to ignore an F-1 antisuit injunction purporting to control litigation in F-2. More fundamentally, he saw no need to reach such controversial questions. Even the majority's holding in *Baker*, after all, rested on much simpler, less debatable principles. Justice Kennedy also quibbled with the majority's articulation of its narrowed down exception. The mere enumeration of F-1 judgments "purport[ing] to accomplish an official act within the exclusive province" of F-2 and F-1 judgments "interfering with the litigation over which the ordering state had no authority" failed to give lower courts sufficient direction on when and how the exception should apply.

Justice Kennedy's resolution of the case turned on his interpretation of Michigan law, which, he concluded, would not give the judgment preclusive effect against the Bakers, who were strangers to the Michigan action. Given that Michigan law would not preclude the Bakers, there was no need to consider whether there was any applicable exception to the Iron Law of Full Faith and Credit.

The several opinions in *Baker* add much needed order to a question that the *Thomas* opinions had muddled badly. All nine justices dismissed the notion of a "roving public policy exception" to the basic rule of preclusion. The five-vote majority would allow for a pared down public policy exception restricted to antisuit injunction cases and quasi-jurisdictional cases like Fall v. Eastin (1909). Although the Court unanimously agreed that its holdings had never explicitly sanctioned the antisuit injunction exception, the principle seems safer than ever given the approving dictum in *Baker* and the numerous state court cases that uphold it.

FULL FAITH AND CREDIT BETWEEN STATE AND FEDERAL COURTS

Full faith and credit is concerned primarily with issues of horizontal (that is, state-state) federalism and thus implicates the tension between individual state policies and the national policy of full intersovereign recognition. But a federated government such as ours also raises issues of vertical (federal-state) federalism, where the policy tensions are more complex. Again there are questions of state policy and national unity, but there are also the policies that motivate particular federal constitutional provisions, legislation, and common law. The recognition of federal judgments in state courts and state judgments in federal courts brings these issues into sharp relief.

State Judgments in Federal Courts

The Source of the Requirement

Requiring only that "Full Faith and Credit . . . be given in each State to the judicial Proceedings of every other State," the Full Faith and Credit Clause does not speak in terms of the federal courts' obligation to recognize and enforce state court judgments. Nevertheless that obligation exists based on the full faith and credit statute (28 U.S.C. § 1738) whose recognition mandate applies to "every court within the United States."[70] That language certainly covers both state and federal courts.

The statutory rather than constitutional source of the full faith and credit obligation, however, does not affect its rigor. The Supreme Court's decision in Parsons Steel, Inc. v. First Alabama Bank (1986) shows that federal courts must give full faith and credit to state court judgments even when those judgments are wrong and even when they fail to recognize prior federal court judgments. Initially, the Parsons had brought two actions against the defendant bank, one in state court based upon common law fraud and another in federal court based on federal legislation. After the federal court rendered judgment in the bank's favor, the bank pled the judgment as res judicata in the state court, which rejected the plea and issued judgment in favor of the Parsons. The bank then filed another suit in federal court to enjoin the Parsons from prosecuting the state action. Relying in part on the state court's improper failure to recognize the first federal court judgment, both the federal district and circuit courts held that there was no obligation to recognize the erroneous state court judgment.

The Supreme Court reversed, however, holding that the second federal court must give full faith and credit to the state court judgment even though it improperly refused recognition to prior federal court judgment. The remedy for the state court's erroneous refusal to recognize the federal court judgment is an appeal in the state courts, not a collateral attack in a second federal-court action.

The case is directly analogous to and every bit as emphatic as Fauntleroy v. Lum (1908)[71] and Treinies v. Sunshine Mining Co. (1939).[72] The federal court's statutory obligation is no less rigorous than the state court's constitutional obligation. In each case the court must give full faith and credit to a state court judgment even when it is incorrect, and even when its error is a refusal to recognize a prior judgment. The upshot is that the basic law of preclusion applies as stringently to federal courts as to state courts.

Exceptions: Exclusive Jurisdiction

The source of the state court's obligation to recognize the judgments of other state courts is constitutional, so Congress cannot alter it. By contrast, the source of the federal courts' full faith and credit obligation is statutory; and the full faith and credit statute, like any other congressional enactment, can be modified or repealed in whole or in part by Congress. Thus Congress could provide for exceptions to the federal courts obligation to recognize state court judgments.[73] There have been few explicit exceptions,[74] but litigants occasionally argue that a particular federal statute has effected an implied partial repeal of the full faith and credit statute and thus permits federal courts to refuse full faith and credit to selected state court judgments. These arguments have seemed strongest when the state court judgment involves matters within the exclusive jurisdiction of federal courts and civil rights cases.[75]

Congress has given the federal courts exclusive jurisdiction over several kinds of cases, cases under the federal antitrust laws, patent infringement cases, and bankruptcy cases, for example. When a federal court exercises jurisdiction in such cases, is it bound by the preclusive effect of prior related state court litigation? The question can arise in the context of claim preclusion or issue preclusion.

Claim Preclusion and Exclusive Jurisdiction

Suppose the plaintiff has both a federal and state antitrust claim against the defendant. After first suing the defendant in state court on the state antitrust claim, the plaintiff then sues the same defendant in federal court on the federal antitrust claim. Should the claim be precluded according to orthodox full faith and credit law, or did Congress intend an implied exception to the full faith and credit statute when it gave the federal courts' exclusive jurisdiction over federal antitrust claims.

The Restatement (Second) of Judgments concludes that the exclusive jurisdiction claim should not be precluded by the prior state court action.[76] For one thing, preclusion might diminish the nationwide uniformity and effectiveness of the federal antitrust scheme that the congressional grant of exclusive jurisdiction sought to assure. Further, it seems unfair to preclude the plaintiff's federal claim when that claim could not possibly have been brought in the state court action.

The Supreme Court refused to reach the question of implied partial repeal in Marrese v. American Academy of Orthopaedic Surgeons (1985). As in the hypothetical, the plaintiff had brought an antitrust action based on state law in state court and then a subsequent suit in federal court based on that court's exclusive antitrust jurisdiction. Instead of addressing the implied partial repeal question, the Supreme Court provided a two-part test for federal courts to use in such cases. The first step requires the federal court to consider whether state preclusion law would preclude the subsequent federal-court action. Many states, after all, fail to preclude claims that could not have been brought in a prior action, and that doctrine might well apply to federal antitrust claims since they are within the exclusive jurisdiction of the federal courts. If, however, the federal court determines that state law would preclude the subsequent federal action, it would then need to proceed to the second step of the analysis and determine whether the exclusive federal antitrust jurisdiction statute had worked an implied partial repeal of § 1738.

When analyzing the second step, the court should treat as determinative the intent of Congress in granting exclusive jurisdiction to the federal courts. Determining congressional intent requires an inquiry into the particular federal statute, the nature of the federal claim, and the policy behind the grant of exclusive jurisdiction. In *Marrese*, there was no need for the court to apply the second step; the case was remanded because the lower courts had not determined the content of state preclusion law. Until it was clear that state preclusion law would preclude the subsequent federal-court antitrust action, there was no need to analyze the implied partial repeal issue.

In Matsushita Electric Industrial Co. v. Epstein (1996), the court found it necessary to reach the second step of the *Marrese* analysis. Matsushita made a tender offer for the stock of the Delaware corporation, which precipitated a Delaware state court class action based on state law claims against the directors of the Delaware corporation, Matsushita, and others. While the Delaware action was pending, another class action was filed against Matsushita in a California federal court based on the exclusive federal jurisdiction provisions of the Security Exchange Act of 1934.[77] The parties to the Delaware suit negotiated a settlement. In return for a global release of all claims arising out of the Matsushita tender offer, the defendants agreed to deposit $2 million into a settlement fund to be distributed to the members of the class. Pursuant to Delaware law, the members of the plaintiff class in the California action (also members of the Delaware class) were notified of the settlement and offered the opportunity to "opt out" of it, but they did not. Matsushita then invoked the Delaware settlement as res judicata in the California action.

Applying the *Marrese* analysis, the Supreme Court upheld the preclusive affect of the Delaware settlement. Step one of the *Marrese* test required the court to determine whether, under Delaware law, the settlement would preclude subsequent assertion of claims that could not have been raised in the Delaware proceeding. Delaware law was not completely clear on the issue, of course, because no Delaware court had faced, nor could face the issue. By hypothesis, the preclusive effect of a state court judgment in a subsequent federal court exclusive jurisdiction action can arise only in a federal court, not in a Delaware state court. Nevertheless, the Court extrapolated from the general principles of Delaware preclusion law and reached the conclusion that it would preclude the California plaintiffs' claims.

Applying step two of the *Marrese* analysis, the Court tried to discern congressional intent on whether the Securities Exchange Act effected an implied partial repeal of § 1738. Not surprisingly, the legislative history and language of the act, which had been adopted in 1934 and been part of a general code revision in 1948, gave no direct indication. Nevertheless the Court determined that the purposes behind the exclusive jurisdiction provision of the act did not require an exception to the general rule of preclusion of § 1738.

Marrese and *Epstein* do not permit a completely confident statement of the law regarding an exclusive-jurisdiction exception to the preclusion principle of § 1738. The court did not reach the issue in *Marrese*, and the purportedly preclusive state court judgment in *Epstein* resulted from a class action settlement rather than a contested litigation. The Court's attitude on the issue, however, seems clear: It will be extremely reluctant to find in the legislative history of an exclusive jurisdiction statute the clear congressional intent required to posit an implied partial repeal of § 1738 and thus an exclusive jurisdiction exception to the general rule of state-federal claim preclusion.

Issue Preclusion and Exclusive Jurisdiction

Issue preclusion also can provide the context for claims of implied partial repeal of § 1738 by subsequent exclusive federal jurisdiction statutes. The leading case, Lyons v. Westinghouse Electric Corp. (1955) was a suit for treble damages under the federal antitrust laws brought in a federal court, which had exclusive jurisdiction over the claim. Westinghouse claimed that the antitrust issue was precluded by the findings in a prior contract action it had brought against Lyons in a state court. Lyons had pleaded as a defense in the state court contract action that the contract had violated the federal antitrust laws, but the court rejected the defense and found the contract legal under the antitrust laws. The Second Circuit in an opinion by Judge Learned Hand stated the preclusion question succinctly:

> Thus the inquiry comes down to whether, when Congress gave exclusive jurisdiction to the district court over wrongs committed under the Anti-Trust Acts, it only meant that the 'person who shall be injured' must sue in the district court to recover damages; or whether it also meant that the district court must have unfettered power to decide the claim, regardless of the findings of any other courts.[78]

Relying on the need for national uniformity in enforcement of the antitrust laws and the quasi-criminal nature of a treble damages action, Judge Hand concluded that Congress intended that issue preclusion should not apply. "In the case at bar it appears to us that the grant to the district courts of exclusive jurisdiction over the action for treble damages should be taken to imply an immunity of their decisions from any prejudgment elsewhere."[79] The Supreme Court denied certiorari review.

Although the Supreme Court has not spoken precisely on the issue, there is reason to believe that it would not uphold the result in *Lyons*. Its claim preclusion holdings in *Marrese* and *Epstein* and its issue preclusion holdings in recent civil rights cases suggest that it would apply the *Marrese* two-step analysis and that it would be unlikely to find in step two of that analysis that Congress, by enacting an exclusive jurisdiction statute, intended an implied partial repeal of § 1738.

An Exception for Civil Rights Cases?

There is a plausible argument for an exception to the general rule of state-to-federal court preclusion in civil rights cases. Congress was motivated in part by distrust of state executive, legislative, and judicial officials in enacting at least some of the civil rights statutes. Given that distrust, it is possible that Congress intended that federal courts hearing civil rights claims not be precluded by prior state court litigation. Once again the discussion can be divided conveniently by the distinction between claim and issue preclusion.

Issue Preclusion and § 1983 Cases

The Court first addressed the issue in the context of a § 1983 claim, Allen v. McCurry (1980). The plaintiff had been convicted in state court for possession of heroin and assault with intent to kill. During the criminal trial, he had moved unsuccessfully to suppress evidence that the police seized from his home during a search; the trial court held a hearing on the motion and ruled that the police had not violated the plaintiff's Fourth Amendment rights.

Subsequently, the plaintiff brought a § 1983 action in federal court against the police department, several individual police officers, and the City of St. Louis based on the claim that the search of his home had violated his rights under the Fourth Amendment. The defendants argued that the findings of the state court in the suppression hearing precluded the issue of the constitutionality of the search. The Supreme Court agreed and held that § 1983 did not work an implied partial repeal of § 1738, and thus state court findings ordinarily should have issue preclusion effect in subsequent § 1983 actions in federal court.

The plaintiffs' argument for an exception to the general rule of preclusion cited the historic distrust by Congress of southern state courts as a principal legislative purpose for enacting § 1983, which, after all, is also known as the Ku Klux Klan Act. The Court's response was that nothing in the language or history of § 1983 could support a general preclusion exception for actions under the statute. A more limited exception might exist, said the Court, when the state court had not permitted "a full and fair opportunity to litigate the claim."

In University of Tennessee v. Elliott (1986), the Supreme Court extended its holding in *Allen* to cover the issue preclusion effect of state administrative proceedings on subsequent § 1983 actions in federal court. After the plaintiff, an African-American employee of the University of Tennessee, was informed that he would be fired, he requested a hearing pursuant to Tennessee administrative law and also filed a civil rights action in federal court.

The state administrative hearing, conducted by a university official acting as an administrative law judge, was extensive, involving 100 witnesses, 150 exhibits, and 5,000 pages of transcript. At its conclusion, the official found that some of the charges were valid and that they were not racially motivated. The plaintiff appealed the findings and penalty—transfer rather than dismissal—to a university vice president who affirmed the hearing officer's recommendation. Rather than seeking review of the administrative action in the state courts, the plaintiff chose to pursue his federal civil rights action instead.

The Supreme Court held that the prior state administrative findings had issue preclusive effect in the later federal court § 1983 action. That effect was not required by the Full Faith and Credit Clause or its implementing statute, which applied only to judicial proceedings. The Court, however, fashioned a rule of federal common law to govern the issue. It held that the state administrative body's resolution of factual issues should have issue preclusion effect in subsequent federal litigation when the state body acted "in a judicial capacity," and the parties had an adequate opportunity to litigate the issue. The Court based its holding upon federalism concerns as well as the standard policies favoring preclusion, the parties' need for repose, and the judicial system's need to conserve resources.

Issue Preclusion and Title VII Cases

In Kremer v. Chemical Construction Corp. (1982), the Supreme Court used the same approach in a Title VII employment discrimination case as it had in the § 1983 cases. The plaintiff filed charges of religious and national origin discrimination against his employer with the federal Equal Employment Opportunity Commission (EEOC), which referred the charges, as required by Title VII, to the appropriate state administrative agency, which conducted an investigation and determined that the defendant had not discriminated against the plaintiff. When the plaintiff sought review in the New York State courts, they upheld the agency's decision.

The plaintiff next pursued his claim with the federal EEOC, which also found against him. When he then brought a Title VII action in federal court, his employer argued that the state administrative and judicial findings precluded the discrimination issue in the federal court action. The Supreme Court ruled in favor of the employer and rejected the plaintiff's argument for an implied partial repeal of the full faith and credit statute by Title VII. The Court found nothing in the language or history of the statute from which to infer congressional intent to exempt Title VII cases from the general rule of preclusion. Nor was the Court impressed by the plaintiff's argument that he had not had "a full and fair opportunity to litigate" the issue in the state court proceeding. In *Allen*, the court had held that preclusion might not apply in such circumstances, but it held that the state fact-finding in *Kremer* easily satisfied the minimum procedural requirements of the Fourteenth Amendment's due process clause.

After *Kremer*, it was clear that a judicially reviewed state administrative fact-finding would have issue preclusive effect in a later federal court Title VII action. Unresolved in *Kremer*, however, was the preclusion effect of an *unreviewed* state administrative fact-finding in such an action. In University of Tennessee v. Elliott (1986), the Supreme Court was willing to create a federal common-law rule providing for issue preclusive effect for state administrative findings in *§ 1983 cases*, but it declined to do the same for Title VII actions. Title VII requires that the EEOC give only "substantial weight" to state agency determinations, and such a limited preclusion rule would make no sense if federal courts were then required by federal common law to give those same determinations full issue preclusion effect.

Claim Preclusion in Civil Rights Cases

The Supreme Court has paid less attention to claim preclusion than issue preclusion in the civil rights context. In Migra v. Warren City School Dist. Bd.

of Education (1984), its only significant decision, the plaintiff, an employee of the defendant board brought concurrent state and federal actions against her employer. Initially, the board had offered her a renewal of her contract, which she accepted; but upon reconsideration, it voted not to renew her. She sued first in state court based on breach of contract and wrongful interference with contract. After prevailing in state court, she sued in federal court under § 1983 on the theory that she had been fired in violation of her First Amendment, due process, and equal protection rights.

The Supreme Court ruled that the federal action was claim precluded. Because the state court judgment would receive full claim preclusion effect in state courts, the same result was compelled in federal court. Plaintiff had argued that permitting concurrent actions in state and federal court would permit each tribunal to adjudicate the claim over which it had greater expertise, but the court rejected the relative expertise argument as inconsistent with the mandate of the full faith and credit statute. Further, the Court held that its claim preclusion holding was compelled by the precedent of *Allen*; congressional suspicion of state court prejudice being insufficient to warrant an exception to the general rule of state-federal issue preclusion, it made little sense to argue that it would be enough to justify such an exception in claim preclusion cases.

Exclusive Jurisdiction, Preclusion, and Preemption

We have considered in prior sections cases that deal with issue and claim preclusion when the second lawsuit comes within the exclusive jurisdiction of the federal court. Nevertheless, the first lawsuit in each of those cases was properly within the subject matter jurisdiction of the state court. Under those circumstances, as we have seen, the Supreme Court has been reluctant to find an exception to the general preclusion rule of § 1738. But what happens when the subject matter of the second suit is within the exclusive jurisdiction of the federal court, and there is no subject matter jurisdiction in the state court over the first lawsuit?

We have already treated this issue earlier in this chapter, when we addressed the Bootstrap Principle. Recall that that concept requires giving issue preclusion effect to a court's determination of its subject matter jurisdiction even when the determination is incorrect. In Kalb v. Feuerstein (1940), the Supreme Court made it clear, however, that the Bootstrap Rule cannot always prevail. In some areas of the law, the federal interest is so crucial that in order to accomplish the purposes behind the exclusive jurisdiction statute, the federal court must be able to adjudicate the case entirely free of the effect of another judgment resulting from the litigation of any prior state court action. In other words, in those important federal areas, the federal policy is strong enough to trump the otherwise universally applicable policies of finality and waiver.

The areas in which the *Kalb* result makes the most sense are those where federal law has completely preempted the field, requiring not only exclusive federal adjudicatory jurisdiction, but also exclusive federal legislative jurisdiction. In those fields, there simply is no room for state regulation of any kind, and similarly no room for state court preclusion of issues that may arise in subsequent federal court exclusive jurisdiction actions. Excellent examples of such are matters of national security and nuclear power regulation. Far more mundane, but much more likely to arise are ERISA cases (litigation involving rights and duties of pension funds), where the Supreme Court has held that federal solutions to any dispute must be nationally uniform.

Federal Judgments in State Courts

Both the Full Faith and Credit Clause and the implementing statute are silent about the recognition due federal court judgments in later state and federal litigation. The clause addresses only the effect of state judgments in the courts of sister States, and the statute addresses that issue as well as the effect of state judgments in federal courts. Neither provision, however, speaks in explicit terms about the recognition due federal court judgments and findings in subsequent state and federal litigation. Notwithstanding the absence of a textual source, however, it is clear, and always has been clear, that state and federal courts must give full faith and credit to the judgments and findings of federal courts.

The exact amount of faith and credit due federal court proceedings is not quite as clear; it depends, of course, upon the preclusion law that the recognizing court will apply to the federal court judgment. Does it apply its own opinions on preclusion law, the preclusion law of the state where the federal court sits, or a set of federal common law preclusion principles? The answer is clear when the rendering federal court has adjudicated issues of federal law; the federal common law of preclusion controls, and all recognizing courts, state or federal, must apply it.[80] Until recently, by contrast, there was no clear answer when the rendering federal court exercised diversity of citizenship jurisdiction.

Commentators disagreed on the question. According to one view, the preclusive effect of all federal judgments—whether based on federal question or diversity jurisdiction—should be controlled by federal law. Determining the scope of its judgments, the argument went, is among the defining characteristics of a court, and any body that lacks that power is not fully a court as that term is understood in Article III of the Constitution.[81] Another school of thought favored numerous specific choice-of-preclusion-law rules, each narrowly tailored to address one of the multiple permutations of substantive and procedural, state and federal policies at stake in the many possible preclusion scenarios.[82]

The Supreme Court ended the debate and settled the issue in Semtek International, Inc. v. Lockheed Martin Corp. (2001). Initially, the plaintiff in *Semtek* sued the defendant in California state court, and the defendant removed to the appropriate California federal court on diversity grounds. When the defendants moved to dismiss the claim based on California's two-year statute of limitations, the federal trial court granted the motion, and the plaintiff then brought suit in a Maryland state court where the limitations period was longer. The Maryland state courts (the case could not be removed to federal court due to a lack of complete diversity) then held that *federal* preclusion principles determined the res judicata effect of the California federal court judgment, and that according to those principles, the Maryland lawsuit was barred. The Supreme Court granted certiorari and reversed.

Initially, the Court in an opinion written by Justice Scalia, held that the rule of Dupasseur v. Rochereau (1874) was obsolete. That case, which had held that forum state law should control the preclusive effect of federal court judgments, was decided under the Conformity Act, which subsequently had been superseded by the Federal Rules of Civil Procedure. The court also determined that Rule 41 (b) of the Federal Rules of Civil Procedure, which deals with the effect of a dismissal, did not supply the answer. While the language of that Rule suggested that California federal court judgment was "upon the merits" and, therefore, subject to preclusive effect, the Court held that the rule was designed only to restrict the plaintiff's opportunity to refile a dismissed action in the dismissing court, not its ability to refile the action elsewhere.

With no controlling precedent and no governing Federal Rule of Civil Procedure, the Supreme Court was free to consider the problem afresh. Noting that the Full Faith and Credit Clause and its implementing statute failed to address the preclusive effect of federal court judgments, the Supreme Court determined that the appropriate solution was to create a rule of federal common law. There was no need for a nationally uniform rule because the substantive law controlling diversity cases is state rather than federal law. Instead, the Court determined that the Erie Railroad Co. v. Tompkins (1938) decision and its policy of discouraging intrastate forum shopping should control. Accordingly, the Court held that the preclusive effect of a judgment of a federal court exercising diversity jurisdiction should be determined by referring to the preclusion law of the state where the federal court sits. Thus, in the case itself, the preclusive effect of the judgment of the California federal trial court (the court that had dismissed on limitations grounds) was to be determined by California state law.

That result seems correct. The goals of the *Erie* decision were to return to the states control over matters of substantive law and also to discourage forum shopping between state and federal courts. A contrary holding in *Semtek* would have frustrated both policies. First, preclusion rules clearly can be substantive, for they can have a profound effect on the outcome of litigation. Moreover, substantive law policies may motivate a state's position on preclusion issues. A state might well retain the common-law mutuality rule in order to protect its mass transit or resort industries from repetitive litigation based on a single disaster, or to protect its manufacturers from sequential product liability actions.

More important, perhaps, a difference between federal and state preclusion law certainly could encourage forum shopping. Mutuality of estoppel again provides a good example. A litigator representing mass disaster or product liability victims might well choose a federal forum that had abandoned the mutuality rule over a state court that had not. A victory for the first plaintiff in the federal court would inure to the benefit of other possible plaintiffs, but a similar victory in the state court would not. Accordingly, we believe that Justice Scalia was correct in *Semtek*. We also note that these policy arguments are not particularly strong; thus, it might be that the best thing that can be said about the decision is that it settled the law in an area where it was more important that the law be settled than it be settled correctly.

NOTES

1. Sun Oil Co. v. Wortman, 486 U.S. 717 (1988); Warner v. Buffalo Drydock Co., 67 F.2d 540 (2d Cir. 1933).
2. *See* American Law Institute, Restatement of the Law, Second, Judgments § 19, comment d (1982).
3. *Id.*
4. *See, e.g.*, ALI, Restatement (Second) of Judgments § 68(1).
5. Federal Rules Civil Procedure 60(b).
6. ALI, *supra* note 2, at § 70.
7. Baker v. General Motors Corp., 522 U.S. at 222 (1998).
8. *Id.* at 234.
9. James v. Grand Trunk Railroad Co., 14 Ill.2d 356, 152 N.E. 2d 858, *cert. denied*, 358 U.S. 915 (1958).
10. *Baker*, 522 U.S. at 236.
11. The most common methods of obtaining valid personal jurisdiction are: consent, domicile or incorporation in the forum, service in the forum, and minimum contacts there.
12. The Supreme Court has fared poorly where it has tried to explain with any greater sophistication or precision the policies behind the personal jurisdiction requirement. *See* William Richman and William Reynolds, Understanding Conflicts of Law § 35 (3d ed., New York: LexisNexus 2002).
13. That case and the requirement established by it and its progeny are discussed more fully in Chapter 4.
14. The phrase comes from Moffatt Hancock, *Equitable Conversion and the Land Taboo in Conflict of Laws*, 17 Stanford L. Rev. 1095 (1965).
15. Formerly, it had been suggested that equity decrees, acting only on the conscience of the defendant were not entitled to full faith and credit, see Willis L. M. Reese, "Full Faith and Credit to Foreign Equity Decrees," 42 Iowa L. Rev. 183 (1957), but that view is no longer the law. See *Baker*, 522 U.S. 222 (1998).
16. *E.g.*, Varone v. Varone, 359 F.2d 769 (7th Cir. 1966); Weesner v. Weesner, 168 Neb. 345, 95 N.W.2d 682 (1959).
17. It is important to distinguish the absence of subject matter jurisdiction from a finding of improper venue. The former goes to the *power* of the court, while the latter goes only to whether the litigation was brought in the proper *location* in a jurisdiction which otherwise had power to render a judgment in the case.
18. There are two kinds of constitutional authority at play in these types of cases. The first type is discussed in the text; the second type is easier to see, perhaps, for it involves the question of whether the federal government has *pre-empted* state authority in the area. To give a simple example, federal law does not permit state courts to exercise authority over claims involving foreign sovereigns. Thus, an Ohio judgment against the United Kingdom is void because no state court can render such a judgment.

19. The phrase comes from Dan B. Dobbs, *The Validation of Void Judgments: The Bootstrap Principle*, 53 Virginia L. Rev. 1003 (Part I) (1967).

20. 375 U.S. 106, 111.

21. The rationale is similar to that of the last-in-time rule for inconsistent judgments discussed earlier.

22. DesMoines Navigation and Railroad Co. v. Iowa Homestead Co., 123 U.S. 532 (1887).

23. Kalb v. Feuerstein, 308 U.S. 433, 444 (1940).

24. Sherrer v. Sherrer, 334 U.S. 343 (1948); Chicot County Drainage Dist. v. Baxter State Bank, 308, U.S. 371 (1940).

25. See ALI, *supra* note 2, at § 12 (listing a set of factors that should control which policy prevails).

26. Kenney v. Supreme Lodge, 252 U.S. 411, 414–15 (1920).

27. 23 U.S. 66, 123.

28. ALI, *supra* note 2, at § 28(4) and comment f, § 85 comment g.

29. *Id.*, §§ 85 (1), (2).

30. Federal Rules of Evidence 803 (22).

31. Milwaukee County v. M. E. White Co., 296 U.S. 268, 271 (1935).

32. *Id.* at 271.

33. *Id.* at 272.

34. *Id.* at 279.

35. State Tax Commission v. Cord, 81 Nev. 403, 404 P.2d 422 (1965); Nelson v. Minnesota Income Tax Div., 429 P.2d 324, 325 (Wyo. Sup. Ct. 1967); Eugene F. Scoles, Peter Hay, Patrick J. Borchers, & Symeon C. Symeonides, Conflict of Laws § 24.23 (3d ed., 2000).

36. See Scoles, Hay, Borchers, & Symeonides § 24.23.

37. International Shoe Co. v. Washington, 326 U.S. 310 (1945) (coincidentally, *Shoe* involved both adjudicative (personal) jurisdiction and (regulatory) jurisdiction to levy an unemployment compensation tax).

38. Wisconsin v. Pelican Ins. Co., 127 U.S. 265, 290 (1888).

39. *Id.* at 299.

40. Huntington v. Attrill, 146 U.S. 657, 673–74 (1892) (emphasis supplied by authors).

41. *Id.* at 676.

42. 296 U.S. 268, 277.

43. See the discussion of this doctrine in Chapter 4.

44. McBride v. General Motors Corp., 737 F. Supp. 1563 (M.D. Ga. 1990).

45. Magnolia Petroleum Co. vs. Hunt, 320 U.S. 430, 444 (1943).

46. Industrial Comm'n of Wisconsin v. McCartin, 330 U.S. 622, 627–28 (1947).

47. *Id.* at 628.

48. Thomas v. Washington Gas Light Co., 448 U.S. 261, 290 (1980).

49. *Id.* at 293.

50. *Id.*

51. *Id.*

52. *Id.* at 296.

53. *Id.*

54. Lower courts have refused to take the bait and expand the scope of the workers' compensation exception to other areas. The leading case is Semler v. Psychiatric Institute of Washington, D.C. 575 F.2d 922 (D.C. Cir. 1978). The plaintiff there had recovered dam-

ages in a wrongful death action in Virginia. She then sought to recover survivor's benefits under District of Columbia law, relying on *McCartin*. Judge Malcolm Wilkey, speaking for the court, expressly rejected the analogy and refused to grant relief.

55. *Fauntleroy* is also discussed in detail *supra*, Chapter 4.

56. Fauntleroy v. Lum, 210 U.S. 230, 237 (1908).

57. *Id.* at 236.

58. *E.g.*, James v. Grand Trunk Western Railroad, 14 Ill. 2d 356, 152 N.E. 2d 858, *cert. denied*, 358 U.S. 915 (1958). This issue is discussed *infra*.

59. Yarborough v. Yarborough, 290 U.S. 202, 214–15 (1933).

60. Industrial Commission of Wisconsin v. McCartin, 330 U.S. 622, 627–28 (1937).

61. *See* Albert A. Ehrenzweig, *The Second Conflicts Restatement: A Last Appeal for Its Withdrawal*, 113 University of Pennsylvania L. Rev. 1230, 1240 (1965) ("There is . . . no authority whatsoever for the startling proposition that 'a judgment . . . need not be recognized or enforced in a sister State if such recognition or enforcement . . . would involve an improper infringement of the interests of the sister State' ").

62. *See* Richman & William, *supra* note 12, at § 117(b).

63. Williams v. North Carolina, 325 U.S. 226, 232 (1945).

64. Baker v. General Motors, 522 U.S. 222, 233–34 (1998).

65. *Id.*

66. *See, e.g.*, James v. Grand Trunk Western Railroad Co., 14 Ill. 2d 356, 152 N.E. 2d 858 (1958).

67. *Baker*, 522 U.S. 222, 235-36.

68. *Id.* at 241.

69. *Id.*

70. 28 U.S.C. § 1738.

71. See discussion in Chapter 4, *supra*.

72. See discussion in Chapter 4, *supra*.

73. Gene R. Shreve, *Preclusion and Federal Choice of Law*, 64 Texas L. Rev. 1209, 1223–24 (1986).

74. *See, e.g.*, 28 U.S.C. § 2254, the federal habeas corpus statute.

75. *See* generally Richman & Reynolds, *supra* note 12, at § 113(b).

76. ALI, *supra* note 2, at § 26(1)(c) and comment c.

77. 15 U.S.C. § 78.

78. Lyons v. Westinghouse Electric Co., 222 F.2d 184, 188 (1955).

79. *Id.* at 189.

80. *See* Parklane Hosiery Co. v. Shore, 439 U.S. 322 (1979) (establishing a federal common-law rule of preclusion that permits offensive nonmutual use of issue preclusion, subject to certain exceptions); Deposit Bank of Frankfort v. Board of Councilmen, 191 U.S. 499 (1903).

81. Ronan E. Degnan, "Federalized Res Judicata," 85 *Yale Law Journal* (1976) 741.

82. Larry L. Teply and Ralph U. Whitten, Civil Procedure 963–68 (2d ed., 2000); Charles A. Wright, Arthur R. Miller, and Edward H. Cooper, Federal Practice and Procedure § 4468 (31 vols., 2000).

6

Family Law: A Special Full Faith and Credit Problem

INTRODUCTION

The courts have read the Full Faith and Credit Clause as having a good deal to say about family law. As is true in other areas, the clause has had little effect with regard to sister states' "public acts," which is to say, choice of law (the sole exception to this statement is the Defense of Marriage Act,[1] discussed later in this chapter), but the clause has had substantial effect on the respect to be given "judicial proceedings" or judgments of other states.

Federal full faith and credit legislation applies here as well, Congress having exercised its implementing powers under the Full Faith and Credit Clause more actively in the family law area than in others. Indeed, family law is the *only* field where Congress has used its powers to implement the clause in a specific area. Until 1980, almost two centuries after the adoption of the Constitution, Congress had exercised its full faith and credit power only once, when it enacted in 1790 (and periodically reenacted) the general full faith and credit implementing statute, 28 U.S.C. § 1738. After 1980, however, Congress became considerably more active with all of its efforts centered on family law issues. The first of the family law full faith and credit statutes dealt with the urgent problem of the abduction of children by their own parents. Since then, Congress has adopted several more statutes designed to deal with interstate family law issues, particularly those involving child custody and support. Finally, Congress adopted the Defense of Marriage Act ("DOMA," 1996), a law authorizing states to decline to recognize same-sex marriages performed elsewhere.

These statutes reflect the central role that the concept of full faith and credit to judicial proceedings plays in contemporary family law. Our highly mobile society has created many problems in the area, problems that are exacerbated by our federal system and the inherent difficulty in effectively enforcing judgments in courts that may be located across a continent. It is fitting, therefore, that Congress, the only legislative body which can deal effectively with both national problems and federal ones, has made use of its power under the Full Faith and

Credit Clause to ameliorate them. The Framers of the clause, after all, intended that Congress use its full faith and credit implementing power to make interstate proceedings both swifter and more just.

This chapter examines both the constitutional and statutory responses to interstate problems involving family law, specifically those responses relating to marriage, divorce, support, and custody.

MARRIAGE

Problems in this area generally involve the question of whether the forum will recognize as valid a marriage entered into legally in another state, but illegal for some reason in the forum. American courts have not generally felt themselves bound by the Full Faith and Credit Clause when the validity of a marriage comes up as an issue in litigation. Because marriage is not a judgment (at least speaking legally), the Iron Law of Full Faith and Credit is not involved. The question, therefore, becomes one of choice of law—whether one state will recognize the consequences of a "public act" (that is, the marriage laws) of another state. The forum is free, then, to apply either its own law or the law of the place where the marriage was "celebrated." (It is very rare to see a choice of law issue involving a third state.)

Expressed somewhat differently, recognition of an out-of-state marriage is a matter of comity, or choice; in practice, however, recognition will be denied only if the foreign marriage violates the basic public policy of the forum. This strong deference to the laws of other states is, of course, unusual, and reflects the compelling social need to validate marriages.

The way that the traditional choice of law rule favors the validity of foreign marriage (both sister-state and foreign-nation) is by applying the law of the place of celebration of the marriage in most cases.[2] In other words, the forum will invalidate a marriage that was valid where celebrated only when it violates a fundamental public policy of the forum. The leading case is In Re May's Estate (N.Y. 1953).[3] There, a couple, both New York residents, had gone to Rhode Island to be married. They did so because they were uncle and niece, and New York law forbade their marriage as incestuous; Rhode Island, on the other hand, had no such prejudices. The Mays returned to New York and lived together there for thirty-four years until Fannie May's death in 1945. During the administration of her estate, the question arose as to whether her marriage to Sam had been valid. Although noting that the general rule is that the validity of a marriage is to be tested under the law of the place where the marriage was celebrated, the court noted that a "positive law" of the forum could lead to a different result. The court, however, rejected the argument that the express statutory prohibition of marriage in New York between "an uncle and niece" required nonrecognition of the Rhode Island marriage. Instead, the court ruled that it could and would be recognized because the marriage between uncle and niece was "not offensive to the public sense of morality to a degree regarded generally with abhorrence and thus was not within the inhibitions of natural law."[4] Unfortunately, the court did not explain how it knew that the challenged marriage was not sufficiently "offensive."

The rule in *May's Estate* has been followed generally. It is easy to understand why. There is a very strong judicial desire to uphold an ostensibly valid marriage because the consequences of not doing so can be quite devastating,[5] especially with respect to children and property. The public policy loophole mentioned in *May's Estate* has had little impact because of the strong push toward validation, and because the marriage rules of the several states do not differ all that significantly. Public policy in this area, at least, has long been converging toward recognition of marriages that appear to be "normal."[6]

Such was the law for the first two centuries of our national existence. Congress, however, was not content with this well-settled state of affairs, and it entered the interstate marriage arena with the passage in 1996 of the DOMA, 28 U.S.C. § 1738C. DOMA was the Congressional reaction to the threatened legalization of same-sex marriages in Hawaii, which caused great consternation among many politicians. Congress worried that the Full Faith and Credit Clause would require other states to recognize same-sex marriages entered into in Hawaii. DOMA provides, therefore, that no state or other American jurisdiction

> shall be required to give effect to any public act, record, or judicial proceeding of any other State . . . respecting a relationship between persons of the same sex that is treated as a marriage under the laws of such other State, . . . or a right or claim arising from such relationship.[7]

Congress, in other words, enacted DOMA in an attempt to deny constitutional protection to same-sex marriage. The states responded to the obvious congressional invitation by adopting legislation denying recognition, to such unions; as of this writing (June 2004), more than two-thirds of the states have done so.

DOMA provided, therefore, an effective weapon for those states that do not wish to respect same-sex marriages entered into elsewhere. It does raise two important questions, however: First, was DOMA necessary to achieve the congressional goals; second, is it constitutional?

As to the first question, DOMA was largely a waste of congressional time for it does nothing but codify existing law; in other words, all that DOMA accomplishes is to tell the states that they are not required to recognize same-sex marriages that were entered into legally under the laws of another state. DOMA, in short, neither compels nor forbids recognition by a state of such marriages. That was precisely the state of the law at the time DOMA was adopted, as *May's Estate* demonstrates.

The history of the Full Faith and Credit Clause makes it easy to conclude that the constitutional obligation it imposes on each state has nothing to do with the recognition, *vel non,* of a marriage entered into in another state. The syllogism works this way: Only judgments are entitled to near automatic recognition (see Chapter 4, *supra*); a marriage is not a "judgment" (at least of the relevant kind), but, rather, it is a state licensed and sanctioned arrangement entered into under the umbrella of a statute. A marriage, therefore, is a sister-state public act, and historically the Supreme Court has not required the states to give full faith and credit to such acts. Expressed somewhat differently, the Full Faith and Credit Clause has never been read to require recognition of the *validity and effect* of a marriage made in another state. Because that was clearly the situation before the adoption of DOMA, the statute, though politically controversial, was legally superfluous.

The second question about DOMA is whether it is constitutional. There can be little doubt that Congress has power under the Full Faith and Credit Clause (and probably under the Commerce Clause of Article I, as well) to regulate the interstate impact of a state's "statutes, or "public acts" (including its marriage laws). The plain language of the Full Faith and Credit Clause supports that interpretation, as does the purpose of the second part of the Full Faith and Credit Clause, which states that "Congress may by general Laws prescribe the Manner in which such Acts . . . shall be proved, and the Effect thereof." That is exactly what DOMA does. It prescribes (or, rather, delegates to each state the decision whether to prescribe) the "effect" of a marriage made in other states. And that conclusion is amply supported by the historical development under the Full Faith and Credit Clause.

It is possible, however, to think of situations in which DOMA might have some effect and might raise serious constitutional questions. A same-sex couple duly married under the laws of Massachusetts might also obtain a divorce there. One (former) partner then takes the divorce decree to another state, say, Texas, and seeks to have it enforced there against the property of the other partner. Must Texas recognize the divorce judgment? Another possibility would be for the Massachusetts couple to ask a court in that state for a declaratory judgment that their marriage was valid. If the declaratory judgment is granted, must Texas recognize it? In both cases, the fact that Texas was asked to recognize a judgment (that is, a judicial decree) rather than a statute would, before DOMA, require recognition under the Iron Law of Full Faith and Credit. Those possibilities, therefore, raise the very serious question whether Congress can authorize a state to ignore the Full Faith and Credit Clause as it has been interpreted by the Supreme Court and refuse to recognize a *judgment* valid (and final) where it was rendered.

That specific question has never been litigated, which may seem surprising but really is not. As mentioned earlier, Congress did not pass specific legislation under the Full Faith and Credit Clause until 1980. That legislation, especially the Parental Kidnapping Prevention Act and the Full Faith and Credit for Child Support Orders Act (discussed below), certainly authorizes, if it does not require, a state to ignore a seemingly valid judgments of other states. Congressional power to require nonrecognition of a judgment that fails to comply with the conditions of those statutes has never been challenged seriously.

It is, however, one thing to say that Congress has the *power* to pass a particular statute and quite another to say that the statute is otherwise constitutional.

Commentators have expressed serious doubts about DOMA and whether it passes muster under equal protection and due process analysis. This book is not the place to analyze that question;[8] it is sufficient for present purposes to conclude that DOMA is otherwise a perfectly acceptable exercise of Congressional power under the Full Faith and Credit Clause.

Divorce

For most of this nation's history, divorces were disfavored and treated with great suspicion by society generally. This attitude was fully reflected in the law of recognition of foreign divorce decrees (that is, divorces granted by courts in other states). Until 1942, the law was that an action to dissolve a marriage was treated as an action in rem—with the *res* that was the subject of the action being the marriage itself.[9] The marriage, in other words, was treated by the law like a piece of property. This conceptual tour de force permitted the courts to pinpoint where jurisdiction to divorce resided. The conceptual magic works this way. Jurisdiction in an action in rem generally lies where the *res* is located; thus, jurisdiction to grant a divorce was proper only in the state of the marital domicile. Because the traditional law of recognition provided that there could be one and only one marital domicile, only that state could divorce the couple.

Historically, therefore a divorce rendered by any state other than the marital domicile was not entitled to recognition under the Full Faith and Credit Clause. Locating the state of the marital domicile presented no problem when the couple lived in the same state, although it certainly did when the two partners lived apart. Ordinarily, in such circumstances the marital domicile was deemed to be the domicile of the husband,[10] but when the husband deserted his wife, his new state of domicile could not issue him a divorce entitled to full faith and credit in the couple's former marital domicile.[11]

That situation was to change, however. In Williams v. North Carolina (1942, *Williams I*), the Supreme Court held that the state of domicile of the *deserting* spouse had an interest in the status of one of its domiciliaries that was sufficiently important to give it jurisdiction to grant a divorce entitled to full faith and credit in all other states. The result was that any state where *one* member of the couple was domiciled had jurisdiction to grant the divorce, thus making a divorce proceeding more like an ordinary transitory action.[12] No longer did the divorce have to take place in the state of the marital domicile for it to be entitled to recognition and enforcement elsewhere.

The *Williams I* case involved two couples from a small town in North Carolina,[13] Mr. and Mrs. Williams and Mr. and Mrs. Hendrix. Mr. Hendrix had worked in Mrs. Williams's store where the two apparently fell in love. The lovestruck duo went to Las Vegas, Nevada, in 1940, and each filed an action for divorce in a Nevada court. Although service was made on one absent spouse by publication and on the other by mail, neither spouse showed up at the Nevada divorce hearing. The Nevada court found that the two divorce seekers met the statutory definition of domicile—continuous residence in the state for six weeks before commencing the action—and each petitioner was then granted a divorce on the ground of "extreme cruelty." The happy duo quickly married each other in Nevada and returned to North Carolina where they were prosecuted for bigamy, presumably for causing a small-town scandal. After their conviction was upheld in the North Carolina courts, the Supreme Court took the case and reversed.

The forceful majority opinion by Justice Douglas listed the dire consequences that would follow from a holding that did not recognize the Nevada divorce: There would be "considerable disaster to innocent persons"; it would "bastardize children hitherto supposed to be the offspring of lawful marriage"; and it would encourage collusive divorces. Justice Douglas then added to those strong and very pragmatic concerns a powerful argument based on the unifying purpose behind the Full Faith and Credit Clause.

> These intensely practical considerations emphasize for us the essential function of the Full Faith and Credit clause in substituting a command for the former principles of comity and in altering the "status of the several states as independent foreign sovereignties" by making them "integral parts of a single nation."[14]

The purpose of the Full Faith and Credit Clause, in other words, was to insure that respect *must* (rather than *might*) be given to the judgments—the "judicial proceedings"—of another state, and that doing so was required of an "integral part of a single nation after the ratification of the Constitution"; the states, after all, were not individual sovereigns, but part of one nation. In short, the Full Faith and Credit Clause removed all elements of discretion from the question of recognition. The Nevada court's decree of divorce, therefore, must be recognized in North Carolina.

The Douglas opinion also held that there had to be a sufficient connection between the divorcing state and the party seeking a divorce. Domicile provided that connection; but both to Justice Douglas and to the rest of the majority it was not the *marital* domicile that counted, but the *petitioner's* own (and current) domicile. That is, only one spouse had to be domiciled in the state for it to have subject matter jurisdiction to enter a divorce. That was truly revolutionary.

The importance of *Williams I* in family law cannot be overstated. Once divorce actions became migratory—that is, once jurisdiction to divorce depended only on the domicile of one spouse—then a spouse trapped in a bad marriage could become domiciled in a new state; that state then could give her a divorce that other states must recognize under the Full Faith and Credit Clause.

The result was to liberate a spouse trapped in an unwelcome marriage in a state with restrictive divorce laws. No longer could a spouse unwilling to enter into divorce veto the action by remaining in a marital domicile that is hostile to divorce. It does not matter if the stay at home spouse does not wish to be divorced; if he wishes to stay married, he must travel to the state hearing the divorce action in order to contest it. That contest may be based on the merits of the petition, or the defendant could argue that the divorce plaintiff had not become a domiciliary of the new state; in that event, the court would lack subject matter jurisdiction to dissolve the marriage. (Making that journey, however, might subject the absent spouse to a whole new set of possible unpleasant happenings, discussed *infra*). Nor does it matter if the new state of domicile grants the divorce on grounds not recognized in the old domicile; the forum always applies its own law in a divorce action.

The revolution sparked by *Williams I* can be understood fully, however, only in light of the ease with which domicile can be changed; legal change of domicile requires only physical presence in the new location along with the subjective intent to make that place the new domicile. In theory and practice, domicile can be changed in a day, or even in a minute. Thus, the unhappy spouse could vest another state with the power to grant her divorce—without having to undergo a lengthy wait. The result was a kind of "Gresham's law" of divorce. (Gresham's law stated that bad money drives out good.) An unhappy spouse living in a state with restrictive divorce laws has a choice after *Williams I*. She can go to a state with more permissive divorce laws, establish a domicile there without having to undergo a long waiting period, and dissolve the marriage. If the change in domicile were basically fictitious, as it often was, then the restrictive divorce laws of the couple's true "home" state, the state with the strongest connection with the couple, were rendered ineffective. Restrictive laws after *Williams I* could not withstand less restrictive ones. Lax divorce laws (bad laws, at least in the view of some), in other words, inevitably drove out stricter ones. Today, virtually all states have "no-fault" divorce laws, and most states impose limited waiting periods before a divorce can be granted.

Divorce, in short, is much easier to obtain today than it was two generations ago. That is a profound social change. Not all of that change, of course, can be traced to the regime of migratory divorce established in *Williams I*. Other social factors also propelled the change. But by making divorce far more practicable (at least for those with the money to travel) *Williams I* surely played a significant role in the divorce revolution. It did not, however, answer all of the questions concerning migratory divorce. Courts, however, worked out the solutions to almost all of those problems fairly quickly. Among the most significant issues were who could challenge the earlier finding of domicile, why should domicile remain a constitutional requirement for divorce recognition, and whether there should be a federal definition of domicile.

Challenging Domicile

The rule in *Williams I* turns on the question of domicile; more particularly, it turns on the acquisition of a new domicile by the traveling spouse. There is no problem, of course, if the forum refuses to find that a bona fide change of domicile occurred. But if the divorcing court does find that the petitioner has acquired a new domicile, does that finding bind other courts? The absent spouse? Third parties? The couple's children? Does the Full Faith and Credit Clause require recognition of the finding by the divorcing court that there has been a true change of domicile?

That was the question faced by the hapless Williams couple after what proved to be their temporary victory in *Williams I*. The prosecutor back in North Carolina, deeply offended by an obviously spectacular small-town scandal, tried again. The first time around the prosecution had not challenged the Nevada court's finding of domicile in that state; in Williams v. North Carolina (1945, "*Williams II*"), the prosecution did make that challenge, and the jury found that there had not been a valid change of domicile. As a result, the Nevada court had lacked subject matter jurisdiction, and its decree, therefore, need not be recognized. Again the state appellate courts upheld the conviction of the couple; but this time around, the Supreme Court also affirmed.

The Court, speaking through Justice Frankfurter, labored its way to a conclusion. The opinion explored the duties each state owed the other in our federal system, and then concluded: "The challenged judgment must satisfy our scrutiny that the reciprocal duty of respect owed by the States to one another's adjudications has been fairly discharged, and has not been evaded under the guise of finding an absence of domicil."[15]

What seemed to bother the majority was the notion that the divorcing court could determine domicile in an uncontested proceeding, where there was no one to challenge the petitioner's assertions concerning where she intended to live. In a footnote, the Court significantly noted that in the case before it, domicile had not been "squarely litigated in a truly adversary proceeding."[16] The finding of a new domicile, therefore, had to be a "real finding"—factually grounded in order for the divorcing state's "interests" to overcome the "interests" of the state of the former marital domicile.

Williams II threatened to undo much that was good about *Williams I*. By making vulnerable the divorcing court's determination of domicile, the second *Williams* case called into question both the finality of any migratory divorce decree and the ability of anyone to rely with confidence on such a decree. *Williams II* raised, therefore, the very real possibility of many prosecutions for bigamy, an occurrence that certainly would have deterred many an unhappy spouse from availing herself of the opportunity offered by *Williams I*. Fortunately, that possibility never materialized, and bigamy prosecutions since *Williams II* have been either rare or nonexistent. Prosecutors surely have appreciated the undesirable consequences Justice Douglas had listed in *Williams I*, including the effect on children born to the new couple, when settled expectations are upset. The wise exercise of prosecutorial discretion, in other words, has prevented any harm to other divorcing parties arising from the second conviction of the unfortunate couple in the *Williams* cases.

As for challenges by the absent spouse to the decree, the Court quickly applied routine preclusion law to that and other similar questions. Thus, it held in Sherrer v. Sherrer[17] that a spouse who appeared in a divorce proceeding was precluded from later attacking its jurisdictional basis. There, the respondent husband had been domiciled in Massachusetts; the wife then moved to Florida, where, after a ninety-day waiting period, she sought a divorce. Her husband retained Florida counsel who entered a general appearance in the case and offered evidence on the issue of child custody, but did not contest the wife's domicile in Florida. The Court treated the question as a routine application of well-settled law: Because the husband had a representative who could have challenged the wife's assertion of domicile on his behalf, the husband was bound under ordinary preclusion principles by the decision of the Florida divorce court.

That holding is not remarkable. After all, the law long has been that a party can not later raise an issue that it could have litigated in F-1 but failed to do so. The law, of course, has a strong interest in fair and economical litigation, and that interest precludes one who ignored the opportunity to litigate an issue from asserting it in a subsequent proceeding. In the context of divorce litigation that means that the mere entrance of an appearance by a party precludes it from ever again raising the issue of jurisdiction (that is, the petitioner's domicile).

That rule has been applied with a vengeance. Thus, the Supreme Court later held in Johnson v. Muelberger (1951),[18] that those in privity with the respondent spouse (that is, those whose rights derive from the respondent spouse) were precluded from challenging the divorce if the spouse would have been precluded. If the stay-at-home spouse could not challenge the divorce, neither could anyone whose claim was derived from or depended upon the claim of that spouse. The holding in *Johnson*, which conforms with the general law of preclusion, effectively cuts off almost all potential challenge to the divorce other than a challenge made by the state of the absent spouse in the form of a bigamy prosecution. And because those rarely, if ever, occur, there is little likelihood of a successful collateral attack on a divorce.

Why Domicile?

The decision in *Williams I*, of course, makes domicile, even if the domicile only of a deserting spouse, the linchpin of modern divorce jurisdiction. And yet, the Court was not very clear about whether domicile is the only constitutional basis for the exercise of subject matter jurisdiction in a divorce action. It is easy to understand why domicile is a sufficient basis for divorce. Domicile is the place where personal jurisdiction is always present; it is, in Justice Holmes's memorable phrase, an individual's "pre-eminent headquarters."[19] But domicile, while a useful proxy for state interests, can be manipulated (as the *Williams* drama shows) because it is highly technical. Are there any other candidates to support subject matter jurisdiction in divorce? Two alternatives come to mind: residence (as opposed to domicile) and consent.

A number of states provide that residence in the state for a stated minimum period of time confers subject matter jurisdiction to grant a divorce to members of the armed forces. Recognition of divorces entered under those statutes has not proved problematic, suggesting perhaps that a lengthy residence in the forum confers enough of a forum interest to confer subject matter jurisdiction to divorce. Of course, another way of looking at these cases is to think of them as recognizing that the benefit to service personnel who might have practical troubles in transferring their domicile, outweigh technical problems associated with nondomiciliary jurisdiction to divorce.

That solution, of course, merely raises another question. If the *Williams I* requirement of domiciliary jurisdiction can be overcome in situations involving armed forces personnel, why not in other cases? Unfortunately, this question has been little discussed in recent years either by courts or commentators.

The most serious judicial discussion of whether there is a constitutionally satisfactory alternative to domicile, now half a century old, held domicile to be a constitutional requirement. That case, Alton v. Alton (1953), occasioned a debate between two renowned circuit court judges, Goodrich and Hastie. It involved a Connecticut couple who both wanted a divorce. The wife traveled to the Virgin Islands where she established her "residence." On the basis of that residence and personal jurisdiction over the husband by consent, the Virgin Islands trial court granted a divorce. That court squarely held that Mrs. Alton was not domiciled in the Virgin Islands. The question for the Third Circuit on appeal, therefore, was whether divorce could be granted, in the absence of domicile, solely on the basis of consent.

The answer was "No."[20] In the majority opinion, Judge Herbert Goodrich, who was also a well-known Conflicts scholar, wrote that domicile was required for a court to enter a divorce decree entitled to recognition "if our states are really to have control over the domestic relations of their citizens."[21] In other words, domicile provides the necessary relationship between the divorce seeker and the forum to make sure that the petition for dissolution is handled by a state with a real "interest" in the matter.

On the other hand, in a highly mobile society like ours, it will often be the case that the partners will live in different states, and that no state will have a superior "interest" in the proceedings. In those circumstances, it is difficult to see why a divorce proceeding should not be treated as any other ambulatory proceeding and brought in any convenient forum. This was essentially Judge William Hastie's point in dissent in *Alton*, although the judge added that domicile was such an "elusive" and "technical" concept that it served as a poor proxy for state interests.

Another way of analyzing the question is to ask why a state needs an "interest" in the couple (or at least half of the couple) before it can grant a divorce. We do not require that such an interest be present before a court can hear other important types of cases, such as product liability or defamation. Is there something special about divorce that requires the presence of such an interest?

It is hard to see what that could be. Treating divorce as a transitory proceeding does not mean that a state need hear all divorce petitions. A state may require a long waiting period before an out-of-stater can bring a divorce action (a requirement permitted in *Sosna*, discussed below), or a court could dismiss the proceeding on *forum non conveniens* grounds. Either alternative would permit states that impose special (and expensive) requirements before granting a divorce—mandatory mediation, for example—to reserve those resources for those parties with whom it does have a substantial and stable connection.

The most likely candidate to replace domicile, of course, is to treat divorce the same as any other transitory action. In that case, the action could be brought anywhere where personal jurisdiction could be obtained over the defendant, and domicile, therefore, would be irrelevant. The difficulty with that solution is that it raises the awkward question of the absent spouse; if divorce were a transitory cause of action, then the divorcing court would need personal jurisdiction over the stay-at-home spouse, presumably subject to the "minimum contacts" test set forth in International Shoe Co. v. Washington.

The problem with that alternative—if it is a problem—is that the divorcing spouse must choose a jurisdiction that can assert jurisdiction over the absent spouse. In other words, the divorcing spouse can no longer use domicile as the ticket into any court that she wants. Expressed differently, the domicile fiction permitted a divorce action to be filed anywhere that a pretense of domicile could be maintained. If domicile no longer conveys subject matter jurisdiction, then the freedom of the divorcing spouse to choose a favorable forum has been seriously circumscribed.

This is not a very active subject. There is almost no case law. In addition, rarely does the academic literature raise the question of replacing the domicile requirement with some other measure—perhaps because the family law professors don't know conflicts law and the conflicts scholars don't know family law.

The Supreme Court has not weighed in on the debate directly in recent years. But in Sosna v. Iowa (1975),[22] the Court observed: "judicial power to grant a divorce—jurisdiction strictly speaking—is founded on domicile."[23] Although that statement is dictum (the case involved the constitutionality of Iowa's one year residency requirement to obtain a divorce), it was made in the context of explaining why Iowa would want such a requirement: The waiting period made Iowa's finding of domicile virtually unassailable factually and, therefore, helped preserve the enforceability of Iowa divorce judgments in other states. Although the reasoning is somewhat strained, the dictum does indicate that the Court saw no reason to question the traditional jurisdictional requirement of domicile.

A Federal Definition of Domicile?

In a footnote to the *Williams II* opinion, the Court suggested that because domicile was a necessary condition to divorce recognition, it was possible that the term should be given a federal definition. That seems logical enough at first glance; if the Court really took seriously the notion that domicile served as an adequate proxy for state interests, it also would have to take seriously the definition of the term. Otherwise, divorce mills with a loose definition of domicile (e.g., Nevada in the *Williams* litigation) could displace the interests of states with more exacting requirements.

Nevertheless, The Supreme Court has not attempted to impose a national definition of domicile, in divorce or, for that matter, anywhere else. One explanation for that lacuna comes readily to mind. The stated definition of domicile—actual presence in the state (however brief) and intent to remain there for the time being—is common throughout the land; the problem lies in the application of that definition. As we have seen in connection with the possibility of using the Full Faith and Credit Clause to police choice of law decisions, a federal definition of domicile would require supervision by the Supreme Court of the various state applications of the federal test, a task the Court surely does not want to undertake.

SPOUSAL SUPPORT

A curious corollary of treating a divorce as an in rem proceeding is that a court can grant a decree entitled to recognition even if it lacks personal jurisdiction over the absent spouse. That is so because jurisdiction in an in rem proceeding depends solely on the presence of the *res* before the court; and the fiction is that the *res* (i.e., the marriage) travels with each spouse to any new domicile. When the divorce seeker becomes domiciled in the new state, therefore, a court in that state has the *res* (the marriage) before it, ready for adjudication and can dissolve the marriage without any participation by the absent spouse as long as there is proper notice under the Due Process Clause. Thus, in *Williams I*, the Supreme Court was quite willing to require recognition of the Nevada divorce decrees, even though the stay-at-home spouses were not personally subject to the jurisdiction of the Nevada court.

One problem with the *Williams I* solution to the divorce jurisdiction problem is that divorce courts often deal with issues beyond mere marital status, such as spousal support, child support, marital property division, and child custody. Can a court that has divorce jurisdiction based solely on the domicile of a migratory spouse adjudicate those important related claims and issues as well? If it could, the result might well be devastating to the stay-at-home spouse. She would face a difficult choice: allow her support and custody rights to be determined ex parte (i.e., without input from her) in a foreign state or incur the financial burden of travel to and litigation in a distant forum. Putting her to such a choice would violate the basic principle of due process that a court cannot deprive a litigant of property rights if it cannot exercise personal jurisdiction over her. Yet in many cases the stay-at-home spouse will lack minimum contacts with the newly acquired domicile of the deserting spouse.

The Supreme Court eventually resolved the divorce/support jurisdiction problem in a curious and elegant way. That solution, which has come to be known as "divisible divorce," first saw the light of day in Estin v. Estin (1948),[24] which involved a couple with a marital domicile in New York. In 1943, the wife obtained a legal separation from a New York court which also ordered the husband to pay permanent alimony. A year later, he went to Nevada where he filed a petition for divorce. Mrs. Estin did not appear in the Nevada proceedings, even though she had been notified of them by mail. The husband hit the jackpot in Nevada—not only did he get the divorce, but he also was not ordered to pay alimony. As a result, he stopped payments under the New York order. When the wife later sued in New York for the arrearages, the husband interposed the Nevada decree as a defense.

The Supreme Court ruled in favor of Mrs. Estin. It treated the issue as one involving a "property interest" that arose from the New York court's alimony order. Such a property interest, under well-settled law, could be extinguished only by a court having personal jurisdiction over the holder of the interest (that is, over Mrs. Estin). Thus, even though the Nevada divorce decree was valid and entitled to full faith and credit, it could not affect every other legal incidence of the marriage. (That explains Justice Jackson's sneer in dissent: "The Court reaches the Solomon-like conclusion that the Nevada decree is half good and half bad under the Full Faith and Credit clause.") The opinion, written by Justice Douglas, concluded that the result makes "the divorce divisible."

Later cases refined the divisible divorce concept. In Vanderbilt v. Vanderbilt (1957),[25] the Court made clear that a court without personal jurisdiction over the obligee spouse could not cut off her right to spousal support. Unlike Mrs. Estin, Mrs. Vanderbilt had not obtained a New York support order before Nevada granted her husband a divorce, nor had New York been the parties' marital domicile. Rather, Mrs. Vanderbilt had moved there before her husband's Nevada divorce. Nevertheless, the Supreme Court upheld the New York support order against the husband's claim that it was precluded by the Nevada divorce. "Since the wife was not subject to its jurisdiction, the Nevada divorce court had no power to extinguish any right which [the wife] had under the law of New York to financial support from her husband."[26] The concept of divisible divorce, thus, made it possible to protect the property rights of the stay at home spouse, while still permitting the divorce to proceed in any state where the deserting spouse could establish a new domicile.

The concept of divisible divorce does not, however, offer complete protection to the stay-at-home spouse. In exceptional circumstances, she can still lose rights in a divorce granted by a court that lacks personal jurisdiction over her. In Simons v. Miami Beach First Nat. Bank (1965),[27] the husband left New York, the marital domicile, for Florida, where he obtained an ex parte divorce. He then remarried. When the husband later died in Florida, his former wife appeared in the Florida probate proceeding and claimed her dower rights under Florida law.

The Supreme Court of the United States agreed with the Florida courts that dower rights are "inchoate" and, therefore, could be extinguished in an ex parte proceeding. Apart from the Court's shoddy reasoning—all property rights in divorce (and indeed, everywhere else) are "inchoate" until a court awards them to someone—the *Simons* decision may have been unavoidable in order to ensure that the title to Mr. Simons's property remained clear and marketable. Consider the mess that would have occurred if there had been *two* Mrs. Simons claiming dower rights. Thus, *Simons* can be seen as a compromise with the basic *Estin* principle, one that was necessary to balance individual economic rights with the state's interest in securing title to property within its borders.

CUSTODY

Child custody decisions in American law have always been heard exclusively in state courts. (Indeed, federal courts, under a judicially declared exception to the otherwise applicable jurisdictional statutes, have long refused to hear family law cases, even when federal jurisdiction is otherwise present.) As a result, when the parties to a custody proceeding all are from the same state, only the law of that state applies. It is a different matter, however, when a judge is asked to enforce a custody order entered by the court of a sister state. At that point, the Full Faith and Credit Clause—and legislation adopted by Congress under the authority given to it by that clause—enter the picture.

This section examines the law governing the enforcement of interstate custody orders. It begins with an analysis of the primary federal law, the Parental Kidnapping Prevention Act, and the relevant Uniform Acts adopted by all fifty states, the Uniform Child Custody Jurisdiction Act, and the Uniform Child Custody Jurisdiction Enforcement Act. There follows a discussion of the special problem of personal jurisdiction in custody matters, and the chapter ends with a short description of custody problems involving Indian tribes, and problems of international custody.

The PKPA and the UCCJA (UCCJEA)

The Parental Kidnapping Prevention Act ("PKPA"), 28 U.S.C. § 1738A, adopted by Congress in 1980, dealt with a very serious problem: conflicting custody orders entered by courts in different states. The problem generally arose when a parent, not satisfied with a custody/visitation order entered in one state would take the child to another state and seek a more favorable order there.[28] The new court generally was in the unhappy parent's home state, and often inclined to favor the local voter and taxpayer, giving that parent a strong "home court" advantage. Afterwards, armed with the new (and more favorable) custody order from a court in his domicile, the newly happy parent would refuse to give the child back, and the result would be a morass of litigation, crisscrossing contempt citations, and so forth.

Although custody disputes would seem to be *the* quintessential problem for state resolution, the federal government's intervention in the area through the adoption of the PKPA was eminently proper for two reasons. First, the problem of interstate custody battles was one that was caused by the very existence of a federal system; no authority other than Congress existed to resolve conflicting custody orders issued by different states. Thus, it was appropriate for Congress to solve a "local" problem at the national level. Second, the problem was made worse by a flaw in the full faith and credit system itself. That flaw is that custody orders can always be modified prospectively; traditionally, therefore, they were never treated as "final" judgments for enforcement purposes. For that reason, courts could (and often did) disregard the custody orders of other states.

Congress solved the interstate custody problem by passing the PKPA pursuant to its implementing authority under the Full Faith and Credit Clause. The act, primarily designed to solve the problem caused by the lack of finality to custody orders, requires certain custody orders be treated as final; because those orders are now considered to be final they are entitled to recognition under the Full Faith and Credit Clause. And because the PKPA was enacted by Congress pursuant to its authority under the Full Faith and Credit Clause, the mandate of the PKPA became the law of the land under the Supremacy Clause. Thus, under the PKPA properly entered custody orders are entitled to the same respect in other states as would an order in any other type of case.

The important question for Congress in adopting the PKPA was to determine which orders required recognition; in doing so, Congress made a very wise decision. The PKPA largely tracks the provisions of the Uniform Child Custody Jurisdiction Act ("UCCJA"). First promulgated in 1968, and eventually adopted in every state, the UCCJA, provides, generally speaking, that the orders of only one court will control establishment and modification of child custody, thus defeating the "snatch and run" strategy employed by disgruntled parents under the prior custody regime. The UCCJA, in other words, established a regime sometimes referred to as the "one controlling order system." That regime can be summarized briefly: When a court with proper subject matter jurisdiction enters a custody order, only that court—and no other—can change the order.

Because a finding of subject matter jurisdiction is so important under the UCCJA, the act establishes a hierarchy of jurisdictional possibilities for entering the original (and controlling) order. The first jurisdictional priority goes either to the state which is the child's "home state" (the state where the child lived for six months before the custody petition was filed) or to a state that both has a "significant connection" with the child and the contestants for custody *and* is the location of substantial evidence relevant to the custody decision. Other possibilities are "residual jurisdiction," which is available when no state meets any of the other criteria, and "temporary emergency jurisdiction," which is exercised when the child is present within the state and is abandoned or threatened with mistreatment. The UCCJA also encourages judges in different states to consult with one another and to refuse to exercise jurisdiction if another court has begun proceedings or is otherwise better able to hear the case.

Finally, and most important, the UCCJA provides that any modifications to the order can be made *only* by the state that entered the order.[29] No longer can there be multiple orders involving the child; instead, there is only "one outstanding order." The combination of "one outstanding order" feature of the

UCCJA with the full faith and credit mandate of the PKPA has largely ended the "snatch and run" abuse and has made interstate postdivorce family life more orderly and humane.

The PKPA illustrates the proper use by Congress of its constitutional power to enforce the Full Faith and Credit Clause. The act addresses a serious national problem created by our federal system, and it attempts to solve that problem by making custody orders final and entitled to recognition. By tracking the UCCJA, the PKPA largely federalizes the Uniform Act.

Thus, the UCCJA performed the state function of regulating family law, and the PKPA performed the federal function of regulating interstate enforcement of judicial orders. The two laws together have helped solve the problems presented by parental "kidnapping" across state lines.

(A final note on interstate custody statutes: The UCCJA was superceded in 1997 by the Uniform Child Custody Jurisdiction and Enforcement Act ("UCCJEA").[30] The new law was designed better to harmonize the state law of custody with the requirements of the PKPA. The UCCJEA, however, does not disturb the basic outline of the UCCJA, especially its one outstanding order requirement.)

Due Process and Custody

The federal and uniform acts do not eliminate all interstate custody problems. One vexing issue that has not yet been resolved is whether the state entering the custody order must have personal jurisdiction over both spouses.

At one time, that was not a problem. Parents did not migrate with children from one state to another, so custody was a purely local concern. When the rare interstate case did arise, the continued indulgence of the historical fiction that the dispute was one in rem (with the child as the *res*) meant that a court with the child before it could adjudicate all interests in the *res*. That meant that the court did not need personal jurisdiction over both spouses in order to render a constitutionally permissible decree.

As our nation became more migratory, however, fairness questions arose over that treatment. Why should a person be forced to come to a distant and perhaps hostile forum in order to protect his rights as a parent? Moreover, by coming to the forum, the absent parent exposed himself to the possibility that the forum would assert personal jurisdiction over him, and thus acquire power to enter child or spousal support orders. This fundamental dilemma—stay out of the forum and lose the child; appear and lose your wallet—mirrors the dilemma faced by the stay-at-home spouse following the decision in *Williams I*. That dilemma, of course, was resolved by the invention of the concept of the "divisible divorce," which preserved the fiction of the *res* (the marriage) thus permitting the ex parte divorce, while still protecting the financial interests of the absent spouse with the personal jurisdiction requirement. A similar concept, which might be styled "divisible custody," has evolved in the custody area.

Divisible custody works this way. Custody orders can be entered by a court at the situs of the *res*—remember that the child is the *res*—that is, the child's "home state," but financial decrees—child support—can be entered only by a court with personal jurisdiction over the putative support obligor. Necessity is the justification for permitting a court without personal jurisdiction to issue a custody order, and the argument is compelling. If the rule were otherwise, a parent who wished to deny effect to a custody order would simply avoid all contact with the forum. As a result, if personal jurisdiction—over both parents—were required, often no court would be able to enter a valid custody order. And that would be a disaster for the child who badly needs stability.

It is not surprising, therefore, that neither the PKPA nor the UCCJA requires personal jurisdiction over both parents as a condition to the entry of a valid order. (In an emergency, any state has the power to issue a temporary order.) Moreover, neither case law nor the commentary of academics shows much enthusiasm for requiring personal jurisdiction over the absent parent. There is only one flaw in this rosy scenario: It is not clear whether the Supreme Court agrees. Twice the Court has had the absent parent issue on its plate, and twice it has punted on the issue.

The first opportunity came in the case of May v. Anderson (1953)[31] in which a Wisconsin court entered an ex parte order giving custody to the father. The father then took the order to Ohio where the children were living with their mother. The Ohio courts gave full faith and credit to the Wisconsin order, and the mother appealed. The case eventually made it all the way to the Supreme Court; that court reversed.

Unfortunately, the holding in *May* is quite murky. The majority opinion by Justice Harold Burton can be read as saying that custody rights are like other property "rights" which can be extinguished only by a court with personal jurisdiction over the defendant. On the other hand, the opinion may simply have said that the Ohio court (F-2) could, but was not required to, recognize the Wisconsin decree; plausible readings of Justice Burton's majority opinion can support either position. Even worse, the concurring and dissenting opinions disagreed as to what the majority had really held in *May*. In short, Justice Burton's opinion in *May* is a real mess.

Thus, with respect to the first possibility—that custody is like any other property right—Justice Burton stated the issue to be whether the Wisconsin court could eliminate the mother's right to custody, "without having jurisdiction over her in personam." Moreover, Burton closed the opinion by noting that "[r]ights far more precious to [the mother] than property rights will be cut off if she is to be bound by the Wisconsin award of custody."

The second possibility—discretionary recognition—derives support from the failure of the majority to mention the Due Process Clause, the source of whatever rights the mother might have had. Further, Justice Burton framed the issue in terms of whether Wisconsin should have the right, "as against Ohio," to decide the mother's custody rights. That is, the majority opinion could have been treating the question as one of *states'* rights rather than one involving *individual* rights. Justice Frankfurter's concurrence also supports the second interpretation, stating explicitly that personal jurisdiction over both parents is not necessary for a court to render an enforceable decree in a custody case.

A generation after *May*, the Supreme Court had an opportunity to clarify the situation. Once again it blew the analysis. Shaffer v. Heitner (1977)[32] was a major opinion on the relation between the Due Process Clause and personal jurisdiction, the first issued by the Court in twenty years. The holding in *Shaffer*, that the personal jurisdiction test ("minimum contacts/fairplay and substantial justice") also applies to attachment jurisdiction has little relevance to custody. Nevertheless, the *Shaffer* Court made an effort to explain the effect of its holdings on other problem areas of jurisdiction. Those efforts, although certainly dicta and made in footnotes, have been taken seriously by courts and commentators.

In footnote 30 to the *Shaffer* opinion, the Court observed: "We do not suggest that jurisdictional doctrines other than those discussed in text, such as the particularized rules governing adjudications of status, are inconsistent with the standard of fairness."[33] In other words, *Shaffer* does not affect "status" determinations such as those made in custody cases, and, therefore, in rem treatment of custody proceedings can survive the holding, although the opinion had invalidated other uses of the in rem fiction in jurisdictional cases. That argument is strengthened by the fact that divorce is still treated as an in rem action, suggesting that the concept of status has not lost all of its utility in cases involving family law. Further, the Court did not refer to *May* at all in footnote 30, a lacuna perhaps suggesting that *Shaffer* does not jeopardize the in rem treatment of custody proceedings.

A final point of persuasion on this issue can be found in the fact that Congress, when it adopted the PKPA, agreed that a valid custody order—one entitled to recognition throughout the nation—does not require jurisdiction over both parties. And a large majority, but not all, of the state courts that have wrestled with the issue have held that custody decisions may be made by a court lacking personal jurisdiction over both parents.

Finally, the state where the child has a real home—the "home state"—has a strong interest as a sovereign in looking out for the best interests of one of its children, the basic test in all custody litigation. When that interest is coupled with the practical need to have at least one court where the custody issue can be authoritatively resolved, we can prophesy that the Supreme Court, when it gets another chance to address the issue, will hold that the forum where the child and one parent are located can resolve a custody dispute without personal jurisdiction over the absent parent.

SUPPORT

Child and spousal support matters, like child custody, historically have been decided under state law. The Full Faith and Credit Clause, however, does play a role in the enforcement of interstate support orders. The law of support follows closely the pattern established with custody orders—a uniform act adopted by the states, which has been given stronger teeth by a federal statute adopted pursuant to congressional authority under the Full Faith and Credit Clause.

The success of the PKPA in the area of interstate custody encouraged Congress to seek statutory solutions for interstate child support orders. As a result, Congress in recent years has passed several major pieces of legislation dealing with interstate enforcement of child support orders.

The first of these laws, known as the "Bradley Amendment," adopted in 1986,[34] brought state child support orders under the Full Faith and Credit Clause. Before the Bradley Amendment took effect, child *support* orders (like *custody* orders before the adoption of the PKPA) were generally held not to be entitled to full faith and credit because they were modifiable, according to state law, both prospectively and retrospectively, and thus were not considered to be "final judgments." The result was that if the noncustodial parent had fallen $1,000 behind on her payments, those arrearages had to be sued upon in another action and reduced to a judgment in order to be sufficiently final to be entitled to preclusive effect in another state. The Bradley amendment changed that cumbersome and difficult process by requiring each state to adopt legislation making child support arrearages nonmodifiable. (A state that did not adopt that legislation could have lost enormous sums of federal money.) Thus, any time the obligor parent falls behind on her support payments, she owes a sum certain to the custodial parent, a sum, which, because of its certainty, can then become the subject of an immediate enforcement action. Although Congress did not use its Full Faith and Credit Clause power when it adopted the Bradley Amendment, the law fits within the spirit of the Clause in making enforcement of support orders across state lines easier to obtain.

More recently, in the Full Faith and Credit for Child Support Orders Act (the Act has a very uneuphonious acronym, "FFCSOA," usually pronounced fic-só-a),[35] Congress placed the Full Faith and Credit Clause squarely behind the enforcement of interstate child support orders. FFCSOA closely resembles—and deliberately so—the enforcement model established by the PKPA. That is, federal law now mandates enforcement of orders entered pursuant to a Uniform Act. That act in the case of child support is the Uniform Interstate Family Support Act ("UIFSA"). UIFSA follows the "one-child, one-order" concept pioneered in the custody field by the UCCJA, and described in the proceeding section.

The basic idea behind UIFSA is that only one court can have the subject matter jurisdiction needed to enter a valid support order; that court is the one in the "home state" of the child, which UIFSA defines as the place where the child lived for the six months before an order was sought. Once home state jurisdiction has been established, an order from a court of that state must be respected: *Only* the court that entered the support order can modify that order, unless either that court has lost jurisdiction because all of the persons involved, both parents and children, have left the state, or the parties have agreed to locate the order elsewhere.

FFCSOA requires the recognition by other courts of an order properly entered under UIFSA. Because the latter served as the basis for the substantive provisions of the former, the practical effect of FFCSOA is to constitutionalize the "one-child, one-controlling-order" regime of UIFSA for purposes of entering a support order entitled to recognition.

FFCSOA, like the PKPA, is a perfectly proper use of the full faith and credit powers given to Congress. First, interstate enforcement of support orders is a major *national* problem, one that only Congress has the power effectively to resolve. Second, uncertainty about multiple orders had made the enforcement of any *order* problematic. Third, Congressional intervention did not require widespread involvement with inherently local activities; the statute is expressly limited to enforcement of orders across state lines. Thus, FFCSOA provides a textbook illustration of the proper use of federal regulatory authority in an area normally reserved for state authority. But that, of course, was what the Full Faith and Credit Clause was all about.

Although the law and practice have come a long way in the past two decades, a major obstacle stands in the way of further progress. That obstacle is the Supreme Court's opinion in Kulko v. Superior Court (1978).[36] In that case, a New York family had entered into a custody agreement, which gave custody of the two children to their father. Later, with his permission, the children moved to California to live with their mother, and she later obtained a California support order. When she sought to enforce the order, the husband resisted, on the ground that the California court lacked personal jurisdiction over him.

The Supreme Court agreed. Justice Marshall's majority opinion applied the well-known "minimum contacts" test concerning personal jurisdiction to the question and found that the test had not been satisfied. In so holding, Justice Marshall made two troubling observations: He first noted that the litigation arose "not from the defendant's commercial transactions in interstate commerce, but rather from his personal, domestic relations." It is difficult to understand the relevance of this attempted distinction. After all, if the children are not properly supported in California they will suffer demonstrable—and foreseeable—harm in that state. When viewed in that light, it is easy to see how the facts of *Kulko* could have been found to satisfy the minimum contacts test. Moreover, the fact that the case involved a "domestic relations" problem rather than a "commercial transaction" argues *in favor of* finding personal jurisdiction. If the type of problem matters, as the majority suggests, than it is hard to understand why commercial matters are more important than domestic ones.

The second point emphasized by Justice Marshall was that California had not "attempted to assert any particularized interest in trying [child support] cases in its courts."[37] Here, Justice Marshall apparently was referring to the fact that California did not have a long-arm statute that expressly provided for specific jurisdiction over support obligors. Although many states have so-called "enumerated" long-arm statutes, which specify the types of problems over which jurisdiction may be asserted, California had a general long-arm statute, which asserts jurisdiction over any matter that the constitution permits. It is extremely difficult to understand why California should be penalized for having a *broader* long-arm statute than most states.

Finally, the Court referred to the fact that the then-existing Uniform Act dealing with interstate child support ("URESA") provided an alternative method for obtaining child support from an out-of-state obligor. That reference makes no sense. URESA was such a cumbersome and ineffective method of obtaining relief that it eventually was discarded in favor of UIFSA, discussed above. It can only be assumed that the Court was thinking that it did not have to address more general issues of long-arm jurisdiction when the petitioner would suffer no harm as the result of the decision. If that was indeed the Court's thinking it was dead wrong; URESA was a poor substitute for obtaining relief directly through long-arm jurisdiction.

The *Kulko* decision has met with heavy resistance in the states. The drafters of UIFSA expressly included a provision for asserting jurisdiction over an out-of-state obligor that is flatly inconsistent with *Kulko*. Section 5 of UIFSA provides that a court may exercise jurisdiction in a support matter if "the child resides in this State as a result of the Acts or directives of the [defendant]."[38]

Obviously, it is widely believed that *Kulko* is both bad policy and likely to be overruled when the Court gets the question again. Both suppositions are correct. *Kulko* certainly is bad policy; it is hard to understand why failure to support a child does not permit the child's state of residence to exercise jurisdiction over the obligor in order to protect the child (as well as the treasury of the state, which will be forced to support the child if the parents do not). Surely that exercise of jurisdiction satisfies the minimum fairness test, which is the basis of all modern exercises of long-arm jurisdiction.

It can safely be assumed, therefore, that when and if the time ever comes, *Kulko* will be consigned to the ash bin of history, and a state will be free to obtain long-arm jurisdiction over a parent who does not properly support a child in that state.

NATIVE AMERICAN CHILDREN

The relations between tribal and state court judgments are extremely complex. Nowhere is that more so than in litigation involving child custody and support. Congress passed the Indian Child Welfare Act,[39] in 1978 in an effort to straighten out the area of required recognition between tribal and state courts. The law under that act is quite complex and will not be reviewed here.

INTERNATIONAL CHILDREN

Because the Full Faith and Credit Clause does not apply to judgments rendered by foreign courts, it has little or no relevance to orders involving children entered by those tribunals. The United States, however, has entered into several treaties (and passed implementing statutes) that attempt to deal with those issues on a global basis. These treaties include the 1961 Hague Convention on the Protection of Minors and the 1980 Hague Convention on Civil Aspects of International Child Abduction.

Although the United States has joined no treaty governing international child support, a number of states have entered into agreements or conventions with foreign governments designed to make the enforcement of support orders easier. These agreements are of doubtful constitutionality given the plenary power of the federal government in foreign affairs. Nevertheless, the agreements have received the active encouragement of the State Department and will likely remain effective until the federal government actively enters the area.

NOTES

1. 28 U.S.C. § 1738B.
2. See American Law Institute, Restatement of the Law of Conflict of Laws §§ 121–22 (1934); American Law Institute, Restatement of the Law, Second: Conflict of Laws § 283 (1971).
3. In Re May's Estate, 305 N.Y. 486 (1953).
4. *Id.* at 492.
5. This "*lex celebrationis*" was one of the few "True Rules" in choice of law identified by Professor Albert Ehrenzweig. See Albert A. Ehrenzweig, *A Proper Law in a Proper Forum: A "Restatement" of the "Lex Fori Approach,"* 18 Oklahoma L. Rev. 340 (1965).
6. Marriages that take place in other countries present a similar problem. Again, the Full Faith and Credit Clause does not apply to international legal problems, and marriages celebrated in other countries are recognized by individual states on the basis of comity. The states show considerable disagreement in this area (concerning what foreign marriages recognize). The cases are very few in number, however.
7. Defense of Marriage Act, 28 U.S.C. §1738C.
8. There is a rich academic literature on this subject. *See generally* Symposium, *Interjurisdictional Marriage Recognition*, 32 Creighton L. Rev. 3 (1998); Larry Kramer, *Same Sex Marriage, Conflict of Laws, and the Unconstitutional Public Policy Exception*, 106 Yale L.J. 1965 (1997). In Lawrence v. Texas, 539 U.S. 558 (2003), the Supreme Court held unconstitutional a Texas law prohibiting consensual sodomy between persons of the same sex. The opinion in *Lawrence* contains broad language which can be read easily to cast doubt on the constitutionality of any discrimination against homosexuals; the opinion also contains language, however, which can be construed as not reaching the issue of same-sex marriage. As of this writing, it is unclear how far that language will be pushed by the Supreme Court.
9. An action in rem centers on the legal status of a particular object, the "res" or thing. It might sound odd to treat personal status as a "thing," but that treatment is of long historical standing. Custody was another status question traditionally decided in an action in rem.
10. ALI, *supra* note 2, at § 27. That resolution, of course, would today be an unconstitutional exercise of gender bias.
11. Haddock v. Haddock, 201 U.S. 562 (1906).

12. A transitory cause of action is any civil action other than one involving real property. It can be brought in any state that has personal jurisdiction over the defendant.

13. The town was Granite Falls, population 2,412. When the new Mr. and Mrs. Williams returned to North Carolina, they "set up housekeeping" in Pineole, population 306. Their prosecution—persecution is not too strong a word—has all of the earmarks of a small-town scandal.

14. Williams v. State of North Carolina, 317 U.S. 287, 301 (1942).

15. Williams v. State of North Carolina, 325 U.S. 226, 233 (1945).

16. *Id.* at 230, n. 6.

17. Sherrer v. Sherrer, 334 U.S. 343 (1948).

18. Johnson v. Muelberger, 340 U.S. 581 (1951).

19. Bergner & Engel Brewing Co. v. Dryfus, 51 N.E. 531, 532 (Mass. 1898).

20. Alton v. Alton, 207 F.2d 667 (3d Cir. 1953). One of the curious things about *Alton* is that the court held the decision below unconstitutional under the Due Process Clause of the Fifth Amendment. This was curious because the husband had consented to the exercise of jurisdiction by the Virgin Islands court. Thus *his* due process rights had not been violated. Apparently, then, the state of Connecticut must have been denied *its* rights under the Due Process Clause. How a constitutional provision, designed to protect individual rights, could be used to protect the rights of a state (Connecticut) is an enduring mystery.

21. *Id.*

22. Sosna v. Iowa, 419 U.S. 393 (1975).

23. *Id.* at 561.

24. Estin v. Estin, 334 U.S. 541 (1948).

25. Vanderbilt v. Vanderbilt, 354 U.S. 416 (1957).

26. *Id.* at 418.

27. Simons v. Miami Beach Nat. Bank, 381 U.S. 81 (1965).

28. The parent's dissatisfaction with the custody order often was coupled with unhappiness over a support order entered on behalf of the child.

29. The rendering court, however, loses subject matter jurisdiction if the parties consent to jurisdiction in another state or if everyone concerned—parents and children—move out of the state.

30. Uniform Laws Annotated 649 (1999).

31. May v. Anderson, 345 U.S. 528 (1953).

32. Shaffer v. Heitner, 433 U.S.186 (1977).

33. *Id.* at 209.

34. 42 U.S.C. § 666 (9).

35. 28 U.S.C. § 1738B.

36. Kulko v. Superior Court, 436 U.S. 84 (1978).

37. *Id.* at 98.

38. UIFSA, § 201 (5), 9B Uniform Laws Annotated 275 (1999). UIFSA contains several other problematic bases for obtaining long-arm jurisdiction. Section 201 (6), for example, provides for personal jurisdiction, "if the individual resided with the child in this State," regardless of when the two lived in the forum.

39. 25 U.S.C. §§1901 *et seq.*

Bibliographic Essay

INTRODUCTION

We know of no work devoted exclusively, or even primarily, to the Full Faith and Credit Clause. Instead, the topic is typically subsumed within larger works on conflict of laws, civil procedure, jurisdiction, or judgments. None of these general treatises, however, covers the topic of interstate comity in depth. Listed below are some key resources in each area—the areas are listed in the order in which they are likely to cover the topic in depth.

Conflicts Treatises

The most serious general writing on the Full Faith and Credit Clause can be found in the writings of scholars whose specialty lies in the area of Conflict of Laws, an area where full faith and credit problems play a significant role. The three leading Conflicts treatises are Eugene F. Scoles, Peter Hay, Patrick J. Borchers, & Symeon C. Symeonides, The Conflict of Laws (3d ed., St. Paul, MN: West Group 2000); Russell J. Weintraub, Commentary on the Conflict of Laws (4th ed., New York: Foundation Press 2001); and Robert A. Leflar, Luther L. McDougal, III, & Robert I. Felix, American, Conflicts Law (4th ed., Charlottesville, VA: Michie Co. 1986). The first of those three works is the most comprehensive in both theory and coverage. The Weintraub treatise is close to comprehensive and provides more than enough cohesive theory to hold the subject together from the author's always thoughtful perspective. The last treatise provides a clear and realistic review of the subject matter. The Restatement (Second) of Conflict of Laws (St. Paul, MN: American Law Institute Publishers 1971) is also thorough, but it was written at a time when the law was in a state of flux. As a result, the Restatement is a bit out of touch with today's law, although it remains influential, especially with the judiciary. Our own views are expressed in a shorter treatise, William M. Richman & William L. Reynolds, Understanding Conflict of Laws (3d ed., Newark, NJ: LexisNexis 2002).

Civil Procedure

Most of the standard works on civil procedure and federal courts touch on interstate comity problems in a general way. The best of these books are: Jack H. Friedenthal, Mary Kay Kane, & Arthur Raphael Miller, Civil Procedure (3d ed., New York: Foundation Press 1999); Fleming James, Jr., Geoffrey C. Hazard, Jr., & John Leubsdorf, Civil Procedure (5th ed., Boston: Little Brown 2001); and Larry L. Teply & Ralph U. Whitten, Civil Procedure (2d ed., Charlottesville, VA: LexisNexis 2000). The only comprehensive treatise on territorial jurisdiction, Robert C. Casad & William M. Richman, Jurisdiction in Civil Actions (3d ed., Charlottesville, VA: LexisNexis 1999), is also a useful source.

Federal Jurisdiction

The law of full faith and credit interacts to some extent with the law of federal jurisdiction. The two basic authorities in this latter area are the magisterial multivolume treatises by Charles Alan Wright, Arthur Raphael Miller, & Edward H. Cooper, Federal Practice and Procedure (St. Paul, MN: West Group 2000); and by James Moore, Moore's Federal Practice (3d ed., New York: LexisNexis 2002). Both commentators and judges rely on these two multivolume works as authoritative. Each gives reliable descriptions of the law, and, although designed primarily for use by practitioners, the discussion is consistently at a high level.

Judgments

Most of the tale of the Full Faith and Credit Clause really concerns the effect that judicial judgments have in another state. Because of that interaction, it is important to understand the more general law of *judgments*. The most influential and useful work in the general area of judgments is the Restatement (Second) of Judgments (St. Paul, MN: American Law Institute Publishers 1982), whose Reporter was Geoffrey Hazard. The Second Restatement of Judgments is a wonderfully concise and well-written description and analysis of the law in the area. It does suffer however from the unavoidable fact that it was written before several key Supreme Court decisions.

CHAPTER 1: HISTORY

The most comprehensive work on the history of the Full Faith and Credit Clause is an unpublished doctoral thesis written for the History Department at the University of Chicago in 1950: Shirley Akerman Bill, *The Meaning and Background of the Interstate Prima Facie Clause of the Federal Constitution* (unpublished 1950, on file with the authors). Although this excellent work has gone unrecognized, it compiles thoughtfully the history (in a large sense) of the Full Faith and

Credit Clause. Bill's dismissive attitude towards legal historians makes for interesting reading. We thank Professor David Bogen for bringing Bill's dissertation to our attention.

There are a number of more conventional sources on the history of the Full Faith and Credit Clause. None of them is particularly controversial or startling. The most important article by a legal historian, as well as the most widely cited, is Kurt Nadelmann, *Full Faith and Credit to Judgments and Public Acts: A Historical-Analytical Reappraisal*, 56 Michigan L. Rev. 33 (1957), on which we have drawn heavily. Ralph U. Whitten, *The Original Understanding of the Full Faith and Credit Clause and the Defense of Marriage Act*, 32 Creighton L. Rev. 255 (1998), also an important resource for this book, provides a contemporary and sensible analysis of the area with a valuable focus on the history of the full faith and credit due statutes. Professor Whitten also reviews critically the debates surrounding the Defense of Marriage Act, discussed in Chapter 3.

Other important articles are George P. Costigan, Jr., *The History of the Adoption of Section I of Article IV of the United States Constitution and a Consideration of the Effect on Judgments of that Section and of Federal Legislation*, 4 Columbia L. Rev. 470 (1904); Max Radin, *The Authenticated Full Faith and Credit Clause: Its History*, 39 Il. L. Rev. 1 (1944); Willis L. M. Reese & Vincent A. Johnson, *The Scope of Full Faith and Credit to Judgments*, 49 Columbia L. Rev. 153 (1949). A recent article setting forth the "debt collection" hypothesis is Michael Finch, *Giving Full Faith and Credit to Punitive Damages Awards: Will Florida Rule the Nation?*, 86 Minnesota L. Rev. 497 (2002).

CHAPTER 2: "PUBLIC RECORDS": THE CLAUSE AND THE STATUTE

As indicated in the text, there is little material for a bibliography on full faith and credit to sister-state records. The most significant of the few cases that treat the clause and the statute are cited in the notes, and there is little if any secondary literature on the subject.

There is, by contrast, a substantial literature on the problem of proof of foreign law, and the solutions offered by the Federal Rules of Civil and Criminal Procedure. On the issue generally, see Eugene F. Scoles, Peter Hay, Patrick J. Borchers, & Symeon C. Symeonides, Conflict of Laws § 12.17 (3d ed., St. Paul, MN: West Group 2000); William M. Richman & William L. Reynolds, Understanding Conflict of Laws 174–76 (3d ed., Newark, NJ: LexisNexis 2002); Gregory S. Alexander, *The Application and Avoidance of Foreign Law in the Law of Conflicts*, 70 Northwestern University L. Rev. 602 (1975).

The federal rules' solution to the problem is treated in 9 Charles A. Wright & Arthur R. Miller, *Federal Practice and Procedure* (31 vols., St. Paul, MN: West Group 1995); Arthur R. Miller, *Federal Rule 44.1 and the "Fact" Approach to Determining Foreign Law: Death Knell for a Die-hard Doctrine*, 65 Michigan L. Rev. 613 (1967). The Uniform Acts are reported at 9A U.L.A. 553 (1965), and 13 U.L.A. 355 (1986). For commentary, see Scoles, Hay, Borchers, & Symeonides, *supra*, at 532–34.

The authoritative multivolume treatises on the Federal Rules of Evidence treat the issues covered in this section. See generally 5 Christopher B. Mueller & Laird C. Kirkpatrick, Federal Evidence (5 vols., 2d ed., Rochester, NY: Lawyers Cooperative Pub. 1994); 3 Stephen A. Saltzburg, Michael M. Martin, & Daniel J. Capra, Federal Rules of Evidence Manual (5 vols., 7th ed., Charlottesville, VA: Lexis Law Pub. 1998); 5 Jack B. Weinstein & Margaret A. Berger, Weinstein's Federal Evidence (6 vols., Joseph M. McLaughlin ed., 2d ed., New York: Mathew Bender 1997–2003); 31 Charles A. Wright & Victor J. Gold, Federal Practice and Procedure (31 vols., St. Paul, MN: West Group 2000). There are also several fine one-volume treatises on the law and practice of evidence: Roger C. Park, David P. Leonard, & Steven H. Goldberg, Evidence Law (2d ed., St. Paul, MN: West Group 2002); Graham C. Lilly, An Introduction to the Law of Evidence (3d ed., St. Paul, MN: West Pub. Co. 1996); Glen Weissenberger, Federal Rules of Evidence: Rules, Legislative History, Commentary and Authority (Cincinnati, OH: Anderson Pub. Co. 1999).

CHAPTER 3: "PUBLIC ACTS"

The literature on choice of law theory is rich, varied, and huge, so a bibliography within the scope of this book must be selective. Good general treatments of the topic appear in William M. Richman & William L. Reynolds, Understanding Conflict of Laws (3d ed., Newark, NJ: LexisNexis 2002); David H. Vernon, Louise Weinberg, William L. Reynolds, & William M. Richman, Conflict of Laws: Cases, Materials and Problems Chapter 4 (Rev. 2d ed., Newark, NJ: LexisNexis 2002); Eugene F. Scoles, Peter Hay, Patrick J. Borchers, & Symeon C. Symeonides, Conflict of Laws Ch. 17–23 (3d ed., St. Paul, MN: West Group 2000); Robert A. Leflar, Luther L. McDougal, & Robert L. Felix, American Conflicts Law Chapter 10 (4th ed., Charlottesville, VA: Michie Co. 1986).

There is great deal of commentary on the traditional system for choice of law embodied in the First Restatement. The definitive works, of course, are the Restatement itself and the nearly contemporaneous multivolume treatise written by the Reporter for the First Restatement, Joseph H. Beale, A Treatise on the Conflict of Laws (3 vols., New York: Baker, Voorhis & Co. 1935). Academic criticism of the Restatement followed almost immediately with works by Walter W. Cook, The Logical and Legal Bases of the Conflict of Laws (Cambridge, MA: Harvard University Press 1942); and David F. Cavers, *A Critique of the Choice-of-Law Problem*, 47 Harvard L. Rev. 173 (1933), and the criticism did not abate. *See* David Cavers, The Choice-of-Law Process (Ann Arbor: University of Michigan Press 1965); Moffatt Hancock, Studies in Modern Choice-of-Law: Torts, Insurance, Land Titles (Buffalo, NY: W.S. Hein Co. 1984); Brainerd Currie, Selected Essays on the Conflict of Laws (Durham, NC: Duke University Press 1963). Contemporary criticism continues. See Richman & Reynolds, Understanding Conflict of Laws; Russell J. Weintraub, Commentary on the Conflict of Laws (4th ed., New York: Foundation Press 2000); Doug Rendleman, McMillan v. McMillan: *Choice of Law in a Sinkhole*, 67 Virginia L. Rev. 315 (1981).

There is no commentary in support of the center of gravity system (a revealing datum). Early cases to abandon the traditional system are Auten v. Auten, 308 N.Y. 155, 124 N.E.2d 99 (N.Y. 1954); Haag v. Barnes, 9 N.Y.2d 554, 216 N.Y.S.2d 65, 175 N.E.2d 441 (N.Y. 1961); Schmidt v. Driscoll Hotel, Inc., 249 Minn. 376, 82 N.W.2d 365 (Minn. 1957). The debate among the courts on whether it is worth abandoning the purported virtues of the traditional system in favor of one of the more modern systems continues. *See* Paul v. National Life, 352 S.E.2d 550 (W.Va. 1986).

The literature on interest analysis also is extensive. The primary sources are a series of law review articles written by Brainerd Currie, beginning in 1958, and collected in Selected Essays, *supra*. For a modern introduction to the method, see William M. Richman, Diagramming Conflicts: *A Graphic Understanding of Interest Analysis*, 43 Ohio State L.J. 317 (1982). For criticism of the method, *see* Lea Brilmayer, *Governmental Interest Analysis: A House without Foundations*, 46 Ohio State L.J. 459 (1985). A Symposium on Interest Analysis appears in 21 University of California at Davis L. Rev. (1990) and contains articles by proponents and critics of the method.

For discussion of Professor Leflar's Choice Influencing Considerations and the Better Law, see Leflar et al., American Conflicts Law; Symposium, *Leflar on Conflicts*, 31 South Carolina L. Rev. 409 (1980); Robert A. Leflar, *Honest Judicial Opinions*, 74 Northwestern University L. Rev. 721 (1979).

The primary sources on the Second Restatement are, of course, that document itself and the writings of its principal Reporter, Professor Willis Reese of the Columbia Law School. *See* Willis L.M. Reese, *Second Restatement of Conflict of Laws Revisited*, 34 Mercer L. Rev. 501 (1983); Willis L.M. Reese, *Conflict of Laws and the Restatement Second*, 28 Law & Contemporary Problems 679 (1963). Modern commentary appears in a Symposium in volume 56 of the Maryland Law Review to honor the silver anniversary of the Second Restatement (with contributions by Professors Borchers, Reynolds, Richman, Riley, Weinberg, and Weintraub). See also Jeffrey M. Shaman, *The Vicissitudes of Choice of Law: The* Restatement *(First, Second) and Interest Analysis*, 45 Buffalo L. Rev. 329 (1997); Michael S. Finch, *Choice-of-Law Problems in Florida Courts: A Retrospective on the* Restatement (Second), 24 Stetson L. Rev. 653 (1995).

The Conflict of Laws treatises are the best sources on the limitations imposed by the Full Faith and Credit and Due Process Clauses of the federal constitution on state choice of law decisions. *See* Richman & Reynolds, Understanding Conflict of Laws, *supra*; Russell J. Weintraub, *supra* at 585–644; Scoles, Hay, Borchers, & Symeonides, *supra* at §§ 3.20–3.30; Leflar, McDougal, & Felix, *supra* at §§ 55–59 (discussion in this excellent treatise is a bit dated).

The law review literature on the topic is extremely rich. A selective sample includes: Douglas Laycock, *Equal Citizens of Equal and Territorial States: The*

Constitutional Foundations of Choice of Law, 92 Columbia L. Rev. 249 (1992); Terry S. Kogan, *Toward a Jurisprudence of Choice of Law: The Priority of Fairness Over Comity*, 62 New York University L. Rev. 651 (1987); Robert A. Sedler, *Constitutional Limitations on Choice of Law: The Perspective of Constitutional Generalism*, 10 Hofstra L. Rev. 59 (1981); Willis L.M. Reese, *Legislative Jurisdiction*, 78 Columbia L. Rev. 1587 (1978). Louise Weinberg, *Choice of Law and Minimal Scrutiny*, 49 University of Chicago L. Rev. 440 (1982), opened our eyes to the virtues of minimal scrutiny.

More specifically, on the relative roles of the Due Process and Full Faith and Credit Clause in reviewing state choice of law decisions, see Ralph U. Whitten, *The Constitutional Limitations on State Choice of Law: Due Process*, 9 Hastings Constitutional Law Quarterly 851 (1982); Ralph U. Whitten, *The Constitutional Limitations of State Choice of Law: Full Faith and Credit*, 12 Memphis State University L. Rev. 1 (1981); Frederic L. Kirgis, Jr., *The Roles of Due Process and Full Faith and Credit in Choice of Law*, 62 Cornell L. Rev. 94 (1976); James A. Martin, *A Reply to Professor Kirgis*, 62 Cornell L. Rev. 151 (1976).

For commentary on *Allstate*, see Gene R. Shreve, *In Search of a Choice-of-Law Reviewing Standard—Reflections on* Allstate Insurance Co. v. Hague, 66 Minnesota L. Rev. 327 (1982); Symposium, *Conflicts-of-Laws Theory after* Allstate Insurance Co. v. Hague, 10 Hofstra L. Rev. 1–211 (1981); Symposium, *A Response to the* Hague *Symposium*, 10 Hofstra L. Rev. 973–1071 (1982); Symposium, *Supreme Court Intervention in Jurisdiction and Choice of Law: From* SHAFFER *to* ALLSTATE, 14 University of California at Davis L. Rev. 837–917 (1981). Commentary criticizing the *Allstate* Court's reliance on the three neglible contacts appears in P. John Kozyris, *Reflections on* Allstate*—The Lessening of Due Process in Choice of Law*, 14 University of California at Davis L. Rev. 889 (1981); Aaron D. Twerski, *On Territoriality and Sovereignty: System Shock and Constitutional Choice of Law*, 10 Hofstra L. Rev. 149 (1981); Arthur T. von Mehren & Donald T. Trautman, *Constitutional Control of Choice of Law: Some Reflections on* Hague, 10 Hofstra L. Rev. 35 (1981). Taking the contrary view, however, is Louise Weinberg, *Conflicts Cases and the Problem of Relevant Time: A Response to the* Hague *Symposium*, 10 Hofstra L. Rev. 1023 (1982). For commentary relevant to the plaintiff's postoccurrence move, see *Note, Post Transaction or Occurrence Events in Conflict of Laws*, 69 Columbia L. Rev. 843 (1969); John K. McNulty, *Corporations and Intertemporal Conflict of Laws*, 55 California L. Rev. 12 (1967).

Commentary on *Shutts* and *Wortman* is less plentiful. On *Shutts*, see Louise Weinberg, *The Place of Trial and the Law Applied: Overhauling Constitutional Theory*, 59 University of Colorado L. Rev. 67 (1988); Gene R. Shreve, *Interest Analysis as Constitutional Law*, 48 Ohio State L.J. 51 (1987); James R. Pielemeier, *Why We Should Worry about Full Faith and Credit to Laws*, 60 Southern California L. Rev. 1299 (1987).

On *Wortman*, see David Seidelson, *1* (Wortman) + *1* (Ferens) = *6 (Years): That Can't Be Right—Can It? Statutes of Limitations and Supreme Court In-*

consistency, 57 Brooklyn L. Rev. 787 (1991); Bruce Posnak, *The Court Doesn't Know Its* Asahi *from its* Wortman: *A Critical View of the Constitutional Constraints on Jurisdiction and Choice of Law*, 41 Syracuse L. Rev. 875 (1990); Louise Weinberg, *Choosing Law: The Limitations Debates*, University of Illinois L. Rev. 683 (1991); Janet Kathleen May, *Constitutionality of a Forum State's Use of Its Own Longer Statute of Limitations When Its Only Contact with the Dispute Is Its Status as a Forum*—Sun Oil Co. v. Wortman, *108 S. Ct. 2117 (1998)*, 64 Washington L. Rev. 741 (1989).

Enthusiastic commentary on other possible constitutional limits on choice of law includes Douglas Laycock, *supra*; Howard W. Horwitz, *The Commerce Clause as a Limitation on State Choice-of-Law Doctrine*, 84 Harvard L. Rev. 806 (1971); and John Hart Ely, *Choice of Law and the State's Interest in Protecting Its Own*, 23 William and Mary L. Rev. 173 (1981).

CHAPTER 4: JUDICIAL PROCEEDINGS: THE BASIC RULE

The full faith and credit scholars have been quite critical of the reciprocity concept. *See* Leflar, McDougal, & Felix, *supra* at § 84; Scoles, Hay, Borchers, & Symeonides, *supra* at § 24.34; Restatement (Second) of Conflict of Laws, *supra* at § 98, comment e. Arthur Lenhoff, *Reciprocity and the Law of Foreign Judgments: A Historical-Critical Analysis*, 16 Louisiana L. Rev. 415 (1956). A good review of the problem of foreign libel judgments (as well as disapproval of the *Telnikof* decision) can be found in The American Law Institute, *International Jurisdiction and Judgments Project*, § 5 (d) (tentative draft: Philadelphia, 2003).

The most encyclopedic treatments of preclusion law appear in the masterful multivolume treatise 18 Charles A. Wright, Arthur R. Miller, & Edward H. Cooper, Federal Practice and Procedure (31 vols., St. Paul, MN: West Group 1981 and 2000 Supp.); and American Law Institute, Restatement of the Law, Second, Judgments Ch. 3 & 4 (St. Paul, MN: American Law Institute Publishers 1982); more compact discussions appear in Gene R. Shreve & Peter Raven-Hansen, Understanding Civil Procedure, Ch. 15 (3d ed., Newark, NJ: LexisNexis 2002); Larry L. Teply & Ralph U. Whitten, Civil Procedure Ch. 13 (2d ed. New York: Foundation Press 2000); Jack H. Friedenthal, Mary Kay Kane, & Arthur R. Miller, Civil Procedure Ch. 14 (3d ed., St. Paul, MN: West Group 1999). A classic treatment that is no longer up to date is *Developments in the Law—Res Judicata*, 65 Harvard L. Rev. 818 (1952).

The best comprehensive treatment of the law of full faith and credit is again in Volume 18 of Wright, Miller, & Cooper, *supra* at §§ 4466–4472; and more compact versions are in David Vernon, Louise Weinberg, William Reynolds, & William Richman, Conflict of Laws: Cases, Materials and Problems §§ 7.02–7.03 (2d ed., Newark, NJ: LexisNexis 2002); Richman & Reynolds, Understanding Conflict, *supra* at § 110; Teply & Whitten, *supra* at p. 949–63; Shreve & Raven-Hansen, *supra* at § 114.

On the history of the Full Faith and Credit Clause, see Chapter 1 *infra*.

The issue of choice of preclusion law has produced some controversy among the scholars. Some agree with the Supreme Court's view that the law of F-1 must control. *See, e.g.*, Ronan E. Degnan, *Federalized Res Judicata*, 85 Yale L.J. 741 (1976); American Law Institute, Restatement of the Law, Second: Conflict of Laws §§ 94–95 (St. Paul: American Law Institute, 1971). Others advocate a more nuanced approach. Wright, Miller, & Cooper, *supra* at § 4467: Teply & Whitten, *supra* at p. 951–52; Sanford N. Caust-Ellenbogen, *False Conflicts and Interstate Preclusion: Moving Beyond a Wooden Reading of the Full Faith and Credit Statute*, 58 Fordham L. Rev. 593 (1990); Robert C. Casad, *Intersystem Issue Preclusion and the Restatement (Second) of Judgments*, 66 Cornell L. Rev. 510, 523 (1981); Jeffrey E. Lewis, *Mutuality in Conflict—Flexibility and Full Faith and Credit*, 23 Drake L. Rev. 364 (1974); Paul D. Carrington, *Collateral Estoppel and Foreign Judgments*, 24 Ohio State L.J. 381 (1963).

Our position is that the area is technical, difficult even for the initiated, and a trap for the unwary among typical litigators. In such areas, a simple and certain solution has much to recommend it. The virtue of the more nuanced approaches is that they sometimes lead to furthering of the interests of F-2 at no cost to those of F-1 or the national unity policies behind full faith and credit. Realistically, however, the F-2 interests that are furthered are seldom very strong nor of concern to anyone but the judiciary of F-2; the risk of unfairness to the unwary litigant seems to us to justify the orthodox law-of-the-rendering-state rule.

The standard conflicts treatises offer useful discussions of interstate enforcement procedures. See William M. Richman & William L. Reynolds, Understanding Conflict of Laws § 110 (b) (3rd ed., Newark, NJ: LexisNexis 2002); Robert A. Leflar, Luther L. McDougal, & Robert L. Felix, American Conflicts Law § 78 (4th ed., Charlottesville, VA: Michie Co. 1986).

The federal registration statute, 28 U.S.C. § 1963 is discussed in Charles A. Wright, Arthur R. Miller, and Mary Kay Kane, Federal Practice and Procedure §§ 2787 and 2865 (St. Paul, MN: West Group 1995). See also Hershel Shanks & Steven A. Standiford, *Schizophrenia in Federal Judgment Enforcement: Registration of Foreign Judgments under 28 U.S.C. § 1963*, 59 Notre Dame L. Rev. 851 (1984).

On the exception for issues concerning methods of enforcement, see Restatement (Second) of Conflict of Laws, *supra* at § 99, 100, 102.

An excellent compact treatment of the territorial jurisdiction of American courts, including the taxonomy referred to in the text, appears in Richman & Reynolds, Understanding Conflict, *supra* at Ch. 3. An exhaustive treatment of the same topic appears in Robert C. Casad & William M. Richman, Jurisdiction in Civil Actions (3d ed., Charlottesville, VA: Lexis Law Pub. 1998).

Again, a compact discussion and of full faith and credit for in rem proceedings can be found in Richman & Reynolds, *supra* at § 111. For a more complete treatment, see Wright, Miller, & Cooper, *supra* at § 4431; American Law Institute, Judgments *supra* at § 30; and American Law Institute, Conflict of Laws *supra* at Ch. 5, Topic 2, Introductory Note.

Combs v. Combs, 249 Ky. 155, 60 S.W.2d 368 (1933), is the leading case dealing with the issue of a court with in rem jurisdiction that exceeds its limited mandate and issues a personal judgment.

The arguments for and against the *Harnischfeger* preclusion principle are analyzed in Wright, Miller, & Cooper, *supra* at § 4431. An older but excellent treatment also appears in Charles W. Taintor II, *Foreign Judgment In Rem: Full Faith and Credit v. Res Judicata in Personam*, 8 Pittsburg L. Rev. 223 (1942). The American Law Institute, correctly in our view, has adopted the *Harnischfeger* rule. The possibility of unfairness to the defendant in specific applications of the *Harnischfeger* principle is discussed in Eugene F. Scoles, *Interstate Preclusion by Prior Litigation*, 74 Northwestern University L. Rev. 742, 755 (1979). The states differ on the *Harnischfeger* issue, so the "more faith and credit" problem can occur here, just as it does with any other preclusion issue. On this possibility, see Michael H. Hoffheimer, *Mississippi Conflict of Laws*, 67 Mississippi L.J. 175, 198 (1997); Robert C. Casad, *supra* at 510.

There is no dearth of secondary literature on the Iron Law. A compact treatment, which, in fact, coined the nickname (certainly not the concept), is William M. Richman & William L. Reynolds, Understanding Conflict of Laws § 114 (3d ed. 2002); see also William L. Reynolds, *The Iron Law of Full Faith and Credit*, 53 Md. L. Rev. 412 (1994); Eugene F. Scoles, Peter Hay, Patrick J. Borchers, & Symeon C. Symeonides, Conflict of Laws §§ 24.2, 24.20 (3d ed. 2000); Robert A. Leflar, Felix L. McDougal, & Robert L. Felix, American Conflicts Law §§ 75, 81 (4th ed. 1986). Forceful statements of the black letter also appear in Restatement (Second) of Conflict of Laws § 106 (mistake of law or fact not a ground for collateral attack) and § 117 (enforcement required even though claim underlying the judgment contrary to public policy of enforcing state) (1971).

For commentary on the application of the rule to inconsistent judgments, see Richman & Reynolds, *supra*; Scoles et al., *supra* at § 24.2, Leflar, McDougal, & Felix § 81; Restatement (Second) of Conflict of Laws § 114 (1971). A more detailed treatment in the periodical literature is Ruth Bader Ginsburg, *Judgments in Search of Full Faith and Credit: The Last-in-Time Rule for Conflicting Judgments*, 82 Harv. L. Rev. 798 (1969).

CHAPTER 5: EXCEPTIONS AND QUALIFICATIONS TO THE RULE OF FINALITY

A brief treatment of the issue of judgments not on the merits in F-1 is William M. Richman & William L. Reynolds, Understanding Conflict of Laws 377–78 (3d ed., Newark, NJ: LexisNexis 2002). For more detail, see Eugene F. Scoles, Peter Hay, Patrick J. Borchers, & Symeon C. Symeonides, Conflict of Laws § 24.24 (3d ed., St. Paul, MN: West Group 2000).

A compact treatment of the issue of fraud is Richman & Reynolds, *supra*. For more detail, see American Law Institute, Restatement of the Law, Second, Judgments § 68, 70 (St. Paul: American Law Institute Publishers 1982); American

Law Institute, Restatement of the Law of Judgments §§ 118–122 (St. Paul, MN: American Law Institute Publishers 1942). A very complete discussion of fraud and irregularities in service of process and in the return of service is contained in Robert C. Casad & William M. Richman, Jurisdiction in Civil Actions § 3–1 (3d ed., Charlottesville, VA: Lexis Law Pub. 1998).

Good discussions of the problems of equity decrees are Polly J. Price, *Full Faith and Credit and the Equity Decree*, 84 Virginia L. Rev. 747 (1998); Willis Reese & Vincent Johnson, *The Scope of Full Faith and Credit to Judgments*, 49 Columbia L. Rev. 153 (1949).

A good short treatment of the Land Taboo problem appears in Richman & Reynolds, *supra* at § 115[e]. More complete discussions can be found in Scoles, Hay, Borchers, & Symeonides, *supra* at § 24.9; Robert A. Leflar, Luther L. McDougal, & Robert L. Felix, American Conflicts Law § 174 (4th ed., Charlottesville, VA: Michie Co. 1986). For a consideration of practical methods for avoiding the result in *Fall* itself, see Brainerd Currie, *Full Faith and Credit to Foreign Land Decrees*, 21 University of Chicago L. Rev. 620 (1954).

On state-court judgments in federal courts, see generally Richman & Reynolds, *supra* at § 113. For a much longer and more detailed discussion, see Charles A. Wright, Arthur R. Miller, & Edward H. Cooper, Federal Practice and Procedure §§ 4468, 4470, 4470.1, 4471.3 (31 vols., St. Paul, MN: West Group 2000); American Law Institute, Judgments, *supra* at § 87.

For commentary on the *Parsons Steel* case, see Richman & Reynolds, *supra* at § 113 [b]. *Marrese* and the problem of exclusive jurisdiction cases as exceptions to § 1738 are the subject of excellent commentary in Wright, Miller, & Cooper, *supra* at § 4470.1; Larry L. Teply & Ralph U. Whitten, Civil Procedure 953–54 (2d ed., New York: Foundation Press 2000); Gene R. Shreve & Peter Raven-Hansen, Understanding Civil Procedure § 15.10[2] (3d ed., Newark, NJ: LexisNexis 2002). For more on *Epstein*, especially with regard to the class action and settlement aspects of the case, see Mollie A. Murphy, *The Intersystem Class Settlement: Of Comity, Consent and Collusion*, 47 University of Kansas L. Rev. 413 (1999).

On an exception to the general rule of § 1738 for civil rights cases, see Robert H. Smith, *Full Faith and Credit and Section 1983: A Reappraisal*, 63 North Carolina L. Rev. 59 (1984).

The problem of issue preclusion for administrative body findings has provoked some controversy. Compare ALI, Judgments, *supra* at § 83 (supporting preclusion) with Marjorie A. Silver, *In Lieu of Preclusion: Reconciling Administrative Decisionmaking and Federal Civil Rights Claims*, 65 Indiana L.J. 367 (1990) (opposite). Our own view is that administrative preclusion makes sense when the decision maker is impartial; that is, it is not a captive of one of the sides to the dispute. Even then, it might make sense if the decision is appealable to a court that does not apply an overly deferential standard of review.

The issue of the appropriate law to apply when recognizing federal court judgments has been the subject of substantial commentary. *See, e.g.*, Gene R. Shreve,

Judgments from a Choice-of-Law Perspective, 40 American Journal Comparative Law 985 (1992); Stephen B. Burbank, *Interjurisdictional Preclusion, Full Faith and Credit and Federal Common Law: A General Approach*, 71 Cornell L. Rev. 733 (1986); Ronan E. Degnan, *Federalized Res Judicata*, 85 Yale L.J. 741 (1976). Commentary on the *Semtek* decision includes Stephen B. Burbank, Semtek, *Forum Shopping and Federal Common Law*, 77 Notre Dame L. Rev. 1027 (2002).

CHAPTER 6: FAMILY LAW: A SPECIAL FULL FAITH AND CREDIT PROBLEM

Good sources on the general rule of *lex celebrationis* for marriages and the traditional exception for marriages that violate natural law are William M. Richman & William L. Reynolds, Understanding Conflict of Laws § 119 (3d ed., Newark, NJ: LexisNexis 2002); Eugene F. Scoles, Peter Hay, Patrick J. Borchers, & Symeon C. Symeonides, Conflict of Laws §§ 13.5–13.14 (3d ed., St. Paul, MN: West Group 2000); Robert A. Leflar, Luther L. McDougal, & Robert L. Felix, American Conflicts Law § 22 (4th ed., Charlottesville, VA: Michie Co. 1986); American Law Institute, Restatement of the Law of Conflict of Laws §§ 121–22 (St. Paul, MN: American Law Institute Publishers 1934); Albert A. Ehrenzweig, A Treatise on the Conflict of Laws 138 (St. Paul, MN: West Pub. Co. 1962); American Law Institute, Restatement of the Law, Second: Conflict of Laws § 283 (St. Paul: American Law Institute Publishers 1971). The periodical literature on these topics is extensive. *See, e.g.*, Rhona Schuz, *When Is a Polygamous Marriage Not a Polygamous Marriage*? 46 Modern L. Rev. 653 (1983); A. E. Gotlieb, *The Incidental Question Revisited—Theory and Practice in the Conflict of Laws*, 26 International and Comparative Law Quarterly 734 (1977); Willis L. M. Reese, *Marriage in American Conflict of Laws*, 26 International and Comparative Law Quarterly 952 (1977).

DOMA, having stirred up political passions, also stirred up a wealth of commentary. *See, e.g.*, Symposium, *Interjurisdictional Marriage Recognition*, 32 Creighton L. Rev. 3 (1998); Andrew Koppelman, *Same-Sex Marriage, Choice of Law, and Public Policy*, 76 Texas L. Rev. 921 (1998); Larry Kramer, *Same-Sex Marriage, Conflict of Laws, and the Unconstitutional Public Policy Exception*, 106 Yale L.J. 1965 (1997); Julie L. B. Johnson, *Note, The Meaning Of "General Laws": The Extent of Congress's Power under The Full Faith and Credit Clause and the Constitutionality of the Defense of Marriage Act*, 145 University of Pennsylvania L. Rev. 1611 (1997); Jennifer Gerarda Brown, *Extraterritorial Recognition of Same Sex Marriage: When Theory Confronts Praxis*, 16 Quinnipiac L. Rev. 1 (1996); Daniel A. Crane, *The Original Understanding of the "Effects Clause" of Article IV, Section 1 and Implication of the Defense of Marriage Act*, 6 George Mason L. Rev. 307 (1998); Joseph W. Hovermill, *A Conflict of Laws and Morals: The Choice of Law Implications of Hawaii's Recognition of Same-Sex Marriages*, 53 Maryland L. Rev. 450 (1994); Mark Strasser, Loving *the*

Romer *out for* Baehr: *On Acts in Defense of Marriage and the Constitution*, 58 University of Pittsburgh L. Rev. 279 (1997).

The congressional hearings on DOMA contained testimony about the ability of Congress to expand and/or contract the Supreme Court's interpretations of the meaning of the Full Faith and Credit Clause. A useful, lucid analysis of that testimony can be found in Emily J. Sack, *Domestic Violence across State Lines: The Full Faith and Credit Clause, Congressional Power, and Interstate Enforcement of Protection Orders*, 98 Northwestern University L. Rev. 827, 888–98 (2004). A comprehensive discussion of jurisdiction in all types of family law disputes appears in Robert C. Casad & William M. Richman, Jurisdiction in Civil Actions § 9–2 (3d ed., Charlottesville, VA: Lexis Law Pub. 1998). Authoritative discussions on divorce jurisdiction and full faith and credit for sister-state divorces appear in Russell J. Weintraub, Commentary on the Conflict of Laws p. 295–307 (4th ed., New York: Foundation Press 2000); Scoles et al., *supra* at §§ 15.1–15.14; Leflar et al., *supra* at §§ 223–26. A more compact treatment is Richman & Reynolds, *supra* at §§ 120–24.

An interesting discussion of the facts of the *Williams* cases is Thomas Reed Powell, *And Repent at Leisure*, 58 Harvard L. Rev. 930 (1945).

On collateral attack on the F-1 divorce, see the landmark article that rationalized the area, David P. Currie, *Suitcase Divorce in the Conflict of Laws*: Simons, Rosenstiel, *and* Borax, 34 University of Chicago L. Rev. 26 (1966). The estoppel that prevents the F-1 plaintiff from collaterally attacking his divorce in F-2 is treated specifically in Homer Clark, "Estoppel against Jurisdictional Attack on Decrees of Divorce," 70 Yale L.J. 45 (1960).

On divorce based on jurisdictional grounds other than domicile, see Helen Garfield, *The Transitory Divorce Action: Jurisdiction in the No-Fault Era*, 58 Texas L. Rev. 501 (1980); Rhonda Wasserman, *Parents, Partners, and Personal Jurisdiction*, 1995 University of Illinois L. Rev. 813 (1995); John F. Hendry, *Conflict of Laws: Limitations on the "Domicile of Choice" of Military Servicemen*, 31 Oklahoma L. Rev. 167 (1978).

Choice of law for divorce is discussed in ALI, Conflict of Laws, *supra* at § 285; Leflar et al., *supra* at § 222.

The status of foreign nation divorces is discussed in Scoles et al., *supra* at §§ 13.5–13.14; Homer H. Clark, The Law of Domestic Relations in the United States 432 (Student ed., 2d ed., St. Paul, MN: West Pub. Co. 1988).

The basic treatises on conflicts provide excellent discussions of the problems of spousal support and divisible divorce. See Richman & Reynolds, *supra* at §§ 126–127; Weintraub, *supra* at p. 307–14; Scoles et al., *supra* at §§ 15.27–15.29; Leflar et al., *supra* at §§ 232–237. Additionally, for treatment in the periodical literature, see David P. Currie, *supra*; and Robert F. Drinan, *What Are the Rights of the Involuntary Divorcee? Reflections on Divisible Divorce*, 53 Kentucky L.J. 209 (1965). On choice of law problems that arise in the division of marital property, see J. Thomas Oldham, *Conflict of Laws and Marital Property Rights*, 39 Baylor L. Rev. 1255 (1987).

There is an extensive literature treating problems of interstate child custody. The standard conflicts and jurisdiction treatises have sections addressing the issue thoroughly. See Richman & Reynolds, *supra* at §§ 130–131; Weintraub, *supra* at 321–45; Scoles et al., *supra* at §§ 15.39–15.43; Casad & Richman, *supra* at § 9–2[5]–[7].

Further, an abundance of law-review commentary treats individual topics within the broad category. On the problems with the traditional law of interstate custody, see Leonard G. Ratner, *Legislative Resolution of the Interstate Child Custody Problem: A Reply to Professor Currie and a Proposed Uniform Act*, 38 Southern California L. Rev. 183 (1965).

The UCCJA is the subject of authoritative commentary by its principal drafter in Brigitte M. Bodenheimer, *Progress under the Uniform Child Custody Jurisdiction Act and Remaining Problems: Punitive Decrees, Joint Custody, and Excessive Modifications*, 65 California L. Rev. 978 (1977). On the relationship between the UCCJA and the PKPA, see Anne B. Goldstein, *The Tragedy of the Interstate Child: A Critical Reexamination of the Uniform Child Custody Jurisdiction Act and the Parental Kidnapping Prevention Act*, 25 University of California at Davis L. Rev. 845 (1992). Patricia M. Hoff, *The ABC's of the UCCJEA: Interstate Child-Custody Practice under the New Act*, 32 Family Law Quarterly 267 (1998), discusses the newer version of the act, the UCCJEA. The due process rights of absent parents under May v. Anderson and Shaffer v. Heitner, is discussed in Wasserman, *supra*; Barbara Ann Atwood, *Child Custody Jurisdiction and Territoriality*, 52 Ohio State L.J. 369 (1991); Helen Garfield, *Due Process Rights of Absent Parents in Interstate Custody Conflicts*, 16 Indiana L. Rev. 445 (1983); Russell M. Coombs, *Interstate Child Custody: Jurisdiction, Recognition, and Enforcement*, 66 Minnesota L. Rev. 735–64 (1982); Brigitte M. Bodenheimer & Janet Neeley-Kvarme, *Jurisdiction over Child Custody and Adoption after* Shaffer *and* Kulko, 12 University of California at Davis L. Rev. 229 (1979).

On international custody issues, see Linda Silberman, *Hague International Child Abduction Convention: A Progress Report*, 57 Law and Contemporary Problems 209 (1994); Adair Dyer, *The Internationalization of Family Law*, 30 University of California at Davis L. Rev. 625 (1997).

Again, the principal texts are useful sources on the interstate recognition of support orders. *See* Richman & Reynolds, *supra* at §§ 127–128; Weintraub, *supra* at p. 307–16; Scoles et al., *supra* at §§ 15.30–15.38; Casad & Richman, *supra* at § 9–2[4]. A more specialized resource is Margaret C. Haynes & Diane Dodson, eds., Interstate Child Support Remedies (Washington, DC: ABA Center on Children and the Law 1989). There is an abundant law review literature on *Kulko* and the constitutional issue it presents. *See, e.g.*, Ann Bradford Stevens, *Is Failure to Support a Minor Child in the State Sufficient Contact with That State to Justify in Personam Jurisdiction?*, 17 Southern Illinois University L.J. 491 (1993); John McDermott, *Personal Jurisdiction: The Hidden Agendas in the Supreme Court Decisions*, 10 Vermont L. Rev. 1 (1985). On the recognition of support orders of foreign nations, see Gloria Folger DeHart, *Comity, Conventions, and the Constitution: State and Federal Initiatives in International Support Enforcement*, 28 Family L. Quarterly 89 (1994). Ms. DeHart, a State Department employee, nonetheless takes an expansive view of the ability of states to enter into arrangements involving custody with foreign countries.

Table of Cases

A

Alaska Packers Association v. Industrial Accident Commission, 294 U.S. 532 (1935)
Allen v. McCurry, 449 U.S. 90 (1980)
Allgeyer v. State of Louisiana, 165 U.S. 578 (1897)
Allstate Ins. Co. v. Hague, 449 U.S. 302 (1981)
Alton v. Alton, 207 F.2d 667 (3d Cir. 1953)
Anglo-American Provision Co. v. Davis Provision Co., 191 U.S. 373 (1903)
Armstrong v. Carson, 2 U.S. (2 Dall.) 302 (Cir. Ct. D. Pa. 1794).
Asahi Metal Industry Co., Ltd. v. Superior Court, 480 U.S. 102 (1987)
Auten v. Auten, 308 N.Y. 155, 124 N.E.2d 99 (N.Y. 1954)

B

Baker v. General Motors Corp., 522 U.S. 222 (1998)
Baldwin v. Iowa State Men's Traveling Ass'n., 283 U.S. 522 (1931)
Bergner & Engel Brewing Co. v. Dreyfus, 172 Mass. 154, 51 N.E. 531 (1898)
Bradford Electric Light Co. v. Clapper, 286 U.S. 145 (1932)
Broderick v. Rosner, 294 U.S. 629 (1935)
Burger King Corp. v. Rudzewicz, 471 U.S. 462 (1985)
Burnham v. Superior Court of California, 495 U.S. 604 (1990)

C

Calder v. Jones, 465 U.S. 783 (1984)
Carroll v. Lanza, 349 U.S. 408 (1955)
Chicot County Drainage District v. Baxter State Bank, 308 U.S. 371 (1940)
Colby v. Colby, 78 Nev. 150, 369 P.2d 1019 (1962)
Combs v. Combs, 249 Ky. 155, 60 S.W.2d 368 (1933)
Crider v. Zurich Ins. Co., 380 U.S. 39 (1965)
CTS Corp. v. Dynamics Corp. of America, 481 U.S. 69 (1987)

D

Deposit Bank of Frankfort v. Board of Councilmen, 191 U.S. 499 (1903)
Des Moines Navigation and Railroad Co. v. Iowa Homestead Co., 123 U.S. 552 (1887)

District of Columbia Court of Appeals v. Feldman, 460 U.S. 462 (1983)
Dupasseur v. Rochereau, 88 U.S. (21 Wall.) 130 (1874)
Durfee v. Duke, 375 U.S. 106, 109 (1963)

E

Erie Railroad Co. v. Tompkins, 304 U.S. 64 (1938)
Erwin v. Thomas, 506 N. W. 494 (Ore. 1964)
Estin v. Estin, 334 U.S. 541 (1948)

F

Fall v. Eastin, 215 U.S. 1 (1909)
Fauntleroy v. Lum, 210 U.S. 230 (1908)
Franchise Tax Board of California v. Hyatt, 538 U.S. 488 (2003)

H

Haag v. Barnes, 9 N.Y.2d 554, 175 N.E.2d 441 (N.Y. 1961)
Haddock v. Haddock, 201 U.S. 562 (1906)
Hampton v. McConnel, 16 U.S. (3 Wheat) 234 (1818)
Hanson v. Denckla, 357 U.S. 235 (1958)
Harnischfeger Sales Corp. v. Sternberg Dredging Co., 189 Miss. 73, 191 So. 94 (1939)
Hilton v. Guyot, 159 U.S. 113 (1895)
Hitchcock v. Aicken, 1 Cai. R. 460 (N.Y. 1804)
Hughes v. Fetter, 341 U.S. 609 (1951)
Huntington v. Attrill, 146 U.S. 657 (1892)

I

In Re May's Estate, 305 N.Y. 486, 114 N.E.2d 4 (1953)
Industrial Comm'n of Wisconsin v. McCartin, 330 U.S. 622 (1947)
Intercontinental Hotels Corp. (Puerto Rico) v. Golden, 15 N.Y.2d 9, 203 N.E.2d 210 (N.Y. 1964)
International Shoe Co. v. Washington, 326 U.S. 310, 316 (1945)

J

James v. Grand Trunk Western Railroad Co., 14 Ill.2d 356, 152 N.E.2d 858 (1958)
James-Dickinson Farm Mortgage Co. v. Harry, 273 U.S. 119 (1927)
Johnson v. Muelberger, 340 U.S. 581 (1951)

K

Kalb v. Feuerstein, 308 U.S. 433, 444 (1940)
Kenney v. Supreme Lodge, 252 U.S. 411 (1920)
Kremer v. Chemical Construction Corp., 456 U.S. 461 (1982)
Kulko v. Superior Court, 436 U.S. 84 (1978)

L

Lawrence v. Texas, 539 U.S. 558 (2003)
Lochner v. New York, 198 U.S. 45 (1905)
Lyons v. Westinghouse Electric Corp., 222 F.2d 184 (2d Cir. 1955)

M

Magnolia Petroleum Co. v. Hunt, 320 U.S. 430 (1943)
Marrese v. American Academy of Orthopaedic Surgeons, 470 U.S. 373 (1985)
Matsushita Electric Industrial Co. v. Epstein, 516 U.S. 367 (1996)
May v. Anderson, 345 U.S. 528 (1953)
McBride v. General Motors Corp., 737 F. Supp. 1563 (M.D. Ga. 1990)
McGee v. International Life Ins. Co., 355 U.S. 220 (1957)
M'Elmoyle v. Cohen, 38 U.S. (13 Pet.) 312 (1839)
Michael D. v. Gerald H., 491 U.S. 110 (1989)
Migra v. Warren City School Dist. Bd. of Education, 465 U.S. 75 (1984)
Mills v. Duryee, 11 U.S. (7 Cranch) 481 (1813)
Milwaukee County v. M.E. White Co., 296 U.S. 268 (1935)
Mitsubishi Motors Corp. v. Soler Chrysler-Plymouth, Inc., 473 U.S. 614 (1985)

N

Nationwide Mutual Ins. Co. v. Black, 656 N.E.2d 1352 (Ohio Ct. App. 1995)
Nelson v. Minnesota Income Tax Div., 429 P.2d 324, 325 (Wyo. Sup. Ct. 1967)
Nevada v. Hall, 440 U.S. 410 (1979)

P

Pacific Employers Ins. Co. v. Industrial Accident Commission of California, 306 U.S. 493 (1939)
Parklane Hoisery Co. v. Shore, 439 U.S. 322 (1979)
Parsons Steel, Inc. v. First Alabama Bank, 474 U.S. 518 (1986)
Paul v. National Life, 177 W.Va. 427, 352 S.E.2d 550 (W.Va. 1986)
Phillips Petroleum Co. v. Shutts, 472 U.S. 797 (1985)

S

Santa Clara Pueblo v. Martinez, 436 U.S. 49 (1978)
Schmidt v. Driscoll Hotel, Inc., 249 Minn. 376, 82 N.W.2d 365 (Minn. 1957)
Semler v. Psychiatric Institute of Washington, D.C. 575 F.2d 922 (D.C. Cir. 1978)
Semtek International Inc. v. Lockheed Martin Corp., 531 U.S. 497 (2001)
Shaffer v. Heitner, 433 U.S. 186 (1977)
Sherrer v. Sherrer, 334 U.S. 343 (1948)
Simons v. Miami Beach First Nat. Bank, 381 U.S. 81 (1965)
Smithsonian Institution v. St. John, 214 U.S. 19 (1909)
Sosna v. Iowa, 419 U.S. 393 (1975)
State Farm Mutual Automobile Ins. Co. v. Campbell, 538 U.S. 408 (2003)
State Tax Commission v. Cord, 81 Nev. 403, 404 P.2d 422 (1965)
Sun Oil Co. v. Wortman, 486 U.S. 717, 722 (1988)
Supreme Court of New Hampshire v. Austin, 470 U.S. 274 (1985)

T

Telnikoff v. Matusevitch, 347 Md. 561, 702 A.2d 230 (1997)
Tennessee Coal, Iron, & Railroad Co. v. George, 233 U.S. 354 (1914)
The Antelope, 23 U.S. (10 Wheat) 66 (1825)
Thomas v. Washington Gas Light Co., 448 U.S. 261 (1980)

Travelers Ins. Co. v. Thompson, 281 Minn. 547, 163 N.W. 2d 289 (1968)
Treinies v. Sunshine Mining Co., 308 U.S. 66 (1939)

U
University of Tennessee v. Elliott, 478 U.S. 788 (1986)

V
Vanderbilt v. Vanderbilt, 354 U.S. 416 (1957)
Varone v. Varone, 359 F.2d 769 (7th Cir. 1966)

W
Walker v. Witter, 99 Eng. Rep 1 (K.B. 1778)
Weesner v. Weesner, 168 Neb. 345, 95 N.W.2d 682 (1959)
Wells v. Simonds Abrasive Co., 345 U.S. 514 (1953)
Williams v. North Carolina, 317 U.S. 287 (1942) ("*Williams I*")
Williams v. North Carolina, 325 U.S. 226 (1945) ("*Williams II*")
Wisconsin v. Pelican Ins. Co., 127 U.S. 265, 290 (1888)
World-Wide Volkswagen Corp. v. Woodson, 444 U.S. 286 (1980)

Y
Yarborough v. Yarborough, 290 U.S. 202 (1933)

Index

About the Authors

WILLIAM L. REYNOLDS has taught at the University of Maryland School of Law since 1971. He has written many articles on appellate decision-making, conflict of laws, and the legal process. He also serves as Counsel to Piper Rudnick LLP.

WILLIAM M. RICHMAN has taught at the University of Toledo since 1976, and has served as a visiting professor at the University of Maryland and the University of Michigan. He has written books and articles on appellate court reform, conflict of laws, and personal jurisdiction.